Date Due

BC 2 Feb 84			
BC 3 Mar 85			

The Second City Book
Studies of urban and suburban Canada

The Second City Book
Studies of urban and suburban Canada

edited by James Lorimer and Evelyn Ross
with the editors of City Magazine

James Lorimer & Company, Publishers
Toronto 1977

ISBN 0-88862-140-X paper
ISBN 0-88862-141-8 cloth

Cover photo and design: Don Fernley

James Lorimer & Company, Publishers
35 Britain Street
Toronto

Printed and bound in Canada

Canadian Cataloguing in Publication Data

Main entry under title:

  The Second city book

Contains a selection of articles which originally appeared in City Magazine.

Includes index.
ISBN 0-88862-141-8 bd. ISBN 0-88862-140-X pa.

1. Cities and towns — Canada — Addresses, essays, lectures. 2. Cities and towns — Planning — Canada — Addresses, essays, lectures. I. Lorimer, James, 1942- II. Ross, Evelyn, 1946-   III. City magazine.

HT169.S42   309.2′62′0971   C77-001261-2

Acknowledgements

We wish to thank the contributors to *City Magazine* for providing us with so many excellent articles and for allowing us to reprint them in this book. We also thank the other editors of the magazine, George Baird, Katharine Bladen, Ron Clark, Kent Gerecke, Donald Gutstein, Audrey Stewart and Valerie Wyatt, for the considerable time and effort they have devoted to the initial organization and production of this material.

J.L.
E.R.

Contents

Introduction

James Lorimer

In many Canadian cities, there is a sense that the continuing battle over planning and power at city hall is toughening up. In cities like Vancouver and Toronto where the first wave of "reform" successes swept through in the early 1970s, the experiments of the moderate middle-of-the-road "reformers" are grinding to a halt. In fact they have been pretty well terminated in Vancouver as of the October 1976 elections, and in Toronto the failure of Mayor David Crombie to ensure the selection of radical reformer John Sewell has been widely interpreted as a sign of his unwillingness to take the reform position seriously. In other cities like Edmonton, Calgary, Winnipeg, Halifax, and Ottawa where "reform" ideas have had a certain hearing at city hall without a clear battle for power being fought between the old-guard developer-oriented politicians and the reform side, there is a sense that an orientation towards citizen interests and a strong sense of civic justice and indignation will not be enough to make a substantial difference in the urban policies and decisions.

For reform-oriented politicians who understand the power of the property industry and who challenge the industry's right to carry on running civic government in Canada, it is clear that a tougher, more precise, and much more detailed analysis is required of the economic and political interests at work in Canada's cities. These interests have to be linked more clearly and concretely to their results in terms of privately initiated development projects and public transportation systems, servicing schemes, land-use controls, and regional planning policies.

A tougher political analysis is required as well, one which accurately describes the many political mechanisms which are used by the property industry and its politicians to maintain their political power and one which leads to strategies which will make it possible for reform politicians to organize politically and take control of city governments from the property industry majorities that have it now. This analysis is likely to lead to different kinds of political initiatives than have taken place in the last decade. Reform politics, which has had its roots in neighbourhood organizing and citizen groups often focussed around a single issue and the need for action on a specific matter, must make the leap into city-wide political organizations that maintain both the grass-roots, democratic procedure of citizen groups and the ability to hold the allegiance of people who consider themselves to hold a wide range of political views. These efforts have to be more carefully considered and produce more results than initial attempts like the reform group who ran in the Winnipeg election in 1974 largely unsuccessfully, or the Reform Caucus that counted on 6 of 23 votes in Toronto from 1975-76 but which failed to make a substantial impact on the 1976 election campaign in Toronto, or the Vancouver reform movement which was not able to make up an effective electoral coalition in 1976.

The Second City Book contains some important contributions to the process of toughening up the reform analysis of the city. Particularly important in this respect is John Sewell's material on the suburbs, which makes up the first four chapters of this book. Sewell's work marks the first comprehensive attempt by a writer with a critical viewpoint to come to grips with suburbia, its causes and consequences. Complementing Sewell's analysis is the material on the suburban land market which sets out the incredible facts about the profits which the large corporate developers are making in the suburbs, the contribution of corporate profits on land to the high price of suburban housing, and the scale of the (mainly tax-free) corporate earnings which are being generated in the process.

Also breaking new analytic ground here is Kent Gerecke's brief but fascinating history of Canadian city planning. Gerecke indicates how city planning was transformed from a utopian and idealistic intellectual discipline to a profession which provides essential routine administration to consolidate the property industry's control of the development patterns of cities.

Along with some analytic material, the second element offered by this book is case studies from a number of different cities and fields which demonstrate that the property industry carries right on implementing successfully projects and policies which have been attacked by citizen groups and reform politicians. These have not been stopped by evidence showing that in many cases they are contrary to the interests of ordinary urban residents and often cause measurable harm to cities.

The section on demolition as a property industry technique offers two particularly offensive examples of this activity. One is Canadian Pacific's demolition of the Laurentien Hotel in Montreal; the other is the Ontario government's demolition of the most important early public building in Ontario, John Howard's 999 Queen Street. In both places, conservationists and others had an irrefutable case that there was economic justification for retention rather than demolition, as well as the many other grounds which make preservation a far more satisfactory urban policy. In both cases, the preservationists lost, and lost badly, with no apparent real likelihood of winning.

The section of the book on politicians and developers offers a case study documenting the steadily growing influence of Genstar Ltd., the land development and construction conglomerate which dominates the suburban land, cement, gypsum wall-board and other industries in Vancouver, Edmonton, Calgary and an expanding number of cities particularly in the West. It details the dealings of the City of Winnipeg with Trizec Corp. over a downtown development project at the corner of Portage and Main where the city's willingness to make unprecedented concessions to the developer ironically failed to get the massive project Trizec promised into construction. Here again, a vigorous and informed citizen opposition made no real dent in the corporate developer's achievement. An account of the fight over an inquiry into the activities of the suburban Toronto municipality of Mississauga shows developer-oriented politicians successfully blocking a well-intentioned reform mayor who wanted to explore relations between the industry and city politics. And a chapter on the politics of Hamilton's harbour demonstrates the almost infinite capacity of the "normal" political process to cover up compromising relationships between business men and politicians at their scandalous worst.

Finally, a chapter which offers a case history of policy-making at Central Mortgage and Housing — the case is native people's housing and a consultative process between CMHC bureaucrats and native organization representatives which led to the unjustified firing of a senior CMHC official for taking "consultation" too seriously — indicates the power of government to carry on in what it considers to be its own best interests while doing little more than paying lip service to the un-vested interests which native people's groups represent, as do the citizen groups and neighbourhood organizations that exist in Canadian cities.

All the case histories here show governments and corporate developers up against more sophisticated, more tenacious, better-informed, more experienced citizen organizations than existed a decade ago. The fights are tougher; that is one point which emerges from the case histories. But the property industry, the corporate developers, and their politicians and planners are still winning most major battles.

So as well as offering some contributions towards a better analysis of urban Canada, this Second City Book indicates in its case studies from across the country useful illustrations of the kinds of issues which are now being battled out, and how these are being resolved.

This book is a sequel to The City Book. As was the case with that volume, what is offered here are chapters which were originally published in City Magazine, an independent Canadian periodical which deals with urban planning, politics, architecture, and policy. Neither this book nor its predecessor is conceived as an analytic work, nor as an extended case study. That function is performed by other books, and the introduction and bibliography to The City Book offers details about where this kind of material can be found. Like its predecessor, The Second City Book is what law students call a case book, a series of materials for students and readers interested in urban Canada.

The success of The City Book has indicated that it is indeed helpful to collect together and make available in book form material which was originally published in a magazine. Where appropriate, the authors of the chapters have updated their original articles. In addition, in response to requests from readers and particularly from high school librarians who have cited its obvious usefulness for high school student readers, this book includes a full index.

The authors of the chapters of this book receive a small fee for their material, and the balance of the royalty income is paid to City Magazine. The magazine continues to increase its readership as word of its existence spreads, and as coverage is expanded to cover fields which have been until now left untouched. For readers who find this book of interest, City Magazine will also certainly be useful and enjoyable reading.

This book, and City Magazine, are the result of a collective effort on the part of a number of people. Editorial duties on the magazine are shared by seven editors from across the country. Contributors to the book — and to the magazine — are very often volunteers who offer to write about news and controversies in their cities. In a very real way, both this book and City Magazine are publications created by the people who read them, and there is always need — and room — for more good material from new contributors across Canada.

I Land and suburbs

Where the suburbs came from

John Sewell

In some respects, the Second World War was a starting point for Canada.* During the latter part of the war, the Canadian government recognized the major changes that were occurring in the economy, and set up committees to recommend new Canadian economic structures and policies. Major shifts would be required to ensure that those returning from the war should have places to live and places to work. Canada was expected to experience a period of strong growth, for which the economy had to prepare itself.

HOUSING IN POST-WAR CANADA

The need for housing appeared to be very great. Reformers were saying that Canada had an obligation to end the cycle of poor housing which led to social problems. This housing had to be replaced. Also the supply of housing units had to increase to accommodate the projected increase in population and new family formation. The Federal Government took early steps in 1944 with a National Housing Act, whose full title was, interestingly enough:

An Act to promote the construction of new houses and the repair and maintenance of existing houses, and improvement of housing and living standards and the expansion of employment in the post-war period.

The two problems of housing and employment were seen as inseparable.

In its report *Housing and Community Planning*, published in 1944, the government's Advisory Committee on Reconstruction calculated that at least 730,000 housing units would be required in the decade commencing in 1946. But even this number of units was considered an underestimate, since it did not take account of the "doubling-up" that the Minister of Reconstruction and Supply

---

*There are tremendous difficulties in writing definitively about the subject of the suburbs in Canada. There is a dearth of material available on who was thinking what 25 years ago. As well, very little of a critical nature has been written about Canadian planning, or the development of planning thought. While a limited number of descriptive documents on Don Mills are available, they are either repetitive (sometimes repeating the same errors), or written by the main actors involved in planning that community. Apart from random newspaper clippings, there is almost no information available on the deliberations of the Council of North York Township about Don Mills. For instance, the Council minutes of the early nineteen fifties (which are typewritten, single spaced, unindexed, and running to 500 or more pages a year), contain almost no references to Council's involvement in the project. Even the minutes of the North York Planning Board reveal little, and the original planning reports (presuming such existed) have been either lost or misplaced.

Thus I have had to make do with what I could turn up in

odd places – journals, government studies, and interviews with some of the personnel involved: Douglas Lee, James Murray, E.G. Faludi, and Macklin Hancock. While I have not quoted directly from those interviewed (except where their own remarks were published elsewhere), I have used the information they provided to draw as coherent a picture as I could of what really happened. My thanks to Vicki Casey of the Municipal Reference Library for locating much of the written reference material.

I would like to thank Susan Richardson for not only helping with the research for this paper, but also for being a part of the development and refinement of the ideas set out here. Also thanks to Robert Hill for obtaining and taking the photographs which appear in the article.

— J.S.

Rental housing units erected in 1946 by the Wartime Housing Ltd. on Queen St. E. in Toronto. Photo: City of Toronto Archives

noted in 1946. His opinion then was that some 480,000 units were required in the next five years. Given that only 260,000 housing units had been built in the ten years prior to the war, it was clear that significant changes would have to occur to meet housing needs as forecast.[1]

Some of these new units were provided by Wartime Housing Limited, a government-controlled corporation providing housing units for rent, a market private companies refused to serve. The record of this company was impressive, completing almost 8,000 rental units in 1946, and 5,000 in 1947.

But most of the housing was not to be produced by government. The Right Hon. C.D. Howe usually concluded his strong statements about housing needs by emphasizing how that need would be met:"It is the policy to ensure that as large a portion as possible of housing be built by private initiative."[2]

Liberal Government policy was to leave housing to private industry. When industry wouldn't supply the appropriate number or types of unit, then the job of government was seen to be to provide help to the industry: improved financing; help with labour and materials; setting targets; and all of the other tools set out in the National Housing Act. Wartime Housing Limited was summarily disbanded by C.D. Howe to give the industry free scope.

Studies were produced which analyzed the cost of the massive housing program. In order to help ensure that private initiative would provide adequate financing (in the form of profit-making investments) the Insurance Act was amended to allow insurance companies to finance land improvements in suburban areas. This, of course, allowed much more capital to flow into housing.[3]

In Ontario, the Planning Act passed in 1946 had the primary effect of regulating the subdivision of land through ministerial approval. While it appears that Planning Act provisions controlling subdivisions might have been a method of government control over the development of land, in fact Ontario was simply bringing the order and stability necessary for substantial investment to a market that was about to explode.

The perceived view of governments and their housing experts in the nineteen forties was that production of new housing by private enterprise was not only desirable, but also necessary for the health of the country. Post-war optimism placed a great deal of faith in the growth and ability of industry to supply housing for the needs of Canada. And governments geared themselves up to help the property industry meet that public need.

HOUSING THAT PEOPLE COULD AFFORD

Soon after the war, the price of building materials jumped rapidly — 38 per cent from 1946 to 1947 alone.[4] Of course, housing costs also began to climb and there was consternation that real housing needs would not be met. One point rapidly became clear: that private developers would not be able to provide housing for those who most needed it. It was the old problem of discovering that the economy did not work for low-income people.

In 1951 Central Mortgage and Housing Corporation published a study entitled *Post-War House Building in Canada* which addressed itself to cost and supply problems. It offered a reassuring, if rather difficult-to-believe, explanation of how this could work to the benefit of all:

11

Humphrey Carver, author of the influential book *Houses for Canadians,* written in 1948. Photo: Courtesy U. of T. Press

In the past new houses have been built mainly for the medium- and upper-income groups in the community. Although some lower-income families may acquire new houses of a modest type, the numbers that do so are not in proportion to the numbers of families at this income level in the whole community. The lower-income groups depend largely on used housing, which is less expensive than new housing. As the pressure of demand for used housing from the lower-income groups increases, the price of residential real estate rises and effects a situation in which members of the medium- and upper-income classes are more apt to build new houses, thus vacating dwellings for successive groups lower down on the income scale. The process by which these groups obtained houses from wealthier members of the community is known as "filtering down."

...There is sufficient evidence to show that the average capital outlay required to obtain a new house is beyond the financial means of many Canadian families.[5]

The study did note that this filtering-down process would not be entirely effective in providing housing for those in the lower-income groups. While government policy under the National Housing Act had been successful in providing housing starts at an unprecedented rate, needs were still not met. For instance, between 1945 and 1950, some 460,000 housing units were built. But there was still a serious housing shortage, and almost half a million families were sharing residences.

The CMHC booklet attempted to analyze the cost components of new housing in order to find out what could be done to reduce housing costs. The study dealt with the cost of labour, the cost of building materials, the cost of money, and developers' profits. The root problem was said to be construction costs. "The fact with the most obvious effect on total costs is the type of structure,"[6] concluded the report.

Two conclusions emerged:

On the supply side there does not appear to be any better way of solving the problem of housing than by reducing construction costs by a change in building techniques. But even with a continuation of traditional building techniques some reductions in house building costs should be within reach of the industry as material supplies become plentiful, trained building tradesmen are available in sufficient numbers, and management uses all its ability to reduce costs even if strong markets reduce competition to a minimum. On the demand side, until a genuine reduction in construction costs is achieved, willingness of families to spend more on housing than they are doing at present would mean more and better housing to be built for many years to come. In this connection, government assistance either in the form of loans and guarantees to families in a position to purchase homes or in the form of capital and rental subsidies along the lines provided in Section 35 of the National Housing Act, 1944, would go a long way to assuring a measure of stability in the house building industry – provided, of course, that such a state of affairs is reconcilable with other demands made on the economy. For example, in a period of rearmament, the proportion of resources going into housing will of necessity depend on the size of defence and defence-supporting programs considered essential for national security.[7]

There are three points to note in this conclusion. First, the problem is seen as a reduction in construction costs as opposed, say, to the reduction in land costs or developers' profits; second, the problem is getting money into the hands of those wishing to buy houses so that demand can be increased, which presumably would be followed by an increase in supply; and third, housing is a sector of the economy that can act as a valve for other fiscal concerns. Interestingly enough, the very same solutions to the very same problems are still being offered.

Perhaps more important was Humphrey Carver's book *Houses for Canadians,* published in 1948. While this book mainly addresses housing problems in the Toronto area, it had seminal influence on both private industry and government in regard to housing policy. Carver again pinpoints the need to reduce housing construction costs. In his mind, the basic cause of high housing costs is one of small builders carrying bits and pieces of materials out to the building site. Carver argues for a rationalized building industry based on large-scale house construction companies:

The small speculative builder undertakes the erection of only a few houses at a time, saving the cost of managerial overhead and office space and protecting himself from market uncertainties by keeping his output in line with the immediate demand of prospective purchasers. Under such circumstances it has been impossible to smooth the process of production. Fundamental changes in the process can only be brought about through the entry of large-scale producers into the housing industry, and they could only enter upon such a business if they could anticipate a continuing market which would justify the necessary capitalization. Since the expectation of such market conditions has never yet seemed justified, the organization of the residential building industry has stagnated.[8]

Bigness, he states, will help ensure cost reductions — big companies, and big projects:

It is only when large-scale projects are planned that there are opportunities to introduce important features of industrial organization aimed to reduce the high labour costs in the building process.[9]

Two of his six conclusions are prophetic for the housing industry in Canada:

Large-scale producers cannot enter the field unless there is the assured continuity of demand which would make it possible to attract capital.

Building projects carried out on a larger scale than is at present customary would provide an opportunity for less stereotyped design and more imaginative planning; this in itself would be likely to stimulate demand for housing.[10]

Carver also deals with the question of land costs, but he assumes that land is *not* the problem. He estimates the cost of an improved lot at $775 or approximately 10 per cent of the cost of the house. Take, for instance, his estimate of the gross monthly payments on a $7,000 housing unit:

Gross Monthly Cost of a $7,000 Housing Unit[11]

	Monthly Payment	Per Cent
a) Building		
Cost of Construction $6,225	$22.94	39
b) Land		
Cost of Improved Lot $775	3.23	6
c) Money		
$2,000 Cash at 3%		
$5,000 N.H.A. Loan at 4½%	15.68	27
d) Maintenance		
At $80 Per Annum	6.66	11
e) Taxes		
At 2% of $7,000	11.66	17
	$60.17	100

Given that the cost of land accounted for such a small part of the monthly payment, there was little reason for governments to assume that any energy should be directed to either the supply of land or its cost. If Carver's analysis was correct, housing costs would fall only if demand were stronger, leading to the creation of larger companies building larger developments so that techniques like prefabrication could be used.

THE SUBURBAN IDEA

Housing in post-war Canada followed patterns of development and physical forms which were in many ways radically different from the ways that cities had been built before 1939. Those new housing and community forms derive their intellectual inspiration from idealized plans worked out by

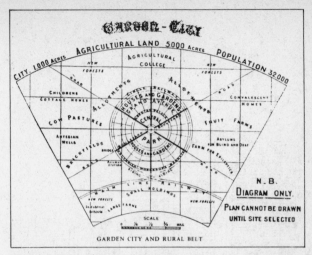

Ebenezer Howards' ideogram for a Garden City, incorporating a favourable and generous ratio between buildings and green spaces. Illustration: *History Builds the Town* by Arthur Korn, Lund Humphries, London, 1953

three urban designers, Ebenezer Howard, Le Corbusier, and Frank Lloyd Wright.

Ebenezer Howard developed his Garden City plan in 1898. Howard attempted to meld the best of the urban and rural environments in a small town of 25,000 people. Le Corbusier's Radiant City scheme proposed a highrise city of a million or more persons in the countryside. To emphasize his vision of the urban environment, Le Corbusier designed his towers on stilts so the landscape could roll under the building and on into the distance. In his Broadacre City scheme, Frank Lloyd Wright tried to join the urban and the rural by sprinkling houses throughout the countryside, with every man, woman and child getting an acre of land.

Canada's post-war suburbs are mostly crude pastiches of these three seminal planning concepts. The highrise apartment tower bears no resemblance to the vision of Le Corbusier. Green strips of land in the suburbs and concreted streams are a mockery of the Garden City concept. And the endless rows of houses on 60 by 100 foot lots only mimic the idea of Broadacre City. Nevertheless all three concepts, in horribly perverted forms, are the intellectual inspiration of contemporary Canadian suburbia.

In the United States, from the early nineteen twenties onwards, planners tackled the problem of trying to turn these urban concepts into reality. Perhaps the most influential was Sunnyside Gardens, built in the mid-nineteen twenties in New York. While Sunnyside Gardens was small by today's standards — less than 60 acres — it introduced the idea of houses set away from the street in a fashion that emphasized the project's garden aspect. It was followed by Radburn, a site of almost two square miles, which was much more ambitious in its attempt to build a garden city. With the

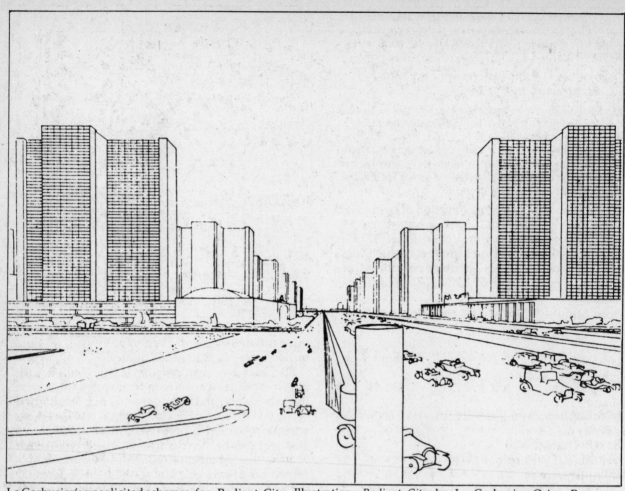

Le Corbusier's unsolicited schemes for Radiant City. Illustration: *Radiant City* by Le Corbusier Orion Press
N.Y.C. 1964

onslaught of the depression, the idea was abandoned after a fifth of it had been built. These concepts were followed by green-belt towns, as their names indicate: Chatham Village, Hillside Houses, Greenbelt, Greenbrook, Greendale, Greenhills, Baldwin Hills.

Clarence Stein and Henry Wright, the American planners involved with Sunnyside and later Radburn, had two ideas about what they were trying to do. First, the evils of tenements and poor housing had to be overcome. That was to be done by the infusion of green space around houses, or alternatively, the scattered placement of houses in a green setting. Second, was the idea of developing whole new communities, that is, putting the residential and other land uses into self-contained community units, not as an extension of existing urban forms. As the Second World War drew to a close, planners again turned to these concepts.

These ideas were first proposed in Canada by the influential Ontario planner E.G. Faludi. Faludi had learned town planning in Italy, where a number of new communities had been attempted. In 1945 he designed Thorncrest Village, a housing development of 100 acres of land on the then outskirts of

Toronto. This development had 180 housing units on 100 acres. Faludi blended two elements: low density housing with much green space; and commercial uses alongside housing in the plan. The result bore some resemblance to a town, a place with some measure of economic self-sufficiency. The greenbelt concept was followed in a number of other subdivisions in Toronto, all of which are summarized in an October 1952 publication of the Toronto Real Estate Board.[12] Faludi edited this booklet. This publication illustrated the new kind of housing which the real estate industry had to market: houses that were single storey (or perhaps one-and-a-half storey), broadside to the street, set on spacious lots, using strong design elements. These ideas were at considerable variance with the match-box bungalows and their mutual drives set row after row on the street line. The large lot was, however, functional: sewer services were not available, and a half-acre lot was necessary to support the septic tank system. But the house design was a matter of principle. Faludi wished to design a house that was set in accordance with topography (rather than lot lines), and at the same time make maximum use of natural light through windows.

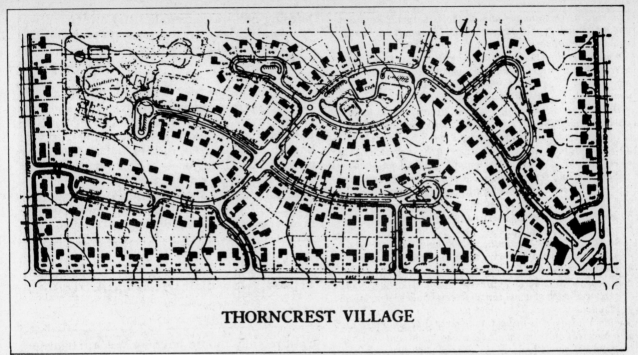

THORNCREST VILLAGE

Thorncrest Village, shown as built in 1948, in the Toronto suburb of Etobicoke. A self-contained community, controlled and regulated by deed restrictions, a property owners association, and by zoning by-laws. Illustration: *A.I.P. Journal, Spring 1950, p. 75*

Combining these ideas with the least expensive building methods (one storey if possible) produced a new house style.

Faludi also introduced building controls. The hundred-acre site was owned by one company, which sold its lots to selected individuals who arranged for their own builders. The company reserved the right to approve house designs and materials used.

Faludi's ideas were innovative, and not repeated immediately. At first these subdivisions served only high-income house purchasers.

The germ of "community planning" as a new approach to housing subdivisions was elaborated on by Humphrey Carver. In his influential 1948 book, *Houses for Canadians*, he outlined what he considered to be the problem of simply building houses, and laid out the direction that Canadian planning thinking has since adopted in rote-like fashion.

Carver thought that any house-building program was inseparable from community planning, not because one was trying to achieve something new, but because the planning process imposed an order to the building process.

In planning the construction of new communities it is necessary not only to lay out the sites but also to determine the sequence of operations. In this sense community planning is similar to the planning of any other kind of industrial process; it may be compared with the designing of the process by which the component parts of automobiles are delivered to the assembly line in a rational sequence so that the finished products can be brought to completion as economically and rapidly as possible....[13]

Carver set out how he thought communities should be planned. He noted that in Toronto city planners viewed the city as a collection of neighbourhoods. And with the neighbourhood as a base, all the component land uses fell into place. In a remarkable two pages, Carver laid out an approach to suburban planning that planners have followed ever since:

... The Planning Board was able to identify seventy-eight neighbourhoods within the city boundaries, varying in size from 150 to 330 acres with an average of about 250 acres. In the older parts of the city there were found to be from 60 to 100 persons per acre – or a population of about 20,000 in a 250 acre neighbourhood. In that more modern part of the city which lies north of the Canadian Pacific Railway North Toronto line there were found to be from 30 to 60 persons per acre – or a population of 7,500 to 15,000 in a 250 acre neighbourhood.

If the density of a development in North Toronto, the most modern section of the city, may be regarded as a reasonable standard, then we may aim to achieve a similar standard in the development of the present housing program. To produce 50,000 houses may therefore be regarded as a community planning program for the creation of about twenty-five neighbourhood communities, each containing a population of about 7,500 people living in about 2,000 housing units (3.75 persons per household). Since, however, a considerable proportion of the program will be absorbed by the filling out of existing incomplete neighbourhood areas it would perhaps be safe to state that twenty (and not twenty-five) new neighbourhood units are required.

A good deal of study of community organization has in recent years been directed towards determining the most desirable size of an operating residential unit or neighbourhood. About 2,000 households appear to provide a well-balanced community. This number of households normally contains about the number of children required to support a school of manageable proportions and buys enough to keep a diversified group of retail stores in business. It is big enough to require its own recreation area and not so big as to make its own shops, schools, and other community services too distant from any house in the neighbourhood.

With its population of 660,000 the City of Toronto has 85 public schools (one per 7,764 population) and 16 secondary schools (one per 41,250 population). On this basis the school district conforms very conveniently with the suggested size of a neighbourhood. Each new community with a population of about 7,500 will require one public school and a secondary school will have to be provided for each group of five neighbourhoods. In all, therefore, the 50,000 unit post-war housing program implies the need for 25 public schools and five secondary schools....

...Residential areas containing 50,000 houses should be provided with about 320 acres of open space. Each neighbourhood should have at least three acres developed as playgrounds for children of pre-school and school age. Five open spaces, each of about thirty acres, should be developed as playfields to serve the young people in a group of neighbourhoods. And in addition to these spaces planned for active recreation there should be a reasonable contribution, perhaps 100 acres, towards the general park system of the metropolitan area, preferably as an integral part of a continuous green belt connected with the ravines and natural landscape areas of the Don and Humber river systems.

Each neighbourhood requires the service of a number of retail stores ....It seems probable that a community of 2,000 households can be quite adequately served by about forty stores which would require about five acres of land or frontage of about 1,400 feet. Considerations of traffic movement and convenient distribution of these little shopping centres will recommend that they should not be strung along traffic arteries but should be located in compact groups at strategic points. In all, not more than 125 acres of land should be required for this purpose.

In addition to these specific requirements other features of residential communities will suggest themselves.

Neighbourhood theatres and churches must be allowed for and there will be a need for a few light industries to provide local employment apart from the areas specifically zoned for industrial use. [14]

Carver's vision was one of building new communities, not just new housing. Up to that time this had only happened in the creation of company towns. Few people in Canada had given serious consideration to the implications of the development of new communities on the fringes of existing settlements.

In fact, of course, company towns are a poor precedent to follow on the outskirts of a city. They are oriented to one specific purpose, usually mining as in Kitimat, Elliot Lake, Arvida, and Inuvik. Houses have no independent market value since the only people who would like to buy them are those who work in the company town. Trying to gear up planning thought to the creation of diverse communities around a city was somewhat more complex. The market one was serving was fragmented; transportation pressures were diverse;

housing mix was uncertain; land ownership was competitive. For Carver these were problems that could and should be overcome.

What was needed was someone to try these ideas out.

In England, the idea of new towns was already being experimented with. Between 1946 and 1950, 14 new towns were undertaken, many just outside London. Carver's writing embodies the reports of English planners who, in 1946, outlined the same type of checklists for new communities. What Carver did *not* do was suggest that, as in England, new communities should be developed by government. As it turned out, they were developed in a manner entirely satisfactory to C.D. Howe.

THE HOUSE-BUILDING INDUSTRY

Until recently, house building was a fragmented industry. It was composed of many very small firms, each producing ten or fifteen houses a year, making a small average profit on each. There was almost no vertical integration. Some companies purchased small parcels of land, put in the servicing and sold off lots. Different companies purchased the serviced lots, built houses and then attempted to sell them. The example of Thorncrest Village is instructive: the company that owned the whole parcel sold off lots to builders and future owners, who carried out construction.

This meant there was substantial and vigorous competition in the housing market. One would buy up land where one could and build on it when one could. One reason for the smallness of firms was that builders sought protection from the vagaries of market forces. Any builder with a large inventory of houses might find that a shift in the market would leave him with an investment he could not market, so builders stayed small and built in response to market demand.

Although no figures are available prior to 1950, the activities in the two decades between 1950 and 1970 give an indication of what was happening. In a study entitled *Subdivision Activity in the Periphery of the Toronto Urban Field,* [15] figures are given of the subdivisions occurring in the outskirts of the Toronto Metropolitan area. From 1950-59, 11,550 acres of land were subdivided for housing purposes; from 1960-69, only 5,500 acres were subdivided. Generally, the lots were large (capable of supporting septic tanks) and no more than 12 persons per acre were housed on this subdivided land. What the figures indicate is that at midcentury there was a relatively high level of subdivision activity, which fell off after 1960 as the need of the building industry changed to conform more to the "efficient model" that Humphrey Carver described. As Gerald Hodge notes:

This is a relatively small volume of subdivided land in the metropolitan region [of Toronto] which is growing by about 60,000 persons per year. It refutes the convenient wisdom that we are vastly oversubdivided. Instead, a sharp slow-down in subdivision activity after 1960 could well be leading to a shortage of land available for urban development outside the urban fringe areas. [16]

One of the people involved in this intensely competitive market prior to 1950 was E.P. Taylor. He had been involved, in a small way, in buying land, servicing it, subdividing it, and then selling off the serviced lots. That was the limit of activity that could be expected from any participant in the housing business. Until, that is, Don Mills. Don Mills radically altered the shape of the housing and property industry, so that instead of having many actors, the industry was reduced to a few gigantic corporations.

1. Humphrey Carver, *Houses for Canadians* (Toronto: University of Toronto Press, 1948), p. 4.
2. *Dominion-Provincial Conference on Reconstruction*, Report of the Plenary Session No. 1, August 6, 1945, p. 6f. Also see *Houses for Canadians*, Chapter 1.
3. *Houses for Canadians*, p. 127.
4. Ibid., p. 8f.
5. *Post-War House Building in Canada*, CMHC, 1951, p. 6.
6. Ibid., p. 57.
7. Ibid., p. 65.
8. *Houses for Canadians*, p. 63.
9. Ibid., p. 64.
10. Ibid., p. 69.
11. Ibid., p.50. Monthly costs would be less if one assumed a down payment of any amount.
12. *Land Development in the Municipal Area of Toronto*, Toronto Real Estate Board, October 1952.
13. *Houses for Canadians*, p. 39-42.
14. Ibid.
15. Gerald Hodge, "Subdivision Activity in the Periphery of the Toronto Urban Field," in *The Form of Cities in Central Canada*, L. Bourne, ed. (Toronto: University of Toronto Press, 1973).
16. Ibid.

Don Mills: E.P. Taylor and Canada's first corporate suburb

John Sewell

In 1947, E.P. Taylor began to purchase farm land to the north and east of Toronto, in the Township of North York. He chose to buy in an area that, although only seven miles from downtown, was remote from other developed land. The site was cut off from Toronto by ravines to the west, south, and east; ravines that contained railways leading into the heart of the city. Roadways had never been constructed across the ravines, and access was limited to York Mills Road to the north and Don Mills Road, which meandered down through the ravine to the south, and up the other side to join with the new subdivisions occurring in East York. At that time, the whole site consisted of 15 or 20 working farms.

In 1947 Taylor was one of Canada's most successful corporate businessmen. His prime success had come from combining small locally-based breweries into a single powerful company which was far more profitable — and hence valuable — than the parts of which it had been made. Taylor exercised his corporate power along with a small group of Toronto-based financiers who owned Argus Corporation.

Taylor purchased land through his company O'Keefe Realty Limited, rather than through one of the Argus companies. His intention, according to many people, was to buy land on which to establish a new plant for O'Keefe Breweries, one of his brewery companies, and then erect housing for workers at the plant.

Although Taylor's previous activities in real estate were limited, they were influential. He had developed the York Mills Plaza, the first regional shopping centre in Canada, just to the north and west of Don Mills. Prior to the successful plaza development — which was implemented just as he began his Don Mills acquisition — he had picked up land in the York Mills area to prevent it being subdivided into small 25-foot lots. He serviced this land, and then subdivided it into large lots known as Wrentham Estates.

In the Wrentham Estates scheme, Taylor had sold off the serviced lots to small builders at $3,200 per lot — a high price in those days. In turn, the builders erected houses which increased the value of the land, and kept the profit for themselves. It is possible that Taylor recognized the money that could be made if somehow controls were established throughout the process of servicing, subdividing, building, and selling, so that the profits at each stage could flow into one pocket rather than two or three.

By 1952, Taylor had purchased 31 parcels of land totalling 2,063 acres; almost all of the island of land created by the ravine system. By that time, the idea of using the land for Taylor's presumed industrial intentions had long been abandoned: the game plan was to develop a new community.

It is not clear just when, and from what source, the idea of a new community came. As Taylor continued to purchase land, it must have been clear to those involved that the early idea of an industrial plant and workers' housing had been superseded. Perhaps it was Carl Fraser, executive assistant to Taylor, who gave birth to the idea. Taylor had only previously employed two persons who might have some inkling of American thinking about new communities, or of the concepts that Humphrey Carver was developing; John Layng, an architect who had worked out the concepts for the York Mills Plaza; and Macklin Hancock, a landscape architect who, through his father's company, Cooksville Nursery, had devised landscape and planning ideas for both the plaza and Wrentham Estates. Layng, however, was more an architect than a planner, and Hancock was still a student more interested in landscaping and the environment than planning.

By 1950, Taylor and Carl Fraser (who was the father-in-law of Hancock) had decided that some comprehensive development was required, perhaps along the line of a new community. By this time, the English were well into the development of their Mark I new towns, but Taylor turned to the Americans for advice. By 1951, consultations had taken place with the Urban Land Institute, an American body consisting of community developers from across the United States. Later, presentations of the community plan proposals were made to the Institute in Seattle and Cincinnati, and members of the Institute visited the site in early 1952 to put their final seal of approval on the scheme.

As the idea of creating a new community took hold, Fraser discussed the idea frequently with his son-in-law, Macklin Hancock. Hancock was then attending Harvard, taking post graduate studies in landscaping and town planning from Sir William Holford, Hadeo Sasacki, and Walter Grophius, all exponents of new town theory. Thus Hancock was in the thick of the discussion about the very proposal which Taylor and Fraser seemed to consider viable for their 2,000-acre parcel.

In 1951, Taylor called the members of the North York Council to a meeting at the Granite Club. He presented a model of a residential development for the site. Faludi, as North York's planning consultant, objected: he wanted industry included in order to help balance the assessment load. Taylor went back to the drawing boards and John Layng proposed a mixed development, incorporating Faludi's wishes.

At this point Fraser and Layng had a falling-out, and Layng either resigned or was fired for reasons that are now obscure. Fraser looked for someone new to coordinate planning. He turned to Hancock, who was still at school. After some reluctance, Hancock agreed to leave his studies at Harvard, and in March 1952, he joined the company. He immediately put together a team of young planners — he was in his mid-twenties — to develop the concept. Assisting him was Douglas Lee,

Carl Fraser, president of Don Mills Development Corp. (left), industrialist James Harris (center rear), and planner Macklin Hancock (right) witness the signature of the first Don Mills housebuilder Arthur Weinstock. Photo: *Architectural Forum*, June 1954.

a student of Sasacki. Later, a couple of young Toronto architects — Henry Feliss and James Murray — were called upon to help sort out architectural problems. By September 1952, the plan was completed in its first draft form.

Up to this point, two names had been considered for the new community: Yorktown (Toronto used to be known as York) and Eptown (presumably after E.P. Taylor himself). Hancock coined Don Mills, since there was a mill at the site on the Don River. The name appeared to satisfy the directors and on May 8, 1952, O'Keefe Realty changed its name to Don Mills Development Corporation.

William Holford, the influential planner of new towns, visited the site in the summer of 1952, and gave his blessing, both to the appropriateness of the site itself and to the concepts underlying the plan. It appears, however, that the model being pursued was more in line with American than British thinking. Perhaps Holford can be credited with the appearance of the semi-detached house in Don Mills, a building form used extensively in Britain, but much out of favour in North America.

Hancock considered that he was on a temporary furlough, and that in a year he would return to school. He requested from his Harvard teachers that his work be treated as a credit to his degree work. They demurred. In their opinion, this attempt to establish a new town of a scope not before

Aerial view of Don Mills in 1958, looking south-east, with 6-storey apartments and shopping plaza at centre, and low-density housing at periphery. Photo: CMHC

seen in North America would soon fail, and Hancock would be back to school in a few months. They never thought Don Mills would be translated from paper to reality.

THE PLANNERS' PLAN

The Hancock team set to work developing concepts for the new community. The plan contained five elements that were new and untried in Canada.

First and most important was the neighbourhood principle. The community would be broken into four neighbourhoods surrounding a regional shopping centre. The hub of each neighbourhood was the elementary school. As Hancock said:

The neighbourhood unit in each case is composed of all the elements which go toward making the elementary school the cultural focus. It is felt that with our present day approach to living, the congregating factor between people who live in groups tends to be the elementary school with its related community activities, such as adult education groups, cultural study groups, hobby and horticultural groups, etc. ... To that end the physical plan developed locates the school at the centre of each neighbourhood, the residential street system focusing toward the school with its related playground and open space. Residents then will be conscious of their neighbourhood identity in the overall scheme of the town.[1]

The neighbourhood, although it had its own elementary schools and its own local store and church, was seen as part of a community. The community consisted of four neighbourhoods which found their common tie in the town centre, where one found a high school, a library, regional shopping facilities including a supermarket, a post office and other such services. Thus a definite structure, expressed in physical plans, was proposed.

The second major element was an attempt to separate vehicular traffic and pedestrians. Pedestrian walkways were established throughout the project leading to the centre of each neighbourhood (the elementary school) and to the activities in the town centre. A hierarchy of streets where the function (arterial, collector, local) was accommodated in design was established, a concept new to Canada at this time. There were two arterial roads, Lawrence and Don Mills, which bisected in the middle of the site. This was the only bisection of two streets: the rest were all T-intersections. Collector and local streets were designed in such a way that through traffic would have great difficulty getting out of the maze created. A ring road separated the town centre from the residential areas. With the extensive walkway system and road system which discouraged traffic, it was thought that vehicles and pedestrians would never meet. To emphasize the point, sidewalks were not provided.

The third great emphasis was placed in planning green spaces. In fact, green space was the major design element in the plan, as reflected in the walkway system, the preservation of many mature trees, and the design of the street system to take advantage of the surrounding ravines. Natural topographic features — such as the rolling land in the south-west quadrant — were designed around, rather than levelled, and to some extent dictated the interior road system. The branch of the Don River in the north-east quadrant was to be dammed to provide a small lake for boating and swimming.

Fourth, work opportunities were to be provided for residents of Don Mills. Thus, large areas were set aside for industry where 5,000 or more workers would be employed. This, of course, meant that the walkways would be used not only by school children, but also by residents coming to and from work. Don Mills was not to be a dormitory suburb. To accomplish this, the planners had to ensure that workers could afford to live in Don Mills. Accordingly, the plan called for a mix of housing types at a range of prices. Inexpensive housing — semi-detached two and three bedroom units — was to be available for sale; rental accommodation both at market rates and by way of government subsidy was to be provided, as well as more expensive housing.

Fifth, great consideration was to be given to architectural and other design elements. In order to ensure a high standard of design, all houses would have to be built by architects approved by the company, and only approved materials could be used. Colour controls would be used to help ensure that the new community had its own special feel in the early stages until residents could impose their own sense of community.

In concept, the plan for Don Mills was revolutionary for Canada. As *Architectural Forum* said, ''The new town of Don Mills is a planner's dream coming true.''[2] This was the first serious attempt to design a real community in a comprehensive way.

Looking back, it is easy to notice some assumptions that are not valid. For instance, Don Mills was not seen as a commuter suburb of Toronto. It was to be a community that was generally self-sufficient. Don Mills was never planned to be a housing estate for upper income people. Instead the planners specifically attempted to ensure that housing was available for all types of people, with all ranges of income. Don Mills was not designed to serve the automobile. The pedestrian's interest was considered paramount, with automobiles being accommodated almost as a necessary evil. The design and colour controls were intended not to dominate people, but to help create a sense of place that people might relate to in the early years. After all, given the choice of house builders or architects deciding on design, materials, and colours, isn't it reasonable to prefer architects?

The approach to house forms was of great significance to the feel of Don Mills, even though it has now become traditional in present day suburban development.

Hancock shunned the North York minimum lot size of 40 by 125 feet in favour of a wider squatter lot of 60 by 100 feet. This allowed him to erect a detached house, set widthwise to the street. The idea of putting the house broadside to the street was relatively new to Canada, and is probably the most noticeable aspect of suburbia. Why was it done? Hancock provides some clues in an article he wrote in 1954:

For single-family houses, lots are designed wider and less deep than is usual in most subdivisions. In the opinion of the designer, elbow room is a desirable characteristic and allows for increased spacial interests and an ability to site houses both broadside to the street and with the narrow dimension to the street. In many subdivisions, too, the rear portion of the lots is poorly maintained and a burden to the homeowner. The more square lot gives insulation between houses...
Because the houses are small, open planning has been encouraged in order to increase the visual space within the units. Individual lot widths have been made an average of 60 feet in order that more space will be provided between the housing units. With more land immediately surrounding the houses, design sitings were directed toward a better use of this land and a closer contact with the land.[3]

21

Don Mills 1949, looking west across Don Valley, with Don Mills Rd. and Lawrence Ave. E. intersection at upper left.

Don Mills 1970, from similar vantage point, with Don Valley Parkway in foreground, and Don Mills Plaza at upper left. Photos: *Boomtown Toronto.* D. Kirkup 1970

It is interesting to note that such an influential decision was made for such value-laden reasons. More practical reasons could have been cited for the choice. First, wide lots allowed everyone to have a separate driveway. No longer would it be necessary to impinge upon one's ownership by having to share a mutual drive. Similarly, the rear lane concept, used extensively until the Second World War in most cities, could also be seen as giving a lack of clarity of ownership. Second, this form of house design helped provide a distinctiveness for Don Mills, important in attempting to market housing in the new community. Even the semi-detached houses employ the same broad-sided approach, although on smaller lots. Third, the wider lot allowed a house to be built with more windows, more natural light. Thus a smaller house could appear to be larger than it was.

Another remarkable feature of the houses is that few were of two-storey design. In most cases they were a ranch-style with a full basement. Since the earliest houses built were modest (1,000-square foot dwellings were common), the planners were attempting to give people basements that could be converted into real living space either as extra bedrooms (the basements were not entirely below grade) or recreation rooms.

The townhouses and apartment units had the same ranch style look about them. This was partly due to the 35-foot height limit the North York Council had imposed on the township, but mainly due to the design approach used.

Design controls went beyond residential units. They applied to industrial buildings (where again an architect was required — something unheard of), and to the shopping centre.

In sum, the plan was very idealistic. It incorporated the best thinking of the day, thinking that was, above all else, directed at providing the best living and working environment possible.

THE CORPORATE STRATEGY

Hancock himself describes the aim of Taylor's company best:

It is the aim of the Development Company to create under the free enterprise system, an integrated new town which will satisfy the requirements of private development and which will also be in accordance with the best principles of town planning. In view of their long-range interest in this project, the Development Company is particularly conscious of the need for long-term worth in such a development.[4]

The question that faced everyone involved was whether good planning was compatible with good business. In the long term, as Hancock notes, the marketability of Don Mills depended on the plan

making sense. If it didn't then there would be no market three or four years later.

Taylor recognized early that the key was control of land prices. The best way to keep control of those prices was by attaching conditions to any land disposed of. Thus, in selling serviced industrial lots, the company wrote in a first option to repurchase for 20 years. If the construction of the factory was not started within three years, then the land would revert to the company at the original selling price.

In regard to residential land, the situation was more complex. Originally Taylor had wanted one contractor to build all the houses: this would allow the development company itself to market the houses and capture any increases accruing because of the success of the project. However, the planning team convinced him — and in fact the lack of any sizeable house building firms in Canada dictated it — that a great variety of builders should be used in order to achieve reasonable diversity in the new community. A strategy had to be devised to keep land prices in the developer's control.

The model used was to sell a few lots to a builder by agreement of purchase and sale requiring 25 per cent down, the balance due in 18 months. This meant that mortgage problems were minimized for the builder, providing he built and sold immediately. It also meant that if the builder's performance was unsatisfactory, then the company could intervene and ensure that the same builder did not get invited to take another ten lots next year, or if he did, then on different terms.

This arrangement had added benefits for the company. Marketing was a responsibility of the builders. Not only would they compete among themselves (in all more than 50 building firms were used), but these firms would not build anywhere else in Toronto in a manner that would be prejudicial to the Don Mills market. As well, the small firms, rather than the company, could arrange their own mortgage financing during construction and for the new owner.

While these benefits meant that the company had to do little of the hard slogging in order to increase land values (which were simply skimmed off), the company did not stay totally aloof since it had an interest in ensuring houses were sold. Two methods were used to help market the product.

First, a large scale model was developed, showing where every road, house, factory, and other building would be. The model was detailed enough to show trees liberally sprinkled across the site. Prospective buyers and mortgage lenders could see for themselves how the plan fitted together.

Second, the company established a mobile information office which moved from site to site as development proceeded. Tied to this was a promotional campaign funded equally by the company

Don Mills 1954, looking east on Lawrence Ave. E., to intersection of Don Mills Rd. Note new Don Mills Information Centre at north-east corner. Photo: Sammon Collection, Toronto Public Library Archive

and the builders by lot levy. As well, the company had its own public relations firm which helped trumpet the good news about Don Mills in the media.

As for the shopping centre, that was a business that Taylor understood well. After his experience with the York Mills Plaza, his strategy was to never dispose of the land. Accordingly, he built all the buildings and leased them out to main tenants, basing rents on gross sales.

The corporate plan was widely successful. So successful, in fact, that in 1955 Taylor began acquiring 6,000 acres of land west of Toronto for the mammoth Erin Mills development which by 1976 was only half built. And, as we shall see, by 1955 the corporate plan overtook the planners' plan, and imposed its own imperative.

The diagram on this page puts the Don Mills plan in graphic form: a town centre at the intersection of Lawrence Avenue East and Don Mills Road surrounded by low-density houses. The breakdown in land use was as follows:

Schools	95 acres
Churches	17 acres
Parks (including a private golf course)	367 acres
Residential	794 acres
Commercial	61 acres
Industrial	310 acres
Public utility and undeveloped	35 acres
Street allowances including railways	374 acres
	2,073 acres

The residential acreage contained 8,121 housing units, of which 4,500 were apartment units. Altogether some 29,000 people were to live in Don Mills. They were served by eight elementary and three secondary schools, as well as nine churches of various denominations.

The town centre containing 36 acres of land (including a curling rink and an arena) operated as a regional shopping centre, with the usual paraphernalia of uses. The shopping centre was planned for two levels, but in fact the second level was never completed. The area within the ring road north of Lawrence consisted entirely of small apartment buildings. Originally the plan called for corner stores and some 17 acres of land were set aside for their development. However, tenants could not be found to operate the stores and they were never built.

On the 310 acres of industrially-designated land (mostly to the south), there are a total of 2.5-million square feet of floor space. This means the floor space index for industry was about 0.2, indicating that factories are set among acres of grass and trees. In all, a total of 63 industrial firms employing 4,500 people are located in Don Mills. Three-storey apartment buildings "buffered" housing from the industry.

Don Mills was built over a period of nine years, beginning in 1953 with the first housing units being made available early in 1954. Following is a summary of the residential program on a cumulative basis:

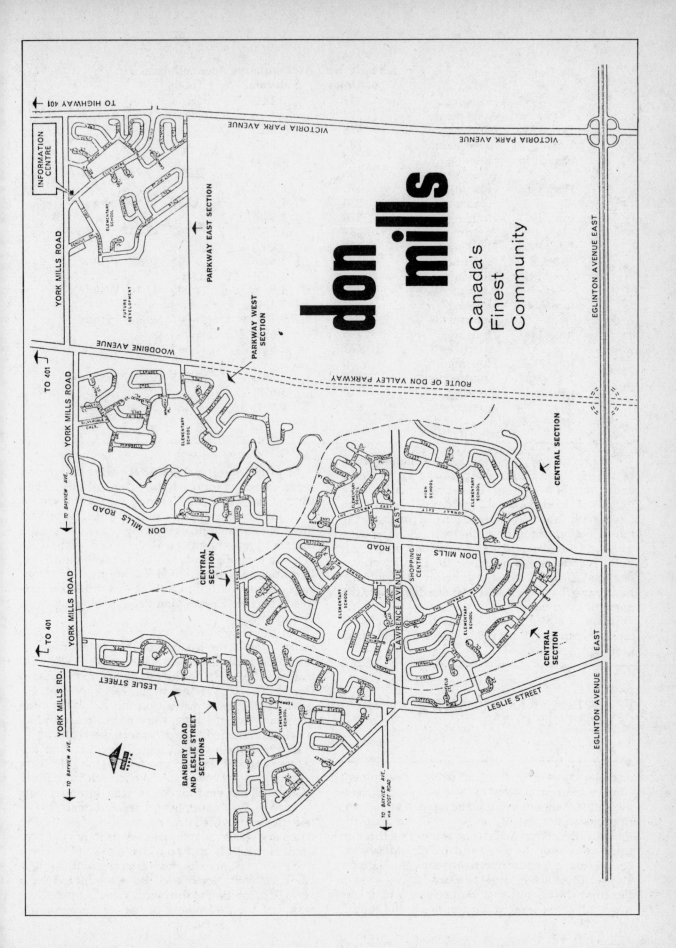

By Date		Yearly No. of Units	Accumulative Sub-total	Accumulative Totals	
Dec. 1953	Housing	144	144)		
	Apartments			144	504 people
Dec. 1954	Housing	658	802)		
	Apartments	287	287)	1,089	3,811 people
Dec. 1955	Housing	732	1,534)		
	Apartments	406	693)	2,227	7,794 people
Dec. 1956	Housing	470	2,004)		
	Apartments	330	1,023)	3,027	10,594 people
Dec. 1957	Housing	376	2,380)		
	Apartments	59	1,082)	3,462	12,117 people
Dec. 1958	Housing	620	3,000)		
	Apartments	563	1,645)	4,645	16,257 people
Apr. 1959	Housing	50	3,060)		
	Apartments	200	1,854)	4,905	17,166 people
June 1960	Housing	374	3,434)		
	Apartments	328	2,173)	5,607	19,625 people
June 1961	Housing	186	3,620)		
	Apartments	641	2,814)	6,434	22,519 people
July 1962	Housing	0	3,630)		
	Apartments	869	3,683)	7,303	25,561 people
Ultimate	Housing	0	3,620)		
	Apartments	818	4,501)	8,121	28,426 people

The private golf course occupied some 140 acres, which left about 240 acres of parkland for residents and workers. Adjacent to every school was a neighbourhood park, and residential areas were laced with walkways (since turned over to the municipality) leading to the schools. The lake proposed for the north-east quadrant never got built. It appears this branch of the Don River was dammed further to the north before the company had begun to make plans to install a dam just to the north of Lawrence.

Today, the plan is so ordinary that it elicits almost no response. But in 1952, it was breaking new ground.

FROM PLANNERS' PLAN TO CORPORATE PLAN

A major concern of the Don Mills Development Corp. was to ensure that the site was properly serviced. Most important, the site needed some connections to the rest of the metropolitan area: the tenuous link of Don Mills Road wandering through the Don Valley to the south and the York Mills Road connection to the north were not enough. Plans for a major Toronto bypass — Highway 401 — were in the final stages, but that expressway was to the north. Hancock wanted connections to the south.

As usual, municipal politicians were obliging in regard to access routes. In the spring of 1953, when Metro Chairman Fred Gardner[5] turned the sod for one of the new industries in Don Mills, he opined that Metro should do everything it could to ensure that Eglinton Avenue was extended easterly in order to provide access just to the south of the site. In spite of Gardner's good intentions, this extension did not get built until the early nineteen sixties, when the Flemingdon Park development was under way.

But there was better luck with connection due south. One of the first items of business the new Metro Council discussed was the Don Valley Expressway, coming up the ravine just to the east of Don Mills. This expressway was approved expeditiously, and construction followed. Thus the necessary external links were put in place by the newly-established Metro Toronto government.

In 1950 North York Council decided that developers would have to pay for internal servicing arrangements in major subdivision schemes. Since Metro was not yet formed, external arrangements — such as water supply and sewage treatment — had to be provided by the township itself. The company was in some quandary as to how to proceed. North York had no water supply of its own, and did not want to finance water trunk-line extensions. As well, North York did not want to fund a sewage plant. Part of the North York Council's fear was that the assessment of the new community would not fund the debt.

A deal was struck. The company would build the sewage treatment plant. (It cost $1.25 million, and was located where the lake had been planned.) As for the water service, the company would buy North York bonds in order to finance the trunk lines. Funds would be placed in escrow by the company to meet the debt service on the bonds in the event the assessment was insufficient to do so.

As it turned out, the funds in escrow were returned to the company. The promised assessment split of 40 per cent industrial/commercial, 60 per cent residential was generally met. Credit for this goes to Carl Fraser. He was able to entice industry to the area beyond everyone's expectation. To some extent he was helped by the earlier decision of IBM to establish its Toronto plant at the corner of Eglinton and Don Mills Road, just to the south of the site. By 1952, IBM had completed a $1.5-million plant, and in 1953, that company began a $2.0-million expansion. By 1953, Fraser had brought in firms that were already putting the finishing touches to the factories. Few of these industries were linked to the Argus group, Taylor's powerful holding company.

Schools had to be provided in the new community. These again were matters of great cost to the municipality. In order to make things a bit easier the company provided a cash grant which allowed the first school to be built. The company used the same controls on resale. Usually, the company sold the land on the condition that the school board was "bound to use said land only as school and playground and not for any other purpose including industrial or commercial purposes." As well, excavation could only occur for a school building and, except for that excavation, no other sand, soil, or gravel could be removed. The third condition was that the school board was not allowed to cut down a living tree unless it was in the area to be excavated.

While the company claimed that it sold school land at cost, one search indicates that land purchased by O'Keefe Realty for $500 per acre was sold to the North York Board of Education for $6,000 per acre some four years later. The company retained the first option to re-purchase for 20 years, and required the Board of Education to build within three years. After the first school was under way, it seems the company had the school board hooked, and no concessions by the company were required: the board could be treated like any other purchaser.

Residential construction began in 1953. Early on, there were problems with the builders who resented having to hire architects, and have their designs and materials approved by the company. As well, mortgage lenders were wary about the new community concept. But as the development began to catch on, the criticism vanished, and both builders and mortgage lenders became cooperative.[6]

Of course, there were interesting sidelines. Taylor disliked blue shingles, and they were excluded from the acceptable colour guidelines. In at least one instance, the architects recommended materials which were supplied only by a non-Argus controlled building contractor. (Argus Corporation had a good share of the building supply market.) Taylor bought out the competitor whose goods the architects were recommending. In all probability Taylor-controlled companies benefitted from Don Mills (one of the first examples of vertical integration in the building industry). But this was probably not planned by Taylor as the way to make the big money: it was simply a happy coincidence.

The north-west quadrant was the first to be developed, and the planners' ideas were followed closely. For example, the edge of the ravine was not occupied by luxury housing, but rather by semi-detached houses, so in the planners' terms, as many people as possible could enjoy the ravine.

But there was consternation over the question of whether good planning was good business. When Carl Fraser died of a heart attack at a board meeting in September 1954, Taylor looked for a replacement who would be hard-headed, with a good business sense, someone who might control the idealism of the planners. He chose Angus McClaskey, then regional manager for Central Mortgage and Housing Corporation.

Taylor need not have worried. The development was proceeding well. But since the opportunity to increase profits was apparent, Taylor took it, even though it interfered with the spirit of the plan. For instance, the company decided not to fight when North York objected to the building of two-bedroom houses. The planners had wanted to have them built so that it was clear housing was readily available to factory workers.

Similarly, the company decided not to conclude an agreement with CMHC for low-income housing. CMHC wished to rent townhouses from the company at $67.50 a month, and then subsidize the rents of those who lived there. The company refused to rent the houses for less than $75.00 a month. Negotiations broke off, and the company rented the houses on the market for more than $100 a month.

The house market was booming. When in the mid-nineteen fifties CMHC removed the funding limit and size restriction on new houses, as well as requiring larger down payments, the company responded by increasing the size of houses, and increasing the price of lots. Taylor's strategy for increasing profits by controlling land had worked. His company had established a valuable commodity in Don Mills, and he had no intention of stifling the market because of the planners' concepts of a heterogeneous community. The following chart gives an indication of price increases as the new community became a success.

Year	No. of Units	Price Range of Don Mills Houses	Average Sale Price of Houses in Toronto (MLS)
1953	144	$12,500-$16,000	$14,400
1954	658	$13,714-$16,000	$14,600
1955	732	$15,000-$45,000	$15,000
1956	470	$17,000-$45,000	$15,000
1957	376	$17,000-$65,000	$15,700
1958	620	$15,000-$26,000	$16,100
1959	50	$15,000-$26,000	$16,600
1960	374	$17,000-$27,000	$16,300
1961	186	$22,000-$45,000	$16,300

Thus the plan was changed, mainly because it was successful beyond anyone's expectation. The intention of providing housing for 50 per cent of the work force was never realized because the market, rather than the plan, became the dominant factor. Today, for instance, less than 5 per cent of the Don Mills work force is resident in Don Mills. With its success, the company was able to forgo other amenities — particularly those of a recreational nature — which it had planned. The corporate plan superseded the planners' plan.

In 1956, Hancock and a number of his associates left the company to form Project Planning Associates, where they could (and did) offer their planning services to the world.

DON MILLS ACROSS CANADA

It is difficult to overestimate the influence of Don Mills on urban development in Canada. Don Mills defined the basic design elements and the business practices now used in contemporary suburban developments. While certain direct refinements have taken place, the form has remained relatively constant.

Some direct descendants of Don Mills are Erin Mills, Meadowvale, and Bramalea, all in the Toronto area; Bow River in Calgary, and Kanata in Ottawa.

Perhaps of more importance is the direct descendant of the Don Mills approach: Canada's suburbia. It is, after all, difficult to assemble very large chunks of land where a new community can be planned by just one development company. Instead, the usual occurrence is for the large developers to own patchwork quilts of one- or two-hundred acre holdings. In this situation, the initiative for an overall plan comes from municipal or regional planning staff. The plan produced is usually a replica of the Don Mills model, altered slightly to accommodate local conditions and individual land holdings.

One good example of this is in Scarborough, a borough within Metro Toronto, which has been divided into communities modelled after Don Mills. For instance, the recently approved Milliken plan (see attached sketch) mimics Don Mills in a sad way. Note the town centre, the ring road, the townhouses buffering the single-detached homes from the highrise apartments and shopping plaza in the town centre. To the east and west of this 1,000-acre parcel are industrial areas. Yet the Milliken plan is no different than the plan for other blocks of Scarborough, where the land mass is divided arbitrarily in communities, each with their own town centre, each with their access to industry.

When the chunks are smaller, and no "community plan" is possible, the ghost of Don Mills still appears. Roadways follow their meandering patterns (even if they do so at the expense of topography), house forms remain similar, and the feel is the same.

The similarities are not difficult to spot since the principles underlying suburban planning remain constant. The following planning principles are worth noting as being common to almost all suburban development since Don Mills:

(i) The planners attempt to devise a residential/industrial assessment split that allows them to consider the new community as somewhat self-sufficient in theory, if not in practice. Thus the new approach of "comprehensive planning" usually includes swatches of industrial land, even if it is not marketable. But while an assessment split is planned which would produce the required number of tax dollars at a reasonable mill rate, if the industrial land is occupied, this assessment split does not allow residents of the new community to work within the community. In almost every case the price of housing is such that an ordinary worker in the local factory could not afford to live there. Thus the assessment split never leads to self-sufficiency.

(ii) Developments are planned with open space as the predominant design element. Thus sites are laced with walkways, bicycle paths, and other forms of open space. Grass is everywhere — around schools, churches, highrise apartments, and roads. So much so, in fact, that one senses land is deliberately being underused.

(iii) A grid system of roadways, the predominant design element in Canadian cities, is never used. Instead, there is a hierarchy of roads separating traffic functions. Arterial roads usually define the boundaries of the site, while the interior consists of a maze of cul-de-sacs and languidly meandering collector and ring roads.

Only non-residents cars are treated like a necessary evil. The design of the roadway system prevents the outside world from intruding into the suburb. But the function of the automobile to drive

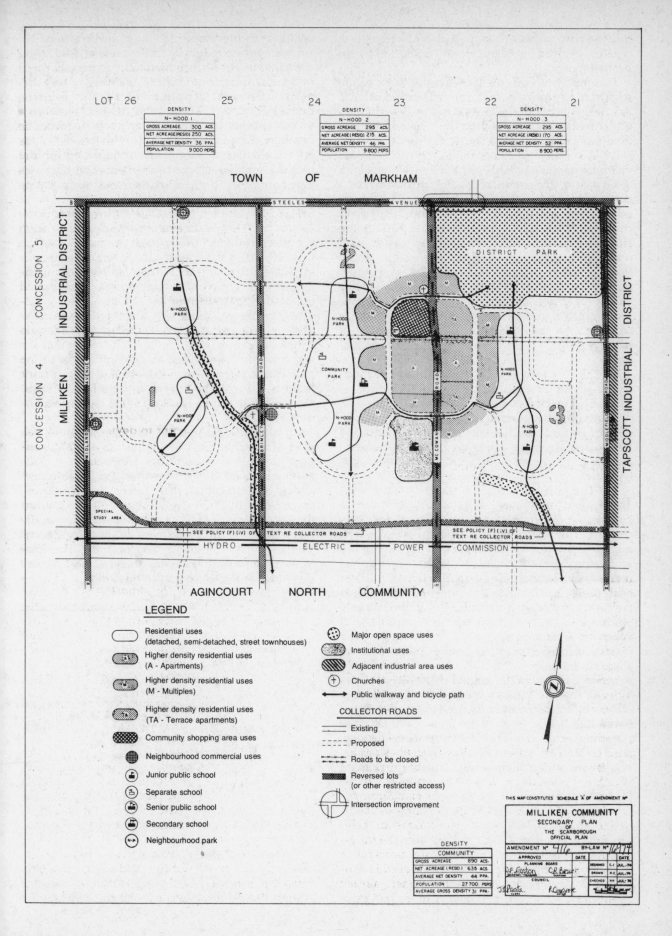

LOT 26 25 24 23 22 21

DENSITY	
N-HOOD 1	
GROSS ACREAGE	300 ACS.
NET ACREAGE (RESID)	250 ACS.
AVERAGE NET DENSITY	36 PPA.
POPULATION	9 000 PERS.

DENSITY	
N-HOOD 2	
GROSS ACREAGE	295 ACS.
NET ACREAGE (RESID)	215 ACS.
AVERAGE NET DENSITY	46 PPA.
POPULATION	9 800 PERS.

DENSITY	
N-HOOD 3	
GROSS ACREAGE	295 ACS.
NET ACREAGE (RESID)	170 ACS.
AVERAGE NET DENSITY	52 PPA.
POPULATION	8 900 PERS.

TOWN OF MARKHAM

STEELES AVENUE

DISTRICT PARK

CONCESSION 5 — INDUSTRIAL DISTRICT

CONCESSION 4 — MILLIKEN

TAPSCOTT INDUSTRIAL DISTRICT

N-HOOD PARK

COMMUNITY PARK

SPECIAL STUDY AREA

SEE POLICY (F)(iv) OF TEXT RE COLLECTOR ROADS

SEE POLICY (F)(iv) OF TEXT RE COLLECTOR ROADS

HYDRO ELECTRIC POWER COMMISSION

AGINCOURT NORTH COMMUNITY

LEGEND

- Residential uses (detached, semi-detached, street townhouses)
- Higher density residential uses (A - Apartments)
- Higher density residential uses (M - Multiples)
- Higher density residential uses (TA - Terrace apartments)
- Community shopping area uses
- Neighbourhood commercial uses
- Junior public school
- Separate school
- Senior public school
- Secondary school
- N-P Neighbourhood park

- Major open space uses
- Institutional uses
- Adjacent industrial area uses
- ⊕ Churches
- ⟷ Public walkway and bicycle path

COLLECTOR ROADS

- —— Existing
- - - - Proposed
- Roads to be closed
- Reversed lots (or other restricted access)
- Intersection improvement

THIS MAP CONSTITUTES SCHEDULE 'A' OF AMENDMENT Nº

DENSITY	
COMMUNITY	
GROSS ACREAGE	890 ACS.
NET ACREAGE (RESID)	635 ACS.
AVERAGE NET DENSITY	44 PPA.
POPULATION	27 700 PERS.
AVERAGE GROSS DENSITY	31 PPA.

MILLIKEN COMMUNITY
SECONDARY PLAN
OF
THE SCARBOROUGH
OFFICIAL PLAN

AMENDMENT Nº 416	BY-LAW Nº 16974
APPROVED	DATE
PLANNING BOARD	
COUNCIL	

29

into the city, to drive to shop, to drive to recreation centres, is clearly recognized and provided for in profusion.

To emphasize the disdain for the automobile within the suburb, houses rarely front on arterial roadways. Instead, the arterial roadways are lined with highback fences, as though the arterial had no function except that of a traffic artery.

(iv) All of the new comprehensively-planned developments have what is euphemistically called a town centre. This centre is usually surrounded by a ring road system within which is a regional shopping centre and high-density housing, usually in the form of highrise apartments. Just outside the ring road system are blocks of street townhouses (row housing) which "buffer" the single family housing from the town centre. The new town centre usually fails to work as such: it is simply a collection of non-residential uses required to provide minimal support services: a supermarket, a restaurant, a few small stores, a high school, a library, perhaps a small office building, a gas station.

(v) The structure usually consists of a "community" made up of a number of "neighbourhoods." The neighbourhoods contain about 6,000 persons, and are centred around one or more public schools, which, in turn, are flanked by a neighbourhood park. This structure exists on paper, but not in reality. Attempts are made to enforce the community feeling by assigning a name to it.

(vi) The house forms in all these developments are similar: split-level, detached houses with a sprinkling of attached houses (either as semi-detached or row housing), plus highrise apartments. There is a strong separation between types of persons who are allowed to live in various places. For instance, single-family housing is not designed to accommodate either roomers or other tenants. Tenants are expected to live in the highrise apartments. Every housing unit is equipped with space for an automobile.

(vii) Business practices have become more sophisticated since Don Mills. Now, an extremely detailed agreement is signed between the developer and the builder specifying when houses will be built, materials to be used, sale price of the house and land, design of the house, and all other relevant matters. The contractual relationship pursued in Don Mills has been superseded by an arrangement where the builder is little more than an agent for the developer, although he is responsible for selling the product he builds. The builder is in a difficult situation since his ability to make a profit is so circumscribed by the controls of the developer. The only opportunity for profit lies in the house being built. Accordingly, there is a tendency to cut corners on construction work in order to generate extra cash. In Ontario, this has led to the enactment of legislation which requires the builder (not the developer, who to all intents and purposes is responsible) to provide a two-year warranty on the new home.

Hard services within the site are provided by the developer. This requirement when originally set in the mid-nineteen fifties was probably seen by municipalities as a way of having someone else pay for necessities. In fact, it has helped permit the large firms, which have easy access to capital, to totally dominate the market.

Marketing practices appear to follow the Don Mills model: part of the advertising costs are paid by the developer (in plugging the development as a whole) and part are paid by the builder (in hiring real estate agents, and advertising his specific homes). Usually the developer pays for the information booth which is set up at the entrance to the new suburb.

It is remarkable that no planning models other than Don Mills exist for suburban Canada. The example of the city, with its compactness and diversity of uses, its grid system, and flexible residency arrangements, has never been followed since Don Mills. One attempt at a different direction — Le Breton Flats in Ottawa — is now under way, but it is an experiment funded by Central Mortgage and Housing Corporation. The Don Mills model was snapped up quickly, and followed slavishly, and the city got left behind.

---

1. *RAIC Journal*, Vol. 31, 1954, p.3.
2. *Architectural Forum*, June 1954, p. 148.
3. *RAIC Journal*, Vol. 31, 1954, p.3f.
4. Ibid.
5. The Municipality of Metropolitan Toronto, a regional government under the guise of a federation of municipalities, was formed January 1, 1953. Metro is responsible for major transportation services, including roads and expressways.
6. See *The Canadian Architect*, March 1956, p.24f

Why suburbia hasn't worked

John Sewell

Suburbia is inhabited by ordinary people. Like most Canadians, suburban residents try to make ends meet and have aspirations for greater economic security and a happier life. The sociology — and the social problems — of the suburbs have attracted a good deal of attention from academics and journalists. Much of this work has made the error of attributing all the characteristics of suburban life to the suburbs, instead of recognizing that people often have problems no matter where they live, and that new settlements take a while to begin to function normally. More serious is the fact that the analysis of the suburbs has concentrated on real or imagined social problems, and ignored the political and economic problems generated by the suburban development pattern for suburbanites and for other urban residents. Some of the problems deserve specific consideration.

THE ECONOMIC AND SOCIAL PROBLEMS

1. High house prices

The cost of housing is increasing dramatically throughout Canada. Since almost all net new housing is being provided in suburbia, it is fair to say that the cost of suburban housing is the major determinant of prices in the housing market generally.

An analysis by a development industry consultant (see figure 1.) indicates the degree of change in house prices and in who can now afford to buy a new house funded under the National Housing Act.[1] What is noticeable from the chart is that while 28 per cent of income earners could afford to buy an NHA house in 1961, by 1971 the figure had dropped to 11 per cent. It is clear that many people are being excluded from the market.

Government figures arrive at the same results. The Government of Ontario in its booklet *Housing Ontario 1974* states:

The income distribution for all 2.3 million households in Ontario in 1972 was such that one-fifth (459,000) of all households had income of less than $5,000. The second fifth (379,000) had incomes between $5,000 and $8,000. The middle fifth (499,000) was between $8,000 and $11,000. The next "quintile" (488,000) was between $11,000 and $15,000 and the top fifth (444,000) of households had incomes in excess of $15,000.[2]

It is difficult to believe — but nevertheless true — that in 1972, only one-fifth of all households in Ontario had incomes over $15,000. In 1976, one-fifth of all households in Ontario had incomes of over $18,000 or $19,000. In other words, 80 per cent of the households in Ontario had incomes of less than about $18,500.

How much income do you need to buy a new house in the suburbs? The general rule of thumb goverments use is that people should spend about 25 per cent of their income on housing. With that assumption, a family with an income of $25,900 can afford to pay $62,000 for a house; a family with an income of $16,000 can afford to pay $39,000 and a

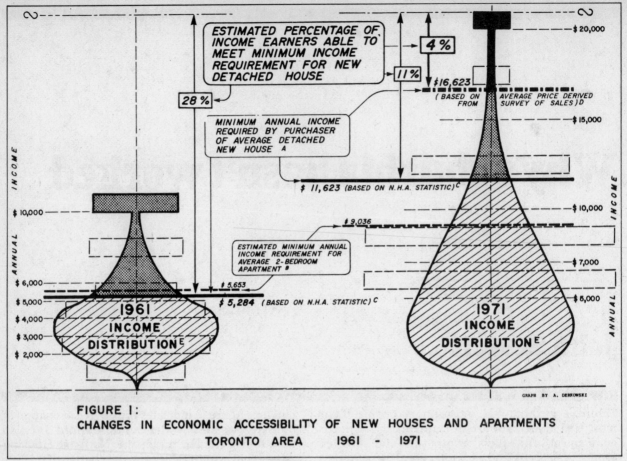

FIGURE 1:

CHANGES IN ECONOMIC ACCESSIBILITY OF NEW HOUSES AND APARTMENTS
TORONTO AREA   1961 - 1971

family with an income of $12,300 can afford to pay $30,000. Obviously, some people are willing to scrimp and save so they can buy a home and such people will put 30 per cent or 35 per cent of their income into housing expenses; families with low incomes find that unless they put 40 per cent or 45 per cent of their incomes into paying for housing they simply won't have anywhere to live.

Using the 25 per cent guideline, here are the incomes required for the new suburban housing at the price levels prevailing in Toronto, other southern Ontario centres, Edmonton, Calgary, Vancouver, and Victoria in 1976:

	Purchase Price $	Annual family income required $
Detached	75,000	30,000
Semi-detached	62,000	25,000
Row	60,000	22,000

It is clear that this new suburban housing cannot be afforded by the vast majority of people. In fact, it is only the top half of the top fifth of the population that can afford to buy this housing. Almost 90 per cent of the households in Ontario are excluded from the new urban subdivisions, and the same figure applies in many other large Canadian cities.

Thus, very few people can afford the benefit of new suburban housing. So the first and most direct problem of the suburbs is that housing there is too expensive. New houses at $60,000 are simply beyond the means of most people.

2. The missing amenities

If you wish to go anywhere in the suburbs, you usually have to drive. This is true even though the major design elements of suburbia, as we have mentioned before, are the open space elements such as parks and walkways. Quite simply, things are spread out so much that it is a long walk to almost any destination you can think of. A quart of milk requires a drive or a long walk. Going to the library is the same, just as is finding nearby recreational opportunities. One development in the Toronto area, Markham Woods, advertises itself as "The community where kids can walk to the hockey rink." The advertisement indicates the difficulties that there are of residents being able to get places without using a car.

It is also difficult to discover informal meeting places in the suburbs. Usually there is one restaurant and one main supermarket and a few other small stores in the "town centre." But a hotel or tavern where one can sit with neighbours and drink is rare — particularly since you will have to drive to get home. These small amenities, taken for granted in cities and towns, are simply not present in suburbia. The result is that people are more

The bland strip retail suburban shopping centre, providing fast service and convenient access by car; at once a retail focus and social vacuum. Photo: Robert Hill

isolated from one another and have to establish formal links, like going to church, in order to get to know neighbours.

As well, it is usually a long way to get to work. People are forced to drive to work, not only because neighbours work in different parts of the metropolis, and therefore can't drive together, but also because public transit cannot adequately serve suburbia.

Suburbia is short of the amenities one expects in an urban area. For people who have difficulty in finding the time or money for an extensive social life, it does not work well.

3. Nowhere is somewhere

A marketing strategy used by the development industry in selling suburbia is the device of putting a name on the new community to indicate that the prospective home buyer will live in a special place. There are three categories of marketing names used. One category attempts to define the new housing as part of a town or village, the second tries to make the development sound like an old English town with a great deal of privacy, and the third attempts to indicate that the house is set well into the country and is surrounded by hills, ravines, rivers, and quite possibly rabbits, foxes, owls, and

beavers. If it were not so sad, it would be laughable. The following names were taken from a Toronto newspaper in March 1976:

Villages
Camelot Village
Johnsview Village
Olde Towne
Village on the Green
Village 77
English towns
Cobble Hill Estates
Millway Gate
Country Club Estates
Glen Leven Estates
John's Gardens
Cedar Mills
Lynde Gardens
Waterdown Estates
Greenmount Gardens
Parkwood Gardens
Country living
Woodstream Meadows
Tall Trees
Erin Mills
Dorset Place
Harbour Hill
Whiteoaks
Seven Oaks
Humberview Hills
Forest Hills
Waverly Hills
Churchill Downs
Thornton Woods
Milton Meadows
Queenston Villas
Woodlands
Meadows of Manvers

But the prospective purchaser gets none of this. Instead he gets a house much like every other suburban house on a street much the same as any other suburban street. The specialness of a house has been reduced to its carpeting and perhaps the colour of its walls. Given the high cost of the house, not only has the homeowner nothing unique, he probably does not even have the security of owning much of what he's bought.

4. Open space that can't be used

Residents of suburbia often think they are surrounded by open space. In one respect this is true: the land is sparsely occupied. But, on the other hand, what real open space is there? Most houses are placed directly in the centre of the lot, with a back yard and front yard of similar size. The two side yards of a 5 or 6 foot width cannot be used for much of anything. It is difficult, for instance, to install a swimming pool or establish a vegetable garden, without eating into the space required for outdoor living.

And, while streets are very wide, there is little that can be done with the space on either side of

Suburban land is under-utilizied because of excessive setbacks and wide lot widths. Note left-over "grass island" in center of curve of road. Photo: Robert Hill

them. Tradition prevents people from actively using the front yard, with its large street allowance in front of the 20-foot minimum setback, and a further five-foot boulevard thrown in. The same is true of the setbacks for schools, or factories, or apartments. The space is so poorly distributed that it is open but of little value.

THE PROBLEMS OF MUNICIPAL GOVERNMENTS

If suburbia has these serious problems for the people who live there, why do municipal governments continue to permit their kind of development with no real effort to change or improve it?

What is it that local government sees in suburbia that allows this development form to be used in an unending fashion? Do the benefits of suburbia to the municipality outweigh the disadvantages to ordinary people? Is suburbia the best form of development to satisfy the requirements of local government?

In fact, suburbs cause problems for municipalities and for all urban residents.

1. Assessment

The example of Don Mills indicated that the development form was thought to be satisfactory if a residential/ industrial split of 60/40 were maintained. It was expected that this would ensure that the residential units did not end up costing the municipality money and that any deficit would be compensated for by the industrial assessment.

Unfortunately, no studies have been done to suggest that the 60/40 split is appropriate. Perhaps 50/50 would be satisfactory, or perhaps 70/30. No one seems to know for sure.

But there are problems with continuing this approach. In fact, these are now revealing themselves where municipalities find their industrially-designated land is remaining idle, and factories built speculatively sit vacant. In Metro Toronto, some 20-million square feet of factory space (that is about 10 per cent of all industrial space) is vacant.

Mail delivery by "suburban service" means a half-mile walk to gang-boxes serviced by private contractors, because the Post Office does not provide door delivery to areas outside regular postal districts. Photo: Robert Hill

Industry is simply not developing to the levels expected. The example of Ontario is instructive in this regard.[3]

According to a recent study by the Ontario Government, in 1951 almost 55 per cent of all employment was in manufacturing and construction, whereas in 1971, this figure had dropped to 40 per cent. Indications are that service employment will continue to grow as a percentage of total employment, and industrial employment will drop. This means than an Ontario municipality's ability to attract industrial assessment to offset low residential assessment has decreased and will continue to do so.

The assessment issue can be looked at in another way. A recent study has been done by the Region of York, just to the north of Toronto, on the financial impact of new suburban communities.[4] The study was specifically directed to the financial ramifications of a provincial housing policy which encouraged low-cost housing by means of various types of government assistance to the developer, the homeowner, and the municipality. Even with all these forms of assistance, the study concludes that each new dwelling built under Ontario Housing Action Program will produce a deficit in tax dollars for the period from 1976-1981. The size of the projected deficit is somewhat frightening. In constant 1974 dollars, the deficit would be a high of $535 per unit in 1976, and a low of $337 per unit in 1981.[5] The Don Mills model was followed with each development, save for the exclusion of industrial uses.

What this means is not that the form of development helps the municipality in its attempt to raise the great sums of money to fund the municipality at a reasonable mill rate; rather, that every housing unit actually costs the municipality money and mill rates must be increased to a level that is probably politically unacceptable. From the point of view of local government, every new suburban house adds to everyone's tax bill.

It would be interesting if cost-benefit studies were undertaken for suburban developments in the same way as they have been undertaken for development alternatives in the city. What the York study seems to indicate is that, from a financial point of view, suburban development is extremely costly for municipalities and taxpayers.

2. Support costs

Maintaining municipal services in suburbia is an expensive job. The crunch really comes in the "soft" services field. Take, for instance, the protective services of fire, ambulance, and police. Each of these functions usually relies on a response time, i.e. if a call is received about a fire, then the fire truck should be on the scene of the fire within three or four minutes. To ensure that this happens, fire stations must be distributed in such a way that the response time is met. Response time does not relate to the number of people who live within the response boundary, but rather to the size of the area. The response boundary will be about the same whether there are 15,000 people living within the boundary, or 5,000. The same is true for police and ambulance services.

The difference, however, comes in per capita costs. If the cost of the fire service in the response boundary is $20,000, then if 10,000 people live within the boundary the cost is $2.00 per person, whereas it is only $1.00 per person with 20,000 people. While the lower density might require slightly lower service levels, in a metropolitan area there is a tendency to ensure equality of service.

A similar situation prevails for "hard" services. Regardless of density, a six-inch water main must be provided for fire fighting purposes, even though a typical suburban street might require only a two-inch service for all residential needs. On a per capita basis, hard service costs are high in the suburbs.

The same situation prevails for facilities which are not highly used because of low population densities: libraries, parks, sports facilities, etc. In many cases, municipalities charge fees in order to allow suburban residents to participate in publicly-run recreational programs. The fee helps to cover a cost which could not be garnered from taxes because tax rates are already high enough. In the Borough of Scarborough, to use a Toronto example, the municipality has decided that local residents must be responsible for equipping local parks with whatever swings, teeter-totters, etc. are demanded by children. Thus the community spends much time and energy fund-raising for expenses that would normally be funded through property taxes.

Maintenance costs of suburbia are higher than people would like. Local government tries to mitigate these costs by raising money in ways that appear less onerous than the property tax, although their effect is probably just the opposite.

From a municipal standpoint, there is probably a density at which services are most economical. Densities that are too high or too low create problems of their own. The low density areas of suburbia increase the costs of municipal government for all taxpayers, suburbanites and urbanites both.

3. Transportation

Perhaps the most significant problem posed by suburbia for government is transportation. Many residents work in downtown offices, some others work in offices not in the downtown, and a few might work in scattered factory buildings. The major transportation need relates to those working in downtown office buildings.

Of course the most efficient and economic form of urban transporation is public transit. This is argued from both an environmental and an economic point of view. Public transit requires enough people going in enough directions in any one time period to make the transit viable economically. Money is supplied both by riders (in the payment of fares) and by government grants. Experience indicates that the fares collected from suburban public transit are so small that massive government grants are required in order to keep a suburban transit system afloat. Unfortunately, few studies are available which give any hard data on this point. However, in the City of Toronto a major transportation study undertaken by Metro and the Provincial Goverment[6] indicated that each suburban rider was subsidized to the tune of $75 per year by each city rider.

In the past, two-zone systems were used in Toronto requiring suburban residents to pay a double fare in order to reach the downtown area. The double fare helped to compensate for the long distances travelled. However, after suburban representation increased in regional governments, the double fare system was abolished. Transit systems in many Canadian cities have found themselves facing major deficits.

In Metro Toronto, for instance, from its formation in the 1920s until 1970, the Toronto Transit Commission paid for itself out of the fare box. The effect of serving suburbia has been dramatic, and in six short years, the TTC deficit has jumped from nil in 1970 to $42 million in 1976. The deficit is a direct result of attempting to provide transit services to the suburbs.[7]

Experiments have been tried in providing transit for suburbia, the most notable of which in Toronto was Dial-A-Bus. In this arrangement, a prospective rider would call bus headquarters and request a bus which would pick him up at his home within 10 or 15 minutes. A flat fee of 50 cents or 75 cents was charged and the rider would be delivered to a subway station. This experiment proved to be extremely costly, with a deficit of approximately $1.75 per rider. Attempts to provide fixed route services and services on demand have both proved to be equally expensive.

It is easy to see why this problem arises. Densities are such that there are simply not enough people living in any particular locale to allow a transit system to work efficiently.[7] Suburban densities range from 15 persons per net residential acre to about 50 persons per net residential acre. Given that a great proportion of the people are housewives or children, who do not travel regularly, the potential ridership is extremely low. As well, the distances to be travelled are very great and

The empty bus in suburbia: a vicious circle of low density, few passengers, enormous deficit, and thus massive subsidies from tax dollars. Photo: Robert Hill

the time involved in a common conveyance vehicle, stopping and starting every two blocks, means that journeys are time-consuming.

Thus suburban areas have usually turned to the automobile as the only viable method of transportation. It allows people a great deal of flexibility in getting where they want to go and its public costs are related only to the capital expenditures and maintenance costs associated with those roadways. The real costs involved in private transportation are paid for by the automobile owner: fuel, insurance, depreciation, and automobile maintenance. Individuals seem much more willing to bear high costs for something they own and control than they are for a public service which in the end might be cheaper.

However, the use of the private automobile leads to the demand for newer and wider roads and for urban expressway systems. These expressways are usually oriented to the place where most people want to go, downtown. Both for the suburban resident and the suburban politician there is no question but that the automobile is the only reasonable way of transporting suburbanites. Public transit is simply too expensive, too infrequent, and too uncomfortable in relation to the private automobile.

This analysis leads to the conclusion that as long as suburbia remains in its present form, all the goodwill in the world will not get people out of their automobiles and into transit. For the suburbanite, public transit doesn't work.

THE EFFECT OF SUBURBS ON CITIES

Suburbs have their implications not just for suburbanites and for municipal governments. They also have a powerful effect on overall urban form: on the rate at which cities use up agricultural land, on the ways in which "urban" land is used or underused and on the density and form of the rest of the city.

Segregation and isolation of land use in the core areas of Canadian cities compounds problems of accessibility, and ultimately eliminates cultural activity during non-business hours. Photo: *Toronto Past and Present* D. Kirkup 1973

There are clear and distinct differences between the form of development in the last 20 years, and the form of urban development in the first half of the twentieth century. For instance, residential densities of the suburbs are much less than the densities of the city cores. Figures that are available for Metro Toronto clearly indicate the extent of the differences. The population per square mile in Metro Toronto as of 1971 averaged 8,633 persons. In the City of Toronto, which is the portion of Metro developed largely before the Second World War, the density is 19,000 persons per square mile, whereas in Etobicoke, a suburb within Metro, largely developed between 1945 and 1970, the density is only 5,908 persons per square mile.[8]

But suburban industrial areas are equally low-density. New industrial estates developed in suburbia have a square foot index of 0.2; for every 10 square feet of land there are only 2 square feet of floor space. This is visible in the extensive green space and parking lots surrounding new industrial buildings in the suburbs, and in the fact that al-

most every new industrial building is only one storey high. In the central city, industrial buildings often have three or more floors, and no green space to speak of. In central Montreal and Toronto, developers are now beginning to build relatively high industrial buildings — 10 or more storeys.

Along with the clear differences in land use densities, the mixture of uses one associates with the city is simply not present in the suburbs. In many inner-city neighbourhoods, there are corner stores; small factories in back lanes; apartments over stores; row houses; semi-detached houses; small apartment buildings; institutional uses. This jumble of uses is what Jane Jacobs praises in both *The Life and Death of Great American Cities*, and *The Economy of Cities*.

In the suburbs, as we have seen, uses are isolated and each has a special place. Some people claim that this means that suburbs are uninteresting and that they will die unless a greater mixture of uses occurs. In fact, the specialization of land use in the suburbs leads to a specialization of land use in the city centre, and perhaps the decline of the city centre itself.

In a landmark study, *The Pickering Impact Study*, the Toronto architectural firm of Diamond and Myers portrayed the problem of specialized uses.[9] The study concludes that the special uses of suburban land for housing and industrial purposes leads directly to a specialization of land use in the central core for office purposes. Further, the specific forms of housing provided in the suburbs (mostly for families) in turn leads to specialized use of residential land downtown for single persons. The study, which also dealt with the effects of the then proposed Toronto Pickering Airport as well as the then proposed North Pickering Community, ends on a note of despair:

The tendencies described in this report exist. They need to be arrested. The construction of the proposed North Pickering Airport and town will only reinforce the tendencies the city wishes to avoid, which are:
- *concentrating office specialization in the core area;*
- *segregating the city into special use areas;*
- *hastening the movement of industry out of the city;*
- *eliminating moderately priced housing and decreasing home ownership;*
- *decreasing densities over the entire urban area;*
- *squandering the use of serviced land;*
- *increasing the problems of accessibility, commuting times and congestion in the core.*[10]

The exact relationship between density or the intensity of land use and land specialization is not entirely clear. It would appear, however, that the less intensely land is used, then the less likelihood there is of a jumble of different activities.

Suburbs can, in fact, be redefined as urban sprawl; controlled sprawl, certainly, but sprawl nevertheless. Suburbia is based on the under-utilization of land accompanied by a specialization of use. Put into these terms, it is easier to see that suburbia is not just an opportunity gone wrong, but actually the cause of many urban problems. Suburbia might have been an appropriate experiment in the case of Don Mills, but the fact that the experiment was highly profitable to the corporate developer should not have meant — even though it did — that Don Mills would be repeated monotonously across Canada to enrich the development industry, leaving urban and suburban residents

and municipal governments to deal with the consequences of this pattern of development whatever they proved to be.

---

1. This chart is taken from *Residential Land Development in Ontario*, prepared for the Urban Development Institute of Ontario, November 1972.
2. *Housing Ontario 1974*, Government of Ontario.
3. *Ontario's Future: Trends and Options*, Ministry of Treasury, Economics and Inter-Government Affairs, March 1976. The information is cited in Table 8.
4. *The Financial Impact of Short-Term Action Housing Programs*, Regional Municipality of York, January 1975. This study was undertaken by Stephenson & Kellogg.
5. The analysis related to two proposed suburban neighbourhoods: Pine Valley Village, a development that would house 20,000 people on 1,000 acres of land, and Milliken Mills, a site of just under 1,000 acres, that would house 22,800 people.
6. *Metropolitan Transportation Plan Review*, 1975. This study consists of 64 volumes and analyzes the major transportation problems and probable solutions in the Toronto area. It is commonly referred to as the Soberman Report, after the director of the study, Richard Soberman.
7. A new study by an American organization, Regional Plan Association, has recently been released, as reported in Regional Plan News, August 1976, No. 99. It notes that suburban densities of seven units per acre can adequately support bus service every half hour — provided there is a government subsidy over and above fares, of 50-75 cents per rider. The study is entitled "Where Transit Works: Urban Densities for Public Transportation." It appears that the problems in the United States are significantly more severe than in Canada.
8. *Soberman Report No. 64*, p.8. This table also compares the density of the central portion of American cities. The following figures represent the population per square mile in the central portion of these cities: Baltimore — 11,568; Boston — 13,936; Chicago — 12,283; Cleveland — 9,893; Detroit — 10,953. It is interesting that the density of the City of Toronto proper is much greater than that of American cities. No one would claim that Toronto proper was overcrowded.
9. *The Pickering Impact Study*, prepared for the City of Toronto Planning Board, June 1974.
10. Ibid., p. 261.

Alternatives to the suburbs

John Sewell

Are there alternative ways in which cities can grow that are more attractive economically, politically, and socially than suburbia? The answer is, of course, yes. The more difficult question is to determine what changes are needed to bring about a switch from suburban to alternative models for city expansion.

Suburbia is now under attack on two fronts, each of which contains the elements of a new approach to development.

CHEAPER HOUSING

One of the attacks is over the matter of house prices. This has been a major concern of ordinary people for many years, but only recently has information been gathered in a systematic fashion, and theories developed which account for the problem.

On the one hand are studies by the Urban Development Institute (usually undertaken by Andrzej Derkowski) and Central Mortgage and Housing Corporation (The Spurr Report)[1]. While UDI claims that high prices are mainly a function of insufficient supply of land caused by the intricacies of a bureaucratic approval process (the "red tape" explanation), Spurr appears to place more emphasis on the high resale prices demanded for older homes. Spurr commits the error of thinking that high house prices arise from the prices demanded by individuals selling *existing* houses on the market

alone, and ignores the crucial role in overall housing supply of the quantity of *new* houses placed on the market by the development industry and the supply and pricing policies followed by the few large corporations that dominate the supply of new lots and houses in most cities.

On the other hand are the theories of James Lorimer, which are based on the documentation found in the Spurr Report.[2] Lorimer theorizes that high housing pricing is a direct result of the control of land by a handful of large companies which control the market in order to maximize profits in both the short and long run. This approach appears to be borne out by the history of Don Mills, where the developer consciously followed policies regarding the quantity of lots supplied and lot pricing to maximize both profits and house prices.

Any attack on house prices ends up being an attack on suburbia, even if it appears at first glance to be peripheral to the question of suburban form. Outrageous prices demand an alternative.

The second approach to the high house price problem relates to the cost of servicing suburban land. In 1973, the Government of Ontario released a little-noticed study[3] which analyzed how servicing requirements might be reduced in order to lower the cost of the hardwear that is buried in suburban land. Like studies of the late nineteen forties and early nineteen fifties, this approach addresses itself to a reduction in construction costs. But it also hints at the necessity for alternatives to suburbia.

Two recent studies have tied together the problems of servicing costs and house prices. Although one study was commissioned by the Ontario

41

Ministry of Housing, and the other by the Urban Development Institute, both argue that it is time to develop a new urban form rather than continue with Don Mills-style suburbia.

The Ontario government study concludes as follows:

(i) Significant cost savings are possible using standards already accepted in various parts of the province. Our studies show that savings in the order of $6,000 to $8,000 per lot are possible. These estimates are based on cost analysis using actual plans of conventionally designed subdivisions and comparable designs using reduced standards which are merely a compendium of the most progressive current practice in the province and, indeed, many of which are minimums recommended by the largest mortgagor of subdivision housing (CMHC). Savings of this magnitude could reduce an owner's monthly mortgage payment by $70 or more. Translated to a broader scale it can be conservatively estimated that $100 million could be saved annually in the province.

(ii) While there are significant savings in reduced engineering standards, more rational site planning standards are the key. Of the total savings identified approximately 75 per cent can be attributed to permitting reduced lot sizes – down to 30 x 80 feet for a single, detached dwelling in the major metropolitan areas, and to 30 x 100 feet elsewhere, together with comparable reductions in lots for other house types. Our studies show that such lots can meet CMHC standards for outdoor space and separation between dwellings and also provide a good quality living environment. In fact, compared to conventional practices, our proposed standards and cost comparisons include increased landscaping and privacy screening, more park space landscaped for children's play, and improved control over design and siting of individual units. The remaining 25 per cent of cost savings can be largely achieved through changes in three key engineering standards – the type of storm drainage system, right-of-way and road widths, and finally the method of connecting sanitary sewage and water service to individual lots.[4]
(Emphasis added.)

This second conclusion requires that residential densities in the suburbs be increased. Generally, the proposal is that the conventional suburban density of 6.46 units per acre be doubled to 12.4 units per acre. This would produce slightly under 50 persons per acre, still significantly less than the 80 persons per acre which appears to be the rule in urban areas developed prior to the Second World War. However, it is interesting that the increasing density is seen to be necessary in order to reduce housing costs. The study does not address itself to the larger problems associated with low densities, so it is only a partial answer to the problems of suburbia.

Unfortunately, the Ontario government study repeats all the assumptions of Don Mills: a non-grid street pattern; specialized land use with no mixture of uses; a separation of pedestrian and vehicle through the use of a walkway system. Presumably (although the study does not deal with this) the same type of community and neighbourhood structure is expected to be followed, with land set aside on the fringes for industry. At best, it calls for a refinement of the Don Mills model.

The second study prepared by the Urban Development Institute is entitled *Lowering the Cost of New Housing.*[5] This study takes the view that the property industry has been prevented by government from providing houses for middle income persons. As the foreword notes:

The following development plan has been prepared in an attempt, once and for all, to set the record straight on three counts: 1) the housing development industry's concern about the problem; 2) the industry's clear ability to solve it; and, 3) the industry's clear ability, given a legitimate opportunity to do so within the context of the current housing and land market – and with the only necessary government assistance being a relaxation of some of the key restrictions that have collectively caused the problem in the first place.

The booklet presents a plan for a 200-acre hypothetical site. According to the study:

The plan would achieve three critical objectives, all of which we believe to be socially and economically desirable; 1) produce quality housing at sale prices far below those which must result from today's development requirements; 2) conserve land and restrain urban sprawl through more efficient land use planning while retaining basic environmental amenities; and 3) minimize long-term transportation and other servicing and tax costs to residents, by improving community compactness.

It is notable that the study addresses the very issue that the provincial study misses: efficient land-use planning.

The hypothetical plan proposes a tripling of net residential density from the traditional density of 35 persons per acre to 101.8 person per acre. This is accomplished by increasing units per acre from 9.6 to 30.4. The study makes it clear that, even with this density, no building, including apartment houses, exceeds three storeys in height. The report claims that such a plan could (depending on land costs) allow three-bedroom, semi-detached houses to sell for $36,000 at 1976 land and construction prices.

Again, the Don Mills model is generally adhered to with the dead-end road systems and separation of uses. The site considered is not large enough to indicate whether or not the neighbourhood and community model, along with the town centre, will be pursued. However, given that the form of this community is similar to the Don Mills model, this is probably the case. There are many problems with the study's proposal. Units are relatively small and access to them is poor, problems that might be resolved if a grid road system was employed along with strip shopping.

However, given these limitations, it is clear that the report is calling for a significant shift in the design of suburbia. If planners could persuade themselves that they need not necessarily follow the Don Mills model, we would see a totally different approach to providing new housing.

The accompanying chart from the report compares the present form of suburbia with the hypothetical plan:

Figure 2   Site Statistics for Traditional Plan

TYPE OF UNITS	NO. OF UNITS		POPULATION
Single Family	594	50%	2257
Semi-Detached	144	12%	547
Street Townhouses	100	8%	380
Multiple Family	120	10%	456
Apartments	240	20%	720
Total	1198		4360

Length of Street   24,820'

ACREAGES

Residential (Single Family-Semi-Detached)	106.5
Street Townhouses	6.1
Multiple Family	8.0
Apartments	4.0
Schools	12.1
Parks	10.0
Watercourse	12.8
Church-Highway Commercial	2.0
Roads	38.5
Total	200.0 AC

Unit Gross Density	6.0 u.p.a.
Population Gross Density	21.8 p.p.a.
Unit Net Density	9.6 u.p.a.
Population Net Density	35.0 p.p.a.

Park Dedication 5%

Figure 3   Site Statistics for Hypothetical Plan

TYPE OF UNITS	NO. OF UNITS		POPULATION
Semi-Detached	466	14%	1631
Quadruplex	616	19%	2156
Duplex	396	12%	1386
Group Housing	1322	40%	4627
Apartments	511	15%	1278
Total	3311		11,078

Length of Street   22,880'

ACREAGES

Residential (Semi-Detached, Quadruplex, Duplex, Group Housing)	108.8
Apartments	10.4
Schools	13.3
Parks	27.6
Watercourse	12.8
Commercial	1.0
Roads	26.1
Total	200.0 AC

Unit Gross Density	16.6 u.p.a.
Population Gross Density	55.4 p.p.a.
Unit Net Density	30.4 u.p.a
Population Net Density	101.8 p.p.a.

Park Dedication 1 acre for 120 units

Source: *Lowering the Cost of New Housing*

Almost three times as much park space is provided in the hypothetical plan, and much less road space is used. The study proposes reducing the traditional 66 foot right-of-way to 40 feet, with a land saving of almost 40 per cent. If roads operate just as well on 40 per cent less land, won't the same thing be true for factories, schools, and retail stores? The report implies that suburban land is grossly underused.

The UDI approach, in spite of its rather startling conclusions regarding cost and amenities, is traditional. It argues that given more flexibility, more opportunity to do what it wants, the industry can produce housing that ordinary people can afford. It is an argument that has been heard for a long time, and given the industry's domination of municipal and (at least in Ontario) provincial governments, one wonders why the industry doesn't use the power it has to do the things it says it can do.

Neither study approaches the larger questions of social costs and benefits. However, according to our earlier analysis, it would appear that the social costs of the higher-density housing contemplated would decrease significantly, and the benefits might indicate a major turn-around from the Don Mills model.

CONSERVING FARM LAND

The second main area of attack on suburbia has come from farmers and environmentalists. They argue, with considerable support from the public at large, that urban Canada cannot continue to sprawl onto otherwise productive farm land. They have popularized the concept that sprawl must stop. In Ontario these arguments were heard persuasively (in conjunction with other arguments) to stop the federal plans for a Pickering airport. They have also been raised in an attempt to save the Niagara fruit belt. In British Columbia, legislation was passed which tries to limit the extent of sprawl so that farm land is protected.

A few years ago, containment of sprawl was seen as the antithesis of growth, and thus involved a head-on challenge to the economic system. Now the argument has softened somewhat so that the question is one of the form of growth. Since growth in the short term seems inevitable, will we continue to develop in the model of Don Mills? Or will we make better use of land?

THE THREE KEY ASSUMPTIONS

If there are to be changes in the way urban growth occurs, the influence of the property industry in deciding what can or can't be done must be faced. Since Don Mills, the industry has so dominated planning that it has been difficult to make any constructive alternatives which are taken seriously. Thus, the North Pickering Project, Toronto's large public land assembly where the Province of

Ontario could explore new directions, is a 1975 version of the same thing that city has seen for the past 20 years. Before we define alternatives, we must first identify the underlying principles which the industry has ingrained so deeply in us.

The property industry in its approach to urban growth makes three assumptions that we have so far refused to question seriously.

The most important of these is that the city has no limits. Canada is a country where there is almost too much land. While we might object to certain parcels of land becoming part of the city (orchards, ravines, farm land) we rarely question the idea (say) of new cities in the Canadian Shield (Richard Rohmer's Mid-Canada Corridor), since no one sees anything in *that* land that might get in the road of a spreading metropolis.

If the city has no limits, then it is only natural for it to spread out and grow.

This concept, though, is relatively new. Cities used to have walls around them for protection. These established definite and clear limits. Land had to be used wisely since its supply was finite. If densities were too low, then the land would have to be developed in a more rational way to keep the city alive. Alternatively, if densities were too high, and social problems of one sort or another began to develop, changes would have to be made. After all, with a walled city, there was nowhere to escape.

Cities today could use the kind of definite limits to their physical size imposed by city walls, and these limits would be a protection for the people who live in them. Not physical walls, but real limits which could not be changed, lines beyond which development in any form was simply not possible. Not only would such an arrangement force a community to make decisions as to how it would allow its finite amount of land to be developed; it would also mean that municipal government, local decision-making, would have a real and fixed locus.

Developers have sold us a dangerous principle in conceiving of cities with no limits. That idea contains a second assumption of the property industry: there is no such concept as the "appropriate" use of land.

In downtown cores, the large developers like Cadillac-Fairview argue that high densities — both residential and commercial — are dictated by the market. If you want more reasonable densities, then you will have to find land that is priced at a rate that allows it. In the suburbs, no arguments of any substance are made about densities, since the Don Mills model is accepted without question.

In fact, most discussions about the intensity of land use revolve around the cost of the land, not the appropriateness of how intensely land is used.[6] Having accepted the bait, many people argue that the lower the density in the suburbs, the better the development, assuming (as is usually the case) that

land is relatively cheap.

But appropriateness of intensity and use does not relate to land cost: it relates to the final results that one wishes to obtain. In an economy where most important decisions are made by people who are concerned mostly about profits and the ability to generate further capital, public decision-making has little real effect. However, land use planning is supposed to bring other criteria to bear on decisions about land use and densities. Strange that no one dares talk about the appropriateness of land use, even if the attempts to establish proper implementation techniques do not always succeed.

Suburbia represents a deliberate underuse of land, as inappropriate as the severe overuses that occur in city centres. The under-development of suburbia raises complex problems which cannot be readily perceived. Using the "appropriateness" approach, perhaps we can begin to develop solutions that avoid problems rather than repeat the actions which cause the problems. That won't happen until the myth that land use should be a function of land values alone is understood as a rationalization by the property industry for making profitability the only criterion for development decisions.

The third assumption is that the country can be assumed into the city. One manifestation of this assumption is the countrified names given to new subdivisions. Another is the idea, rarely challenged, of the satellite city, the new community (Don Mills is a good example of 20 years ago) that will either be linked to, or appended to, the city.

It is a subtle concept. It contains elements of the ideas of Ebenezer Howard and Frank Lloyd Wright which attempt to tie together the city and the country. It leads to the belief that four houses on an acre of land is somehow "better" than 15 houses, perhaps for the same value-laden reasons Macklin Hancock used to explain house design and lot size in Don Mills.

The development industry has employed the muddled distinction between city and country to great effect, although it is hardly noticed. The best example of the industry's diligence is seen in the leapfrog use of land. This occurs where development proceeds first on the portion of land owned that is most distant from the urban fringe, and slowly the land in between is built up. Whereas the strategy behind the technique is to either ensure or increase the value of the land leapfrogged, the strategy takes on a respectable air as we somehow assume that the new development is closer to being part of the country.

The Toronto area has a number of examples of leapfrogging: Meadowvale, which is sold as a suburb in the country, when in fact it is simply the development of the most distant portion of a very large land assembly; and the North Pickering project. The latter is fascinating, since it is to be built

More housing on developer-owned land, now at a higher density, but still based on the Don Mills model — this is the solution proposed in the UDI study *Lowering the Cost of New Housing*, Toronto, 1976. Photo: UDI

on land assembled by the government of Ontario. Provincial reports make it clear that the major purpose of the proposal is to attract development to the east of Toronto. While rural aspects of the proposal are prominent (keeping working farms and long-established towns), the idea of a satellite Don Mills-type community is really what is intended.

Acceptance of these proposals stems from the acceptance of the belief that the country can be assumed into the city. The country/city muddle has confused the judgements that are made about this matter.

The three assumptions — that the city has no limits; there is no such concept as "appropriate" use of land; the country can be assumed into the city — are very deeply ingrained and are rarely made explicit.

They are pushed by the development industry for good reason. As Taylor learned in Don Mills, giant profits come from making farm land part of the city. That can only happen if assumptions such as the above are generally accepted. If the city had limits, then the amount of farm land available for speculation and ultimate development would be limited, and that limits profits in the long run. Given that Erin Mills in Toronto was purchased a full 15 years before it was developed, and that it is still only half completed, one can realize the time frame that the industry has in mind.

If land had to be used at an "appropriate" intensity for housing, industry and other commercial uses, in all likelihood most suburban densities would have to increase. The growing population of cities would be accommodated on less land than is now being gobbled up. That, too, would reduce long-term profits to be made by the large corporate property owners since they would own a relatively small fraction of the land whose densities were increasing.

If ever the decision (which seems inherent in the concepts of both Howard and Wright) was made that there is a clear distinction between the city and the country, then the problems inherent in all of the Camelot Villages, and Cobble Hill Estates and Woodstream Meadows of Canada would not be tolerated. We would reject these approaches in the same way that many of us reject highrise apartment towers as the sign of a healthy city.

The three assumptions are key to the operation of the property industry and its continued ability to turn farm land into part of the urban complex. Because of the relatively few numbers of companies which control suburban and other land on the fringes of the city, those companies can proceed at their own speed, in ways they want, to ensure maximum profits in the long run. While they could sell more houses today by increasing densities slightly, that is not in the long-term interest of the industry.

And in this, of course, lies the absurdity of the UDI report. Given the control of the industry over local councils, it would be easy enough for planning criteria to be changed to accommodate experiments. Given the desire everyone has for cheaper housing, it would be easy for the industry to change the rules in order to produce it. However, both points run contrary to the imperatives of the industry, and will be implemented only if the industry sees no alternative ways to protect its preeminence in the urban growth process.

ALTERNATIVES: START WITH REASONABLE HOUSE PRICES AND LIMITS TO URBAN GROWTH

The important question is not *how much* growth, but rather *what kind* of growth for Canadian cities. Attacking suburbia as a symbol of growth will attract little public support, and in fact will not help to clarify the argument.

Instead, the keys to a successful critique of the status quo lie in the questions of city limits and housing costs.

The second matter, housing costs, appears to be a subject of great public interest. If that interest can be harnessed, then alternatives to suburbia can begin to emerge in a popular way.

The secret of Don Mills, after all, was that gigantic profits lay in the land. If land could be controlled, then the industry would fare well. As the Spurr report points out, a few large firms control almost all of the land on the fringes of almost all Canadian cities. Using data collected by Spurr, Lorimer estimates that in the Toronto area alone, annual profits made by turning farm land into subdivisions exceed $150 million.[7]

Public land banking does not reduce these profits to any noticeable degree so long as the public

land bank supplies only a small percentage of the total number of new lots developed in an urban area. As Spurr shows in his exhaustive review of all public land banking in Canada, this is true in almost every case — Saskatoon, Red Deer, and Hamilton are the only notable exceptions. Now that the industry controls the suburban land market, it sets the prices. Nor will a tax on speculative profit be of much use. In Ontario, the Land Speculation Tax Act, enacted in 1974, has been extremely ineffective. In 1975 a mere $2 million was collected by way of this tax throughout the province. Speculation, it seems, is difficult to define in a manner that produces tax revenues.

The only reasonable course to control suburban land prices and profits is to allow governments to expropriate land at purchase price as of some day, say June 1976. In fact, to soften the blow, one could include a small profit on equity invested (say at 10 per cent) so that the developer/investor would consider an investment in land as no better or worse than, say, an investment in Canadian Savings Bonds. This type of approach would make it perfectly clear that the housing industry was not to be allowed to use farm land as the way to develop massive profits.

An expropriation act set in these terms would end the dreams that the industry has of continuing to build Don Mills again and again.

Support for such a legislative change would not be difficult to muster. Community groups, and social planning groups throughout Canada would seize on any reasonable opportunity to significantly reduce housing costs. As we have noted, in the late nineteen forties, the land component was some 10 per cent of the purchase price of a new home. It now amounts to 40 per cent or more. An approach such as the one outlined here would put land in its proper perspective.

But simply allowing a government to own developable land, even if purchased at a reasonable price, isn't good enough. Ontario's North Pickering Project is the best example of this fallacy. Governments, too, are caught in the Don Mills planning model, and somehow must be shaken from it.

The only reasonable course of action is to set firm and distinct limits to cities, limits that will not be transgressed. As noted earlier, support for such a move is developing among farming and environmental organizations.[8] The setting of limits will develop slowly, as orchards or ravines or marshes are under attack. But the concept of limits can be furthered if people in cities begin to define them geographically, and then begin to use energies opposing servicing schemes designed to open up more of the hinterland.

Without such limits, the suburban form will continue with all of its drawbacks.

Of course, there are variations on these approaches. They will arise from local conditions, just as the political pressure that is mounted will depend on the politics of the particular community. Attacks on suburbia, and the keys to its demise, lie in removing the profit element from land development on the fringes, and defining in clear and absolute terms what the limits of the city will be.

---

1. Peter Spurr, *Land and Urban Development* (Toronto, James Lorimer and Company, 1976). This study was originally completed for CMHC in 1974.
2. James Lorimer, "Their Land, Your Money" and "Your House and Native Land," *Weekend Magazine*, May 22 and 29, 1976.
3. Recommended *Guidelines for Residential Servicing in Ontario*, Ontario Housing Advisory Committee, December 1973.
4. *Urban Development Standards, A Demonstration of the Potential for Reducing Costs*, Ontario Ministry of Housing, March 1976, p. i-ii.
5. *Lowering the Cost of New Housing*, a report for the Urban Development Institute, prepared by John Bousfield Associates and Paul Theil Associates Ltd., 1976.
6. In its recent report, the Science Council of Canada states: "Despite its obvious shortcomings, we persist in the myth that the 'market place' is always the best means of determining our priorities." The Council urges higher densities for suburban land. See *Population, Technology and Resources*, Report No. 25, p. 40-41.
7. See brief by James Lorimer to the Bryce Commission on Corporate Concentration.
8. Farming organizations pose a problem, since farmers are after the goodies of high land prices to compensate for the low incomes they have received. This problem must be resolved.

Bibliography

Materials referred to in the text:
Carver, Humphrey, *Houses for Canadians*. Toronto: University of Toronto Press, 1948.
Central Mortgage and Housing Corporation, *Post-War House Building in Canada*. Ottawa, 1951.
Faludi, E.G., ed., *Land Development in the Municipal Area of Toronto*. Toronto: Toronto Real Estate Board, October 1952.
Hodge, Gerald, "Subdivision Activity in the Periphery of the Toronto Urban Field," in *The Form of Cities in Central Canada*, L. Bourne, ed. (Toronto: University of Toronto Press, 1973).
Hancock, Macklin and Douglas Lee, article in *Journal of the Royal Architectural Institute of Canada*, Vol. 31, 1954, p. 3f.
"Business Builds a City," *Architectural Forum*, June 1954.
"The Architect and the Merchant Builder," *The Canadian Architect*, March 1956, p. 24.
Urban Development Institute of Ontario, Andrzej Derkowski, consultant, *Residential Land Development in Canada*, a submission to the Premier of Ontario, November 1972.

Ministry of Housing, *Housing Ontario 1974*. Government of Ontario, 1974.
Ministry of Treasury, Economics and Intergovernmental Affairs, Regional Planning Branch, *Ontario's Future: Trends and Options*. Government of Ontario, March 1976.
Regional Municipality of York, Stevenson and Kellogg, Ltd., consultants, *Financial Impact of Short-Term Housing Action Programs*. Newmarket, Ontario, January 1975.
Municipality of Metropolitan Toronto, Toronto Transit Commission and Ontario Ministry of Transportation and Communications, *Metropolitan Toronto Transportation Plan Review*. This study in 64 volumes was published from 1973 to 1975 and headed up by Richard Soberman.
Sewell, John, "Commuter Set-Up Knocks the TTC to its Knees," *Globe & Mail*, Toronto, August 16, 1975, p. 7.
City of Toronto Planning Board, Diamond and Myers, Architects and Planners, *Pickering Impact Study*. Toronto, June 1974.
Derkowski, Andrzej, *Costs in the Land Development Process*. Toronto: Housing and Urban Development Association of Canada, December 1975.
Ministry of Housing, Local Planning Policy Branch, *Urban Development Standards*. Government of Ontario, March 1976.
Science Council of Canada, *Population, Technology and Resources*.
Resources. Report No. 25, Ottawa, July 1976.
Bousfield, John Associates and Paul Thiel Associates Ltd., *Lowering the Cost of New Housing*. Urban Development Institute, 1976.
Spurr, Peter, *Land and Urban Development*. Toronto: James Lorimer and Company, 1976.
Lorimer, James, "Their Land, Your Money" and "Your House and Native Land," *Weekend Magazine*, May 22 and 29, 1976.
Ministry of Housing, *Recommended Guidelines for Residential Servicing in Ontario*. Government of Ontario, December 1973.

Other material of interest:
Carver, Humphrey, *Cities in the Suburbs*. Toronto: University of Toronto Press, 1962.
Hancock, Macklin, "Planning Progress in Canada," *Town and Country Planning*, 1952, p. 279-283.
Pressman, Norman E.P., "Planning New Communities in Canada," a paper delivered at the School of Urban and Regional Planning, University of Waterloo, November 1974.
"Start Made on Don Mills Development," *Industrial Canada*, April 1953.
"Industry in a Planned Community," *Plant Administration*, April 1953, p. 57.
"Don Mills 'Today's New Town'," *Town and Country Planning*, Vol. XXIX, No. 2, February 1961, p. 66f.
Plantown Consultants Ltd., *Community Design: New Towns Reviewed*, a study for the North Pickering Project, Ministry of Housing, Government of Ontario, June 1974.
"Where Transit Works: Urban Densities for Public Transportation," *Regional Plan News*, No. 99, August 1976.

47

Housing and land:
Two sides of the story

James Lorimer

Land and Urban Development: A preliminary study by Peter Spurr. James Lorimer & Company, Toronto, 1976, 438 pp. Paper $6.95, Cloth $16.

Costs in the Land Development Process by Andrzej Derkowski. Housing and Urban Development Association of Canada, Toronto, 1975. $10.

In the last three years there has been a price revolution in housing in Canada. Construction costs for the average NHA detached house have risen substantially — by 7 per cent in 1972, 14 per cent in 1973, 27 per cent in 1974 and 18 per cent in 1975. In four years they have gone up 67 per cent. Land prices have risen even faster, and account for a growing percentage of the final price of a new home. There are no reliable and useful indicators of new house lot prices by city, so examples have to serve. At the beginning of 1974, a 50-foot lot in Calgary was selling for $9,000. By the end of 1975, the price was $20,000 and rising. In Toronto, a lot in a new subdivision inside Metro was selling for $11,000 in 1972. In 1975, the price was $36,000.

This price revolution follows a reorganization of the housing and land development industry which began in the 1950s and gathered momentum in the 1960s. In the years just following the second world war, suburban lots were produced by municipal governments (who opened up new land with streets and services, charging the cost to new homeowners through local improvement taxes) and houses were built by large numbers of small housebuilders. In most central and western cities, this arrangement has disappeared almost completely. In its place are a few massive corporate land developers who produce house lots out of vacant farmland using their own financial resources, and who also construct a rapidly growing percentage of

the new houses that go up on this land. Once a bastion of small entrepreneurs, the land development and house construction industry has rapidly been integrated both vertically and horizontally. Small firms are being squeezed out, and medium ones are rushing to find a friendly giant to merge with. The structure of industry we will soon have if governments do not intervene is now clear. There will be a few large subsidiaries of foreign-owned multinationals (Genstar-BACM and two or three of the largest British-owned firms), and three or four giant Canadian concerns each linked to one of the major pools of Canadian finance capital. Bronfman family firms will probably emerge as the largest group; the Bronfmans already dominate Cadillac-Fairview, sit on the board of Trizec which is currently controlled by British interests, and have links to medium-sized firms like S. B. McLaughlin Associates.

As Peter Spurr correctly notes in his report, now published in book form under the title *Land and Urban Development: A preliminary study*, all this has happened with remarkably little concern being shown by government bodies with some responsibility for the industry. There has of course been some work done by independent researchers critical of the industry, but they have been hampered by lack of access to decent data and by a lack of resources as well. Spurr's description of the industry, though it has some analytic weaknesses and though it relies on incomplete data in many places, is a reasonably comprehensive picture of what is happening that includes some discussion of the advantages and disadvantages of corporate concentration and oligopoly in the housing and land development industry. Ironically the research was paid for by CMHC, whose policies permitted and indeed encouraged this concentration apparently with no real consideration of the implications for the public interest, and Spurr's work comes when the process appears to have gone much too far to be reversed.

A DECLARATION OF INTEREST

Before I go further with an evaluation of Spurr's report and to a companion report by Andrzej Derkowski, a declaration of interest is in order. Like many other people, I learned of the existence of Spurr's work from an article in the *Globe and Mail* last September by Graham Fraser. Though the report hadn't been published by CMHC, a hundred copies had been circulated to academics for their comments. It wasn't hard to locate one of those hundred gathering dust alongside lots of other government reports in a Toronto professor's office.

An excerpt of the report was then published in *City Magazine*; some of Spurr's findings were used as the basis for a brief I submitted in December to the Royal Commission on Corporate Concentration; letters began arriving at the magazine and at CMHC asking for copies of the report; and finally urban affairs minister Barney Danson was asked about releasing it at a meeting in North Bay. CMHC remained adamant about not publishing the report itself, but did agree to return all rights to the author. I made an offer to Peter Spurr to publish the report exactly as it was, using the same typescript that had been the basis for the many bootleg xerox copies being passed from hand to hand across the country, and he accepted. Publishing the report is doing CMHC's work for it, a function which was also performed a few years ago by Alan Samuel of the firm of Samuel, Stevens and Hakkert when he brought out Michael Dennis and Susan Fish's *Program in Search of a Policy*, another major research paper CMHC tried to keep under wraps. My decision to publish the report might be seen as an indication that I agree with its analysis and findings. Not so. It arose out of a much simpler attitude: that those of us outside CMHC who are interested in this subject should be able to have easy access to Spurr's data and conclusions. Given my own interest in this field, I thought it would be appropriate to write a commentary on Spurr's work and on Derkowski's recent parallel efforts.

PETER SPURR'S DATA BOOK

Peter Spurr accurately describes his work as a "data book", a document "intended to assist others in their analysis rather than propounding any particular conclusion or solution." The information it contains is certainly its strength. Three major related areas are dealt with. The first is the urban development process itself in Canada. Spurr presents a range of statistical information, and identifies what he considers to be the most important trends: the very rapid rate at which the supply of urban accommodation is being expanded; the trend away from low to higher density development in some cities; the move away from home ownership.

The second major subject area is the land development industry in Canada as of 1973. Spurr provides a brief history of the industry, identifies the major firms, provides basic data about their assets, activities and declared profits, identifies ownership where this can be done, and separates the industry into Canadian- and foreign-owned sectors. There is a table listing the land assemblies of these firms city by city. Though it misses some important parcels and has been altered by events since, this is the first comprehensive attempt to show how a few firms already dominate the supply of new development land in many cities, and are likely to increase and extend this domination in the future. There is also the first discussion I know of which deals realistically with the profits from these land assemblies. Spurr shows that, as of 1972-3, speculative profit made up 60-70 per cent of the final price of a house lot in the highest-price cities — Toronto, Ottawa and Vancouver. Supplementing this overall description of the development industry at work are brief accounts of the land market in Ottawa-Hull, Toronto, Kitchener-Waterloo, Winnipeg, Edmonton and Vancouver.

The third major part of Spurr's work deals with public land development activity in Canada. There are comprehensive and exhaustive tables dealing with all public land assembly projects financed through the National Housing Act since this activity began in 1949. Even more interesting are the five case studies of public land banks in Kingston, Peterborough, Hamilton, Saskatoon and Red Deer. It's clear from Spurr's information that public land banks have had a major impact in some cities, whereas there are also cases (Hamilton is one) where major public involvement in the land market has not hindered the private market from pushing prices and profits sky-high.

Spurr is clear-headed and minces no words in much of his analysis of this material. He concludes his discussion of the role of developer assemblies and public planning policies in the Toronto region, for instance, by saying: "This starkly demonstrates the public sector's ability to create monopoly conditions for a few land developers."

Or consider this summary of the way the development industry is changing: "The small builder, revered in the mythology of housing, is an anachronism — the residential construction industry in metropolitan Canada can be recognized as paralleling the structure of the automobile industry during the 1920s, or the aircraft industry in the 1940s.''

WHO SETS HOUSE PRICES?

Given the strength and importance of his data and the clarity of his analysis on some points, it is surprising to see that on a few key matters Spurr comes to conclusions that are quite at variance with his own data and with the obvious facts about how the land market works.

Perhaps the most vital of these confusions concerns the way that house price levels are set in a market. Spurr notes that in most cities sales of existing house units are greater in number than the quantity of new house units coming onto the market, and that existing house prices have been rising faster than new house prices. This leads him to regard the sellers of *existing* houses as the price-setters in the market. As he explains at one point: ''The increasing prices charged by the relatively small proportion of homeowners who sell each year drives up the market value of all houses, new and existing'' (p.48). Somehow for Spurr it is the individuals who have existing houses to sell who set higher and higher house prices. The large development and housing corporations, who have hundreds of units to sell every year in the same market, in his version have no option but to follow along behind these aggressive homeowners in putting prices up.

In a city with little or no growth, there's no doubt that the prices wanted by the sellers of existing houses would be a major determinant of house prices. But in cities where a considerable supply of new housing is required to keep up with demand, where a few large developers are developing much of the land and building a lot of the houses, and where it is these large firms and not individual homeowners selling who have the best feel for the market, it is impossible to believe Spurr's view of the selling homeowner as the price-setter and the development corporation as price-taker. Emphasizing that there are more existing than new houses sold in a year in a particular city ignores the fact that it is the quantity supplied of *new* houses and the prices set for those *new* houses by their developers which determines the tone of the local housing market, and sets the context in which prices will rise, fall or remain constant.

This may seem a relatively obscure and academic point, but it is of some importance because Spurr's idiosyncratic notion of how the housing market works prevents him from seeing the large development corporations using the monopolistic position they have achieved in the land develop-

ment business (a position Spurr himself documents fully) to act in the way all large corporations do: that is, to set high prices that generate excess profits, to supply whatever quantity of output is bought at those high prices, and to use artificially-created shortages and any other possible excuse to put prices up even higher.

Far more plausible than Spurr's analysis is this view which puts the large development corporations in the role of price-setters, and which involves them keeping the supply of lots reasonably close to anticipated demand, putting up prices even further whenever demand temporarily outstrips supply. It leaves the existing house market as one comprised of price-takers, where sellers are scrambling to keep up with the price increases which are going on in the suburbs, and where smart operators like the two real estate agents described by Donald Gutstein in *Vancouver Ltd.** can make a killing by buying underpriced central-city houses and pushing their prices up to a level commensurate with prices of new homes.

Spurr documents the basis of the market power of the large developers. He also points out the enormous speculative profits they are making in their land development activities. But he sees no use being made of their market power by the developers, and he ascribes their monopoly profit to the greed of small-time homeowners selling their present houses.

PROFITS AND TAXES

There are two other flaws in Spurr's otherwise-impressive description of the land development industry. Both have to do with the distinction between the reported and real circumstances of the industry, and result from Spurr repeating uncritically what the industry says about its operations.

The first concerns his discussion of industry profit levels. He compares profits of small real estate investors, which ranged from 50-57 per cent in one study, to those reported by the large public real estate corporations which, he says, ''averaged only 19.2 per cent per annum.'' An examination of several annual reports from such large developers leads Spurr to conclude that on their rental properties these firms have a ''pre-tax rate of profit on gross income . . . in the range of 5-18 per cent and [it] appears to be falling. The pre-tax rate of return on invested capital (not necessarily equity capital) is in the 1-3 per cent range . . . It appears, then, that the corporate strategy for income property is to seek longer term gains through capital appreciation while maintaining the investment through modest current returns'' (p.234). Spurr recognizes the large profits made by these same firms in their

Profits of 20 of the largest land development corporations, 1974

Firm name	Assets 1974	Net revenue	Deferred income tax	Total deferred tax (millions)	Depreciation	"Appraisal surplus" estimate	True profit	Shareholders equity	% return on equity	Income taxes paid*
Trizec	857	6,050,000	6,118,000		6,251,000	20,075,000	38,467,000	110,025,000	34%	264,000
Cadillac-Fairview	921	13,044,000	14,810,000	46.2	6,588,000	34,037,000	67,759,000	118,774,000	57%	440,000
Campeau	422	(8,379,000)	5,668,624	29.5	3,277,000	12,580,000	30,202,000	47,445,000	63%	113,606
MEPC	178	4,731,000	1,756,000	8.9	2.0 (est)	3,875,000	12,438,000	32,290,000	38%	199,000
Bramalea	164	2,447,000	3,135,000	10.0	1.0 (est)	6,352,000	12,934,000	30,777,000	42%	1,100,000
McLaughlin	226	2,254,000	1,777,000	16.9	1,139,000	12,594,000	18,826,000	28,947,000	65%	376,000
Markborough	133	3,528,000	(279,000)	10.1	683,000	7,508,000	11,440,000	34,140,000	33%	4,175,000
Allarco	93	1,489,000	710,000	4.2	1,366,000	1,704,000	5,252,000	14,108,000	37%	140,000
Block	135	3,634,000	877,000	4.4	762,000	5,659,000	10,932,000	21,291,000	51%	2,757,000
Y&R (73)	82	1,581,000	1,515,000	3.4	442,000	1,881,000	4,943,000	18,203,000	27%	(26,000)
Nu-West	138	7,562,000	668,000	4.8	401,000	7,352,000	15,983,000	23,799,000	67%	5,700,000
Orlando	91	1,711,000	1,837,000	8.1	464,000	3,015,000	7,027,000	11,214,000	62%	23,000
Halifax	47	151,000	156,000	.1	384,000	1,102,000	1,793,000	8,372,000	21%	--
Daon	184	3,096,000	3,574,000	8.6	294,000	8,064,000	15,029,000	12,984,000	124%	--
Wall & Redekop	49	433,000	257,000	2.7	369,000	443,000	1,502,000	5,650,000	26%	123,000
Imperial	54	1,222,000	867,000	3.3	23,000	1,378,000	3,490,000	10,482,000	33%	--
Monarch	62	2,308,000	823,000	.8	416,000	3,967,000	6,270,000	14,444,000	43%	1,531,000
Costain	77	2,697,000	1,056,000	4.7	100,000 (est)	4,378,000	8,231,000	10,486,000	78%	2,021,000
Consolidated	91	4,602,000	2,300,000	6.4	233,000	4,028,000	11,513,000	16,385,000	68%	3,100,000
Major	26	1,118,000	224,000	1.8	63,000	1,425,000	2,830,000	4,391,000	64%	--
TOTALS	4,030	55,297,000	47,849,624	195.9	26,245,000	141,417,000	286,860,000	547,187,000	52%	22,036,606

SOURCE: *The Real Estate Development Annual, 1975.* The annual compiles financial statements of public real estate companies. Items in the table were calculated from these figures using the method described in the text.

*Figures in the *Income tax paid* column are based on the figures published in the annual reports of these corporations.

land development operations, but says that these are more than counterbalanced by low returns in rental and other activities. His conclusions about corporate profits: "While land operations are clearly big moneymakers, it appears these large developers have sufficient costs in other sectors that their total returns are relatively modest."

There are three difficulties involved in relying on corporate reports of after-tax profits (which Spurr does) and in concluding that profit rates are modest. The first, a relatively minor matter, is that the conservative accounting practices of these firms lead them to charge a depreciation expense on their rental properties, even though with rising construction costs and high levels of maintenance no such depreciation is occurring. In a survey I conducted of the financial reports of 20 large development firms reporting after-tax profits of $55.3-million, eliminating this non-existent expense added $26.2-million to profit.

The second weakness of reported profits, one which Spurr recognizes but fails to give proper emphasis to, is that no allowance is made in reports of current profits for the increase in the capital value of land owned by these companies. Spurr notes this fact in the passage quoted above, terming it "capital appreciation." Developers themselves are very aware that the land they own is going up in value, and that this increase is not shown on their financial statements. It is termed "appraisal surplus" by the industry. One company, Daon Developments of Vancouver, regularly draws attention to this figure and reports on it separately from its financial statements. Using crude but conservative techniques, I estimated the appraisal surplus for the same 20 firms accruing in 1974 at $141-million.

A third difficulty about the reported profits of land developers is that company financial statements always deduct the income tax which their auditors calculate should be paid on their profits for the year. Yet two major tax loopholes permit most of these firms to pay little or no income tax every year. The tax item in most companies' statements is for *deferred* tax, and deferred tax is the amount that company auditors figure would be paid if the federal government taxed at normal rates and did not allow these loopholes to the industry. I estimated the total of deferred, unpaid income tax for the 20 firms surveyed for 1974 at $46.9-million, and added that item as well to profits.

The result of these adjustments is that companies which reported after-tax profits of $55.3-million in 1974 actually earned total profits after tax paid of $287-million. That is a rate of return of 52 per cent on shareholders' equity for the industry, a figure much closer to the one reported for small investors in real estate.

Had Spurr paid attention to the deferred tax loophole, taken note of the unrealism of depreciation expenses in the current state of the industry, and made an attempt to estimate the value to corporate developers of the increases occurring in the value of their land holdings, he would have reached quite different — and much less sanguine — conclusions about the profitability of the industry. He might also have gone on to note how Ottawa's extraordinarily generous tax provisions for development corporations have greatly assisted in speeding the process of concentration in the industry, and permitted the assembly of the large privately-held land assemblies which he carefully details.

POLICY OPTIONS

After his long analysis of the development process and the development industry, Spurr's discussion of land policy options is rather brief. He pays little attention to the approach of public ownership of urban land, arguing that rents are necessary and without them the economy would break down. He is unhappy about price controls on land. And, extraordinarily enough, he argues against capital gains taxation on land profits without recognizing that the largest operators in the land market, the large development corporations, are currently paying close to a zero tax rate on the enormous profits they are making in their land operations.

Spurr's policy proposal is for public ownership of development land. This would not be for the purpose of reducing house prices — set by individual homeowners, remember, not large developers — but would rather be a method of ensuring that 100 per cent of the speculative profits being made in land development are received by the public treasury. The method of purchase which Spurr suggests is giving public authorities the right of first refusal to buy any development land coming on the market while zoning on all of it is frozen. He estimates the cost of buying in the 1970s all the land needed for urban development in the 1980s at $110-million a year, an amount which is well within the financial capability of Ottawa and the provinces. He admits that this measure will have no immediate effect: "This reform would not improve the land market immediately." But, unaccountably, he goes on to say: "This is not a valid criticism as there is no reform which can meet this criterion."

Spurr thus ignores a most attractive scheme of having an immediate and far-reaching effect on the land market: immediate expropriation by public authorities of the large private land banks owned by corporate developers at cost plus a fair profit allowance of 10 per cent. With such a measure, provincial governments could acquire the best-located urban development land around major cities at prices which would permit the development of lots at no more than one-third their present price in large cities like Toronto, Calgary and Vancouver. Alternatively, public authorities could carry on selling land at its current sky-high prices and collect most of the speculative profit which is now going, virtually untaxed, to a few large development corporations.

Spurr's own policy proposal would have dramatic effects eventually, and offers a medium-term policy to combine with the short-term approach of expropriating the private land banks. Both measures would have a considerable effect in bringing under control the large corporate developers who have achieved their stranglehold on the supply of housing in most medium and large Canadian cities free until now from the kind of scrutiny which Spurr brings to bear on them.

Spurr's work is valuable not so much for its analytic insights; indeed it has to be read with its analytic weaknesses firmly in mind. Its importance lies in exactly the function which Spurr himself claims for it; it is a "data book", a mine of information for all of us who don't have access to CMHC's files and the internal records of large developers. It takes us a long way forward in understanding the basics of this complex, rich, powerful industry.

DERKOWSKI ON LAND SERVICING

Andrzej Derkowski's report titled *Costs in the Land Development Process*, commissioned by the Housing and Urban Development Association of Canada (HUDAC) and paid for in part by the people who funded and then refused to publish Spurr's report, CMHC, is another matter. The ostensible purpose of Derkowski's work is to offer accurate information on the costs of land development, and indeed some useful data are provided. There are, however, some problems with the figures and the content of the report is very much influenced by Derkowski's desire to show that profits in land development are quite modest, that public land banks never do any good and often do harm, that municipalities and government regulation are the real villain behind high land prices, and that the best market is one where businessmen can go about their business free from government interference. The latter is an old song, often sung by the champions of free competition that hide out at Imperial Oil, Inco and Argus Corp., and the only twist in Derkowski's rendition is that he does make plaintive mention of the many small housebuilders that are being squeezed out of existence by the development corporate giants.

Derkowski, like Spurr, looks at the costs and selling prices of suburban house lots in Canada. Spurr offers figures for nine cities in 1972-73; Derkowski analyzes eleven in 1974. The cost figures provided tally reasonably well with each other, and with information available from other sources, but must be cross-checked and verified before they can be used with any confidence for any particular city. Servicing, municipal levies and engineering, planning and surveying consultants cost between $5,750 and $6,300 in most of the cities analyzed. The Calgary figure, for instance, is $6,300, assuming 4.4 lots per gross acre, and that tallies with what I was able to find independently early in 1976 making allowance for almost two years of cost increases.

But Derkowski's servicing cost figure for Toronto, $10,900 per lot or $38,780 per acre, is substantially higher than actual figures of $25,541 per acre in 1975 for the same general area reported in an excellently-documented unpublished study by Region of Peel planners. The Ottawa figure of $11,200 a lot for services and consultants also seems very high in comparison to other cities. The Vancouver figure is $10,800 per lot which might not be unreasonable for hillside development but seems very high for the flat delta lands of Surrey it refers to.

Strangely enough, the cities where Derkowski's servicing costs seem high are also the cities where lot prices in 1974 were high, so the result is to show smaller profit margins than probably existed.

Derkowski began his research with some assumptions about profit which tend to minimize the figures he produced. Rather than sticking with a simple measure of the profit involved in buying, holding, and then developing land into house lots he makes a distinction between what he calls "land ownership profit" and "development profit." Land ownership profit is the money you make between the time you buy land for $2,000 an acre in 1964 and the time when the land is worth $40,000 an acre and servicing work is just around the corner. Derkowski doesn't attempt to measure "land ownership profit"; he treats it as a *cost* to his land developer. Peter Spurr points out, and Derkowski certainly knows, that most of the large development corporations assembled the land they were developing in 1974 many years earlier. To exclude the gains made during the time the land was held from a measure of the profit involved in this process has no justification except for its effect of reducing apparent profits. In any case, it is not hard to make allowance for what Derkowski calls land ownership profit in his figures. The simplest way to do it is to assume that the land being developed was purchased in 1964 at $2,000 an acre, taxed at the average rate of $20 per acre per year, with carrying costs totalling $2,000 over the 10-year period. For a 4-lot per gross acre development, that yields an estimate of land acquisition, carrying costs and taxes of $1,050 per lot for the holding period.

Adjusting to include all profit in the figures, Derkowski's costs indicate a profit of $12,200 on a $23,000 lot in Toronto, $6,300 on a $19,000 lot in Ottawa, and $9,500 on a $22,000 lot in Vancouver. For other cities, the profits would range from zero to $2,500, with a maximum mark-up of about 50 per cent on relatively low lot prices. Adjusting the servicing cost for Toronto down to the level shown by the Peel study for 1975, however, adds $3,000 to the $12,200 figure and would increase the Ottawa and Vancouver profits by a similar amount. That is $15,200 per lot for Toronto, not far from the $17,200 per lot figure indicated by Spurr's 1972-73 analysis. It confirms that total speculative profit on land in 1975 was running at two-thirds of the price of a lot for developers who assembled when land prices were relatively low in the 1960s.

While Derkowski fingers Ottawa, Toronto and Vancouver as high-profit cities in 1974, Edmonton and Calgary deserve to be added to the list from the ten he surveyed. Derkowski reports a minimum NHA house as selling for $30,000 in Calgary in 1974, with construction costs of $20,750 and a lot price of $9,250. Servicing costs and consultants for that lot cost $6,000, carrying costs were $300, and my estimate of acquisition and holding costs is $1,050. (Derkowski's is $1,364.) That includes a profit of $1,900 per lot.

Less than two years later, in early 1976, the price of a minimum NHA bungalow in Calgary was $54,000. Construction cost including profit was $33,600. The price for the lot was $20,400. Servicing had increased somewhat but the lot for the house I analyzed was 10 feet narrower, so the result was the same cost for servicing, $6,000. The land in my example in Genstar-BACM's Marlborough Park subdivision cost $138 per lot when it was bought in 1964, and $220 for carrying costs and taxes. Carrying costs on servicing add another $1,400 to the developer's costs. Total cost of the lot was $7,758, not much different than the total for the bigger 1974 lot. But this time after prices in Calgary had gone through the roof in less than two years, profit on the lot was up from $1,900 to $11,500.

The thrust of Derkowski's analysis of his data is to argue against public land banking, shift the blame for high land prices from developers, demonstrate that profits are not excessive, and press for fewer restrictions on developers and an increase in the quantity of new lots being developed. He makes no bones about his stress on supply, and on arguing that governments should concentrate on this matter and forget about land banks. He says, in italics and capitals: *"It does not matter so much WHO produces the lots – and even less who owns the raw land – as HOW MANY are produced relative to demand."* But when profits of $10,000 to

$20,000 per lot are being made by the lucky owners of suburban land being developed in some cities, it probably does matter to them that they own the land. It matters to the rest of us, too, since at present those profits are largely untaxed, whereas if the land was owned by a public land bank the entire profit element would go to public authorities.

MONTREAL AS A MODEL

Derkowski does have an illustration of the kind of land development world he would like to see, and it is intriguing — though I think most of us would see it as a vignette from the past, rather than an achievable model of how things could be done. Derkowski's ideal is Montreal, and no wonder. His figures show that the average sale price of a suburban house lot in 1974 was $2,400 — about one-tenth the price in Toronto. The cost of construction of a small NHA bungalow on that lot was just $23,500, yielding a sale price of $25,900. A year later, according to CMHC statistics, the construction cost of the average NHA house in Montreal had increased somewhat and lot prices had gone up by $350, so that a house and lot cost $29,584. On top of this price, a home buyer in Montreal must pay local improvement taxes for the $5,500 in services installed on his lot by the local municipality. Even with this added in, the price of housing in Montreal is far lower than in other large and medium Canadian cities, and the profit on land is only a few hundred dollars per lot.

Derkowski points out that in Montreal, servicing is still done by municipalities instead of developers. The result is that small entrepreneurs, speculators and builders can be involved in owning vacant land. Moreover municipalities vie with each other to open up new land in their jurisdictions, thus ensuring an ample supply and keeping prices from rising. Derkowski attributes this to the fine pro-development mentality of the people and politicians of Montreal. I would be more inclined to attribute it to competitiveness between the small builders who have their local small municipal councils in their pockets, and who want to ensure that the land they own is developed. There are many municipalities with vacant, developable land in the Montreal region and no overall authority to control them.

WHO'S IN CHARGE?

Once large corporate developers have a major position in a local market, and once municipalities have become used to having services financed by de-velopers and not the municipality, no one is likely to turn the clock back. There is no longer a question about whether there should be large land assemblies; in most cities, they exist. The question becomes who should own them, and what their operating policies should be. Derkowski recognizes that once there is regulation of the supply of new lots, and once scarcity exists or can be created so as to generate monopoly profits of the kind his report documents, large corporate developers will consciously choose a relatively slow rate of development for their holdings which generates high prices and high profits. He puts the argument in terms of builders, but it applies equally well to them and to developers.

Derkowski's contention, vigorously argued through his report, is that the people with their hand on the tap, regulating the flow of development of new lots, are municipal politicians and planners. He cites and rejects what he calls the "developers' conspiracy theory," that it is the developers who have their hand on the tap. Indeed he portrays land development as a struggle between giants: the developers on one side, planners and citizens on the other. He recognizes that it is developers who generate the flow of land for development in the first place; all the planners and their allies can do is regulate the speed with which the land flows through the regulatory system.

What Derkowski fails to do is to look to see who actually owns that hand on the tap. Who are the governmental authorities that regulate the development industry? The answer, at the provincial, regional, and municipal level, usually is that it is the industry that is busy regulating itself. And the bigger the government, the wider its jurisdiction, the more influential are the large corporate developers compared to the small HUDAC-member builders who would like to see lower profits and more production in the industry. It's not for nothing that Cadillac-Fairview keeps Fast Eddie Goodman, the provincial and federal Tory Party bagman, on their board of directors. When you've got to get through to a Conservative Party cabinet minister in Ontario, there's no one better to have on your end of the phone than Eddie.

And it is in those parts of the country where the development industry does not have this kind of influence that tentative steps to get the industry and its profits under control have been taken. The NDP government in Manitoba has put together a land bank whose logic isn't clear to the local industry, but whose size worries them considerably. Before its defeat, the British Columbia NDP government was on its way to ensuring that public land banks had a dominant position in the Vancouver housing market.

If it were an independent research report on the land question, Derkowski's study could be considered misguided and even misleading on certain key points, but offering a core of useful if not always reliable information on the costs of suburban land servicing in a dozen cities.

In fact, however, its data are the least important part of Derkowski's report. Its most critical aspects are its analyses of land policy measures like public land banking and its conclusions about housing profits and prices. The report was commissioned by HUDAC, the housing industry's lobby, to serve its political purposes and to counter the findings of less partial researchers like Spurr. Its purpose was to shift the blame for high house prices from the industry to government, to try to argue away the enormous profits the industry is making in its development activities, and to make a case for less government control of the industry as a counter to calls for measures like public land banking. Reading the report, one is left with the impression that its author started knowing the conclusions he was going to reach. What had to be done was to work back from those conclusions to find data that would support them. Hence the development of the curious and artificial distinction between "land ownership" and "development" profits. Hence the constant, clumsy attempts to argue that public land banks are of no actual or potential benefit. Hence perhaps also the failure to provide realistic service cost figures in the two or three cities where even the arbitrary method used to calculate developers' profits would have yielded a very high per-lot figure.

Derkowski's report is, in the end, propaganda masquerading as research. That may not have been intentional on Derkowski's part; he may be presenting the data exactly as he sees them. But HUDAC certainly knows what it is doing, and knows how useful a report like this can be in the public debate over housing profits and prices. How convenient that CMHC should be prepared to underwrite some of the costs (the report neglects to mention this figure) of the research.

In spite of its confusion on some key analytic questions, it is fortunate that Peter Spurr's more reliable and broad-ranging work was done. It's ironic but hardly surprising that the same federal agency that would fund Derkowski's research would not want to publish Spurr's report. With it available, anyone interested in the land question can put Spurr side by side with Derkowski and reach their own conclusions about what's going on in suburban land development.

If the new and better understanding of the workings of the industry offered by Spurr leads to a more realistic notion of the causes of high prices and profits in housing and of the alternatives open to us, it may be wrong to picture an unstoppable movement towards a housing industry organized around Genstar-BACM, Cadillac-Fairview, and a few other corporate giants. Now we know quite clearly what is going on; the problem is to let other people in on the story, and to create the political pressure that will force government action to change things. Fast Eddie, wherever you are, keep that telephone handy; you're going to need it.

---

* *Vancouver Ltd.* by Donald Gutstein. James Lorimer & Company, Toronto, 1976.

The high cost of suburban housing

James Lorimer

In 1972, a small three-bedroom house on a 50-foot lot in the suburbs of Calgary cost $25,000. A family with an income of $12,000, slightly higher than average for Calgary that year, could afford to buy that house.

Today, not quite five years later, a basic three-bedroom new house on a 40-foot lot on Calgary's suburban fringe costs $54,000. That's an increase of more than 100 per cent. To buy that house requires an income of $21,600 a year and a down payment of $8,689.

Calgary isn't the most expensive city for housing in Canada. Edmonton, Hamilton, Kitchener, Ottawa, Thunder Bay, Toronto, Vancouver and Victoria are all more expensive, according to the most recent published figures. That $54,000 house in Calgary costs $60,000 in Vancouver and about $65,000 in Toronto.

Why? Why is housing so expensive and why has it increased so dramatically in price in the last four years? Is it construction wages? Or the rising cost of building materials? High servicing costs for new suburban land? The often-mentioned costs of delay, while city halls quibble with developers over approvals for their projects and local residents object?

Or is it profiteering by the development industry?

In early 1976 I surveyed the housing market in four Canadian cities: Toronto, Thunder Bay, Calgary and Vancouver. Armed with as much information and as many views as I could find, I looked at a representative new house for sale in each city and analyzed what lay behind the final sale price.

I went with an idea of what the answer might be. This came from a report prepared for the federal government housing agency, Central Mortgage and Housing Corporation (CHMC), by researcher Peter Spurr and since published as *Land and Urban Development: A preliminary study*. Making full use of his access to CMHC's vast collection of data on the operations of the land development industry, Spurr pointed out that many corporations in the business of turning farm land into suburban house lots are making enormous profits out of the high prices they charge for those lots. There was strong circumstantial evidence that Spurr's conclusion about profits was true in the Toronto area. I went to see whether the analysis held up in typical cases across the country.

The results? Housing prices have gone up in part because the construction costs of new houses have risen considerably since 1972. In Calgary they've almost doubled. That new house priced at $25,000 in 1972 cost $18,352 for building materials and labour. Today it costs $33,600; the figure is almost twice as much for basically the same house.

An even more dramatic factor in rising house prices is the increase in the cost of land. The average price of a lot in Calgary in 1972 was $6,320, much lower than Hamilton's record high of $11,796 in the same year, but above the nation-wide average of $5,535.

The price of a somewhat smaller lot in Calgary in early 1976 was $20,400. That's three times the 1972 figure.

And what makes that suburban house lot so expensive? Profit. Speculative profit earned by the developer who bought the land from a farmer in 1964, held it for 12 years, and is now servicing the land and turning it into 40-foot lots.

The developer's profit on that $20,400 lot turns out to be $12,642. That's what he has left over after he has paid all the costs of buying, holding and servicing the land. The profit on the lot is almost two-thirds of its price and it is 23 per cent of the final purchase price of that $54,000 house.

Investigation in Thunder Bay, Vancouver and Toronto produced remarkably similar figures for prices, costs and profits to those of the Calgary example.

- In Vancouver I analyzed a comfortable three-bedroom, 1-1/2-bathroom house on a 66-foot lot in suburban Coquitlam. The house was built by Engineered Homes Ltd., a subsidiary of one of western Canada's major land development and construction companies, BACM Limited, itself a subsidiary of a foreign-controlled conglomerate, Genstar Limited. The price tag on the house and its lot: $68,000. Price of the lot alone: $30,800. My estimate of the profit to the developer on the lot: $14,847. Eliminating that profit from the final price of the house would bring it down by 21 per cent.

- In Toronto, two- and three-bedroom town-houses of widely varying size, stacked on top of one another, were selling in early 1976 in suburban Mississauga for $61,900. The interior finish of the townhouses is luxurious, with six appliances, lots of cupboards and balconies, and air conditioning. That partially compensates for the fact that the units have no extra land of their own, have no gardens and open onto a common interior corridor and a large parking garage; and for the fact that so many of them — 20 units per acre — are grouped close together. The full cost to the developer, S.B. McLaughlin Associates Limited, of buying, holding and servicing the land for each unit was about $2,697. The difference between this cost of the land and its selling price is $9,232 on one large sample unit analyzed, and $16,510 on a second, smaller unit.

- In Thunder Bay, modest, new three-bedroom detached houses were selling for $52,000 in February, 1976, if you could find one. I estimate that the speculative profit on lots in the County Park subdivision is $6,900 to $9,700.

Similar large profits are included in the price of every new house being sold in most medium and large Canadian cities.

Later in 1976, I analyzed the suburban housing market in Victoria, Edmonton, Winnipeg, Halifax, and Charlottetown. This later work confirmed that the structure of the market, and the high house prices which result, are similar in virtually every Canadian city. Only Montreal and other centres in Quebec are substantially different. In Charlottetown prices were relatively lower, but pressures were developing which would lead to the same kind of high-price situation existing in most other Canadian cities.

A CALGARY CASE STUDY

A typical example of costs, prices and profits for the large corporate land developers is a three-bedroom bungalow in Calgary's suburban Marlborough Park area. The price tag on the house, built and sold in 1976, was $54,000. The profit the developer, Genstar Limited, will make on the sale of the lot that the house sits on is $12,642.

That's a cool 23 per cent of the sale price of the total package. The sale price of the lot is $20,400. The cost to Genstar for that lot is just $7,758. So the markup on the cost of the lot is 262 per cent.

As a conglomerate enterprise involved in many aspects of construction, development and real estate in Canada, Genstar and its many subsidiaries could build this house themselves. A Genstar company, Consolidated Concrete Limited, supplied concrete for foundations. Another subsidiary, Truroc Gypsum Products Ltd., supplied wall-board. Genstar's subsidiaries also supplied lumber, kitchen cabinets, windows, concrete blocks and other materials. Engineered Homes, a Genstar company, did the general contracting and sold the home. On all these construction materials and contracting work, Genstar's companies made the usual profits for such work. The $12,642 is profit on the land alone, less than the total amount of money Genstar and its subsidiaries made on the construction and sale of the house.

Genstar's land profit was 12 years in the making. The history of this house began in 1964 when according to land title documents another Genstar subsidiary, BACM, purchased two half sections of farmland for $238,515 each through a company called Arcadian. The total purchase price for the 640 acres was $477,030. That works out to $745 an acre. One acre of raw land can be made into 5.4 of our 40- by 100-foot house lots. Therefore the cost of raw land was $138.

BACM has held the land since 1964 and paid municipal taxes on it since then. Mortgage interest rates in 1964 were relatively low, about seven per cent. By the early 1970s the rate reached nine per cent and recently it has gone even higher, but a reasonable estimate for the interest over 12 years is $160. Taxes on undeveloped land in Calgary have been estimated at $5 per lot per year. Thus total carrying costs, interest and taxes from 1964 to 1976 have amounted to about $220.

To turn that land into a house lot, BACM had to install and pay for services such as sewers, water, roads, street lights, sidewalks and every other

The $54,000 Calgary House.

amenity suburban residents have come to expect and that city councils demand. Developers also have to pay municipal levies imposed to cover the cost of facilities like trunk sewers, water mains and expressways which have to be provided to accommodate new subdivisions. BACM has told the Calgary office of CMHC that the cost of these levies and services in the section of the Marlborough Park subdivision where our house is located is $150 per frontage foot. That corresponds with what others in the development business in Calgary say is the current cost of services and levies, but then of course the figure varies somewhat from area to area. The cost on our 40-foot lot was $6,000.

There are a host of other expenses which a land developer must pay, including consultant fees, land title and mortgage costs, carrying expenses and salesmen's fees. A reasonable allowance for these expenses is $1,400.

Altogether, the total cost to the developer for the lot was $7,758.

When you pay your $54,000, of course, you also buy a 1,120 square-foot house which BACM's subsidiary, Engineered Homes, calls the Monterey.

The Monterey has broadloom in the living room, vinyl tile in the kitchen, a full bathroom off the hall, a half bathroom off the largest bedroom and an unfinished basement. The cost of constructing this house in Calgary in spring 1976, including the

builder's profit, is $30 a square foot. That figure comes from three sources: a private mortgage lender in Calgary, a local builder and a CMHC official. For our 1,120 square-foot house that comes to $33,600.

Add it all up: the house costs the developer $33,600 and the lot costs him $7,758. If the house and lot sell for $54,000 that leaves a healthy $12,642 as profit.

There were 167 lots developed by BACM in stage 14 of its Marlborough Park subdivision. The lots cover 30.97 acres of which 10.32 acres are being used for roads and park reserves. If BACM and Genstar made a $12,642 profit on each of those lots, they made a total profit of $2,111,214 on that part of this subdivision. That's not a bad return on the $23,072 it cost to buy the land back in 1964.

When it closed the books on the lot on which the $54,000 house sits, BACM may have discovered it made slightly more or slightly less than our estimate of $12,642. Without access to all the records of the company, an outsider can only gather up the cost figures that are on public record and make reasonable estimates of the ones that aren't. So there's a certain margin of error in the profit estimate made here.

But BACM and Engineered Homes have left a margin for error, too. The salesman who showed me the show home told me that it would probably cost $54,000. But, he said, it could be $56,000. He wasn't quite sure. He offered to put me on his list and call me as soon as the final price was settled.

THE CORPORATE DEVELOPERS' LAND BANKS

More and more of the new suburban houses being built in Canada are going up on large land assemblies put together five, ten, fifteen, or even twenty years ago by a few corporate developers. The largest Canadian land development corporations are in the land banking and land development business on a very big scale indeed. Information collected by Peter Spurr for 1973 showed a total of 119,192 acres owned by 47 different development corporations around 21 different Canadian cities. These private land banks are large enough in many instances to supply all the new land required for housing for the next five years.

Around Ottawa and Hull, for example, nine corporations were found to own 9,416 acres. That's almost 15 square miles of land, and it's an eight-year supply at current new-house densities and projected growth rates.

Around Toronto, 24 firms were listed as owning 41,198 acres, and just nine large firms held 87 per cent of this land. That's 64 square miles, one-quarter of the present area of Metropolitan Toronto, and, again at current densities and growth rates, an 11-year supply.

The most remarkable case in the CMHC report was that of Thunder Bay, where only one corporate land assembly was found. One local large development corporation, Headway Corporation, was recorded as owning 1,190 acres, a nine-year supply.

The figures for Calgary showed that a private land bank totalling 10,920 acres was owned by eight development corporations, a 10-year supply.

Development industry spokesmen have challenged the accuracy and completeness of the 1973 survey and there have been significant changes in the situation around many cities since then. But in all the complaints about details of the survey no one has taken serious issue with the main conclusion: that there are large land banks around most Canadian cities, owned by a few large development corporations capable of supplying most or all new suburban lots needed in the near future. As their lands are developed, these corporations add to and increase their stock of farm land so that, if anything, their domination of the development business is likely to increase. Again, Montreal is the only exception among large cities.

In most localities, comprehensive statistics are not kept to show which firms supply newly serviced lots. Calgary, however, is a welcome exception. There, a meticulous count has been kept since 1973 of every new house lot placed on the market. The 1973 Spurr survey showed that eight firms owned 10,920 acres of Calgary land. Two of the largest owners identified were Carma Developers Ltd., a local firm with 4,500 acres, and Daon Development Corp., with 1,400. Missing completely from Spurr's survey is a third very important development operation, the Genstar conglomerate, whose subsidiaries BACM, Keith Construction Company Ltd., Kelwood Corporation Limited and Engineered Homes are all active in Calgary. A report prepared in 1973 for the city identified approximately 3,180 acres as owned or controlled through purchase options by the Genstar group. In 1974, Genstar announced that it held 3,882 acres in the Calgary area.

The Calgary statistics on new house lots show that these three large land bankers, Genstar-BACM, Carma and Daon, have together dominated the business of supplying new lots in Calgary since 1973. From January, 1973 to December, 1975, 10,107 registered house lots out of a total of 13,578 have come from those three firms: Daon with 2,481, Genstar with 3,752, and Carma with 3,824. The other 3,471 lots have been registered by the remaining 19 firms active in land development. Each of the big three is about as large as all of the other firms combined, and the three together have supplied 75 per cent of all Calgary's registered house lots during the past three years.

Do these large private land banks, and the major role of their owners in developing new house lots, have any connection with high land prices and enormous speculative profits?

The developers themselves say no, vehemently. They admit that there is a restricted supply of new house lots in many cities and argue that if more lots were put on the market the price would be driven down. They claim that they are anxious to develop all the land they own, but they're prevented by planning regulations and city hall red tape. A Calgary builder, speaking to a service club in January, 1975, said that government restrictions were responsible for high land costs and the shortage of lots. "By placing limitations on the amount of land available for development, a scarcity . . . has been artificially created," he argued.

The response of many city planners and politicians to this is that in the end it's the developers who determine how many acres of land get turned into house lots every year. Everyone agrees that the approval process takes time, but planners point out that developers know the time requirements well and often have approvals for lots which they haven't proceeded to develop.

For instance, in the same month that the builder was speaking to the service club, there were 3,218 house lots fully approved and registered by

Calgary's city hall, which had not yet been built upon. That's more than six months' supply; in 1975, there were 5,751 single and semi-detached housing starts in Calgary. These figures indicate that there is an adequate supply of lots being approved by city hall to meet demand at $20,000 per lot.

The developers' claim that government is responsible for the quantity of lots being developed, and for high and rising prices, ignores the way that the land development system works. The initiative to develop rests with the large private land bank owners. Permission to develop land cannot be given by the authorities at a greater rate than developers request it. And no city hall can force a developer to turn approved land into house lots faster than he wants to.

Development industry spokesmen often talk about city hall as if it were a completely separate and independent entity, totally beyond their influence and control. But the history of city politics in most Canadian cities in the past several years has demonstrated amply that developers have many friends and allies on city councils, planning boards and development authorities. In many cities, a substantial percentage of the local politicians are in the real estate and land development business themselves. Many more expect — and get — campaign contributions from developers. Other close links often emerge:

- In Calgary, the city's economic development committee was accused last September of being dominated by developers. A committee member, John Schmal, charged that nine of the 13 members were directly or indirectly involved in the real estate and development business, and that three members represented firms that wanted the city to annex land that they owned. Schmal was not reappointed to the committee.
- In the Toronto suburb of Etobicoke, local alderman Donald Kerr did not vote on a controversial highrise development scheme, proposed by developer S.B. McLaughlin, because he works for the real estate firm that obtained the options on the land for McLaughlin.
- For three months in 1972 Ed McKitka, an alderman in the Vancouver suburb of Surrey, had a Cadillac convertible rented for him by developer Walter Link. A public inquiry revealed the developer was assembling land, seeking rezonings and constructing apartments in the municipality where McKitka is alderman. The inquiry later determined that McKitka gained no personal profit from land or rezoning applications involving Link.

The consequence of the many links between the industry and city councils is a friendly working relationship between two groups. The reality is quite different from the relationship of constant conflict which developers often emphasize.

In a nutshell, then, the large, developer-owned land banks and the present system for turning farm land into house lots produces high and rising land prices. The way this system works, land prices can move in one direction only: upward. Whenever the local housing market is tight, as it is right now in Calgary and Thunder Bay, the large developers who are putting the bulk of the new lots on the market respond by marking up land prices. Small house-builders have no choice but to pay the asking price if they want to stay in business.

When the local market is soft, as it is right now in Vancouver and Toronto, where houses often stand incomplete for months waiting for a buyer who can afford the asking price, the big land development firms have no incentive to cut prices on the houses they've got to sell, or on the lots they're developing. Why should they? They can afford to wait for the market to absorb the houses they have already built, and if they have to slow up the process of developing their land banks today, they'll still be able to develop the land tomorrow. And tomorrow's prices and profits may well be higher than today's.

Small builders who have unsold houses at high prices may want to cut prices in order to sell them, but they can't afford to. They have already paid the developer a high price for the lot, and their margin on house construction is small. Price cutting would be a sure route to quick bankruptcy.

The crucial element in this system is clearly the large, well-financed land development corporation, which, with a few other similar corporations, supplies a high proportion of new house lots in many Canadian cities. Of course these companies are building houses as well as developing land, and no doubt they would be happy to make the same kind of profit in construction as they now make in land development. But house-building is not yet the exclusive domain of giant corporations. Large builder-developers have more than doubled their share of new house construction in many cities, according to one estimate, while the small builders' share has declined dramatically. The big firms have an enormous advantage because they can cut their costs by buying out suppliers and by operating on an almost mass-production scale, so their construction profits on a house are higher than those of a small firm. But the willingness of small builders to work on a profit margin of six or seven per cent of construction costs (an estimate made by housing planners in a recent suburban Toronto study) puts a ceiling on the markup the large corporations can make in building. Competition from small builders ensures that there is still some relationship between cost and price on new house construction, although that relationship has disappeared in determining house lot prices.

A high-price, high-profit housing industry is a terrible problem for families who want to own a

Photo: Ontario Ministry of Housing

house of their own in the suburbs and can't afford one. But every other interest involved is quite well served by this kind of industry.

A limited supply of new house lots and high prices which cut back on the number of families who can afford a house suits most municipal governments. It means they have to borrow less money when capital is scarce and expensive to finance new trunk sewers, water treatment plants, expressways, fire stations and schools. The strain on provincial governments, which often finance part of the capital costs of these expensive services, is also moderated.

The federal government too is reasonably well served by the present system. Housing has a voracious appetite for capital; investment by mortgage lenders in housing has rocketed from $2.7 billion in 1969 to $10.7 billion in 1975. High house prices and high interest rates help keep demand for mortgage money in check by keeping down the number of buyers.

It is important to remember that part of Ottawa's responsibility is to ensure that the total capital funds each year are parcelled out properly for different uses. Funds that are used to finance new housing are not available for other construction projects like the Mackenzie Valley pipeline. Cheaper houses would mean smaller mortgages per house and to that extent they would reduce mortgage borrowing. But cheaper houses would also unleash tremendous pent-up demand for new

houses from families that just can't afford them now.

For anyone who doubts the role big developers play in the rising price of housing, the case of Montreal should serve as a clinching argument. There the supply of new house lots is not in the hands of a few large firms and no substantial land banks have been identified. The price of house lots is incredibly low, averaging $2,709 in 1975, and even though construction costs are as high as in most cities, in 1975 a modest three-bedroom detached house sold in Montreal for $29,584. That's less than half the price of a similar house in Toronto. Part of the reason that lot prices and hence house prices are so low in Montreal is that services are installed by the local municipality, not the developer, and home buyers pay the cost through local improvement taxes. But it is mainly the absence of enormous speculative land profits that keeps house prices at a reasonable level.

With the exception of a few cities like Montreal, the real winners in the present system of land development in Canada are the large corporations. But they don't often discuss their profits. A rare exception came in January, 1976, in a comment made by Ross Howard, the president of Calgary's Britannia Homes. He admitted to a Globe and Mail reporter that there were "fantastic profits" being made on land.

As we've seen, that's no overstatement. If the average speculative profit on each lot sold in Calgary in the last three years was $5,000, a total profit of $65,000,000 has been made in that city alone since January, 1973.

No one has even attempted to calculate the total profit made very year on new house lots in Canada. Taking a relatively low estimate of $3,000 per lot for every single and semi-detached house built in 1975, profit for that year alone would total $291,000,000.

PROFITS AND TAXES: A CASE HISTORY

Accepting that enormous profits are being made out of the high price of suburban housing, one reassuring thought would be that the public gets a share of the action in the form of corporate income taxes on the large development corporations. At the usual corporate tax rate of 48-50 per cent on profits, taxes on the suburban land development business should produce substantial revenues for provincial and federal governments.

Astonishingly enough in the amazing world of land development, this is not the case. Many of the large corporate developers pay absolutely no corporate income tax at present. Many others pay a token amount of tax, a few hundred thousand dollars on profits of many millions. Only a few pay substantial corporate taxes.

One consequence of the low or zero rate of taxation of land developers is, of course, that the rate at which these firms are able to increase their role in the suburban housing market is higher because they are able to keep most of their profits and use the money to finance expansions, land acquisitions, and of course takeovers of smaller firms in the business.

The easiest way of explaining how it is that these corporations avoid taxation legally is to use an example. A case in point is the Vancouver-based development firm, Daon Developments.

In mid-1975, the shareholders of Daon Developments received a glossy annual report which showed that their company had made a profit in 1974 of $3,096,000.

It also showed shareholders who read the report carefully that Daon had paid no corporate income tax whatever to Ottawa or to British Columbia on that profit.

Why?

There is a simple explanation for this situation. When large land development corporations fill out their tax returns for Ottawa, they set out revenues for the year *and* expenses. And generally their expenses are almost as large as revenues. Thus: little or no tax.

As far as Revenue Canada is concerned, these large corporations are break-even or minimum-profit operations.

There are two reasons why Ottawa sees things this way. The first is the result of something people in the development industry call the CCA, which stands for capital cost allowance.

In calculating their expenses for a year, land development corporations are able to deduct up to five per cent of the construction cost of all the apartment buildings, shopping centres, office buildings and other properties they own. The capital cost allowance deduction is intended to cover the depreciation in value of those buildings over the year. The logic of the CCA seems to be that buildings made of brick, steel and concrete are depreciating by five per cent every year.

Daon Developments owned income-producing properties in 1974 valued at $80,890,000. Of the total value, $52,831,000 was for properties already built and $28,059,000 was for income properties under construction at year end. That total included both the cost of the buildings and the cost of the land they were built on. The CCA is calculated on the value of the building alone.

Without access to Daon's income tax return, it's impossible to know exactly what expense was claimed for capital cost allowance in 1974 but, from figures made public in the annual report to shareholders, it was very likely $3 million to $4 million. That alone could reduce substantially the company's profit in Ottawa's eyes.

A second reason why Ottawa saw this company as a break-even operation concerns the costs to Daon of carrying its 8,969-acre land bank. Land bank acreage produces no income for the developer between the time it is purchased and the time it is developed, unless it can be rented out as farm land. But it costs money to pay municipal tax levies and the interest on the mortgages on the land. Until May 6, 1974, the federal government allowed land developers to deduct the carrying cost of land banks as an expense. This meant that their land banks were money-losing operations, producing losses which could be deducted from profits made in other aspects of the business. Daon's net carrying cost on their land bank in 1974 was $2,139,000.

In the 1974 federal budget, this tax law was changed and Ottawa no longer permitted development companies to consider carrying costs as a current expense. The effect? As S.B. McLaughlin Associates delicately phrased it in a 1975 prospectus: "Income taxes will become payable on a current basis to a greater extent than in prior years."

All was not black for the developers, however. At least one province, Ontario, permitted the continuation of deductions for provincial corporate tax purposes.

Using the CCA provision and the deduction of carrying costs, Daon Development's expenses as shown in their corporate income tax return to Ottawa exactly equalled their income in 1974. Hence

Photo: Ontario Ministry of Housing

the company paid no income tax.

But when the company's accountants and auditors reported to their shareholders on 1974, they presented quite a different picture.

When the accountants and auditors looked at Daon's revenue-producing apartment buildings and office buildings, they calculated what they considered to be a fair and accurate cost of depreciation for those buildings in 1974. Their expense for depreciation: $117,000. Far, far less than the probable $3 million to $4 million permitted by Ottawa's tax laws. But the Daon figure is not an underestimate, because the company's auditors are under a strict obligation to ensure that such expenses as depreciation are accurately reported to the shareholders.

Carrying costs of Daon's land bank are also dealt with differently by the company and its auditors. They are added to the book value of the land — "capitalized" is the accountant's word for it — on the reasonable assumption that the carrying costs are not an expense, but rather an investment. This too is a fair and accurate description of what carrying costs on land banks really are.

So when the company and its auditors added up the figures for the shareholders, they didn't count carrying costs in the company's expenses for the year at all. And depreciation on revenue-producing buildings was a tiny $117,000. The result: a profit for Daon of $6,670,000. That's a long way from a break-even operation, and on sales of $64,631,000 that's not a bad rate of profit. It looks even better alongside shareholders' equity in the company, which at the beginning of 1974 was $8,476,000.

So Daon itself considers that it earned a profit of $6.6 million in 1974. Had Ottawa's tax regulations forced it to treat carrying costs as the company itself considers they should be treated and to depreciate buildings at the same rate as the company thinks is accurate, Daon's corporate income tax for 1974 would have been $3,574,000.

In order not to lead shareholders astray about how profitable the company is, Daon and its auditors have made a provision of $3,574,000 for income taxes on the 1974 annual report. The result is that the figures show a before-tax profit of $6,670,000, and an after-tax profit of $3,096,000.

Look a bit further in the annual report, however, under the heading Expenses not Requiring an Outlay of Cash, and you will see an item: Deferred Income Taxes . . . $3,574,000. So although Daon considers that an accurate reporting of its income and expenses would make it liable for that amount in income taxes, it did not have to pay the money. The expense was deferred. And as we have already seen, no income tax was paid by Daon in 1974.

In making full use of Ottawa's tax laws and deducting a capital cost allowance much larger than its actual depreciation expense, and by considering carrying costs an expense and not an investment, Daon was following normal business practice of minimizing the amount of income tax it pays. Paying income tax which a company is not obliged to pay would be considered irresponsible in business circles. If the company had paid such tax, Daon president Jack Poole, who owns 21.8 per cent of the company's outstanding shares, would have come under considerable fire from the other shareholders.

Every large land development corporation that reports zero or minimum profits to Ottawa every year also carefully calculates the amount of corporate income tax it would have to pay if Ottawa demanded the same treatment of company income and expenses as the company's auditors. Every corporation also keeps track of the total amount of deferred income tax in the past. For Daon, this total of unpaid taxes is a relatively modest $8,695,000. For Cadillac-Fairview, as of two years ago, it was $46,236,000. For 20 of the largest firms in the industry, the total amount of unpaid income tax at the end of 1974 was $195 million.

If these income tax loopholes were abolished, the tax authorities could probably collect that $195 million from the industry for past years. Government revenue thereafter from real estate corporations would likely be a minimum of $100 million a year. Considering the high profits earned in real estate, and considering too the burden of income taxes, sales taxes and property taxes on ordinary taxpayers, it is astonishing that the land development industry gets away with paying so little.

HOUSE PRICE POLICIES THAT HAVEN'T WORKED

It's clear that "fantastic profits" on land and fantastic house prices go hand in hand. The question is, can anything be done about it? Can houses ever come down in price? Or is the dream of most Canadian families, that of owning a home of their own, permanently beyond the reach of those who haven't already achieved it?

There is no shortage of good ideas on how the current high prices of new houses in Canada could be reduced. Everyone in the housing business has suggestions about how the other guy's prices could be lowered. For example:

W.D.H. Gardiner, deputy chairman of The Royal Bank of Canada, suggested in early 1976 that the high prices charged by developers for serviced lots could be cut by flooding the market with an abundant supply of new lots.

Vancouver land banker Jack Poole, president of Daon Developments, suggested in June, 1975, that every family should have the right to borrow mortgage money at six per cent, presumably from chartered banks and other lending institutions.

Builders often point out that lots could be cheaper if city planners didn't demand "gold-plated" services, sidewalks on both sides of the street, underground wiring, 66-foot road allowances and so on.

City planners argue that builders could charge less if they didn't include extra features like fireplaces, broadloom, second bathrooms and a complete set of appliances.

Many ways to reduce house prices have been tried. Ottawa offers a complicated subsidy program for new home buyers. In 1974, the federal government halved its sales tax on building materials. Many provinces and municipalities have taken the advice of land experts and got into the public land bank business. Yet house prices remain high, and continue to increase.

Why don't these ideas work? Is there nothing that can be done to bring house prices down to the level where families earning $8,000 or $10,000 a year can afford a home of their own?

Three ways to make new housing cheaper have been tried recently. The first method involves bringing down the price of the land component by reducing the size of house lots and reducing the standards of services installed in new subdivisions.

In the typical suburb it takes an acre to provide five standard house lots and for every two acres actually used as lots, one more is used for roads, sidewalks and parks. Architects, planners and builders often have shown how land could be used more efficiently without seriously affecting the prerequisites of suburban living: the gardens, the front yards, the detached or semi-detached houses, the living at ground level. The use of more house lots per acre and less land for roads can be combined with straighter streets, houses closer to the road, and fewer expensive servicing extras.

Toronto's housebuilders, goaded by attacks on their profits and their wasteful ways of using land, produced a report in 1976 which says that higher densities and lower servicing requirements could cut house prices in Toronto suburbs by as much as one-third. Though their report doesn't say so, these reductions would be accomplished while leaving the speculative profit on land at its present per-acre level.

Some municipal councils have in fact adopted this method, usually because the developer argues that the result will be lower prices for the finished houses.

Calgary's Carma Developments persuaded that city's Development Appeal Board in early 1975 to allow it to build 41 townhouses in a 71-house project on lots just 1,760 square feet in size. That's one-third of the size of a normal suburban lot. Carma explained that the project was intended to come under the federal government's Assisted Home Ownership Program (AHOP), and to reduce final house prices the lots had to be reduced in size and price.

But the cost of new house lots to large land-banking developers like Carma is now relatively low. And that cost bears no relationship whatever to the high prices which are being charged for those lots. If city councils permit suburban developers to reduce their costs by allowing smaller lots and less expensive services, there is no guarantee that all or even some of those savings will be passed along to house buyers. Of course a 25-foot lot will always be worth something less than a 50-foot lot. But it's quite conceivable that developers now charging and getting $20,000 for a 50-foot lot could get $15,000 for a 25-foot lot. The result of using this method to reduce house prices would be a small reduction in the selling price of units on smaller lots — and a large increase in the already enormous profits developers are making on every acre of land they own.

A second way of making new housing more affordable attempts not to reduce prices but rather to make it easier for people to pay those high prices.

Mortgages were once paid off over 20 years. Recently, however, the pay-back period has been lengthened to 25 and even 30 years. For the same payment per month, a family can take on a larger mortgage. But the future consequences — five or ten more years of those same mortgage payments — would be very costly to the home buyer.

Ceilings are imposed by Central Mortgage and Housing Corporation (CMHC) on the total amount of money a family can spend on shelter. The maximum on federally insured mortgages used to be 25 per cent of family income. It's now up to 30 per cent.

The obvious beneficiaries of these changes in mortgage regulations are the developers. Now that more people can afford $55,000 and $60,000 houses, it has become easier for developers to ask, and get, $20,000 or $25,000 for a conventional house lot.

Governments have added to the ability of some home buyers to pay high prices in another way too — by offering them a whole range of subsidies:

- Direct grants to buyers of new homes. Ottawa, through the provinces, ran such a scheme until the end of 1975. Probably the most generous deal was that offered by Prince Edward Island, which made grants of up to $4,000 to new home buyers until April, 1975.
- Lending government mortgage money to home buyers at low interest or none at all. New Brunswick, for instance, had a scheme offering $7,500 second mortgages to home buyers, interest free.
- Subsidies for interest payments on mortgages. Ottawa's complicated AHOP program reduces the effective current cost of mortgage money to eight per cent for families buying moderately priced housing, but some of the subsidy money eventually has to be paid back.
- Indirect subsidies. Particularly the federal

scheme which permits taxpayers who do not own a home, and who can afford to save $1,000 a year, to pay no income tax on that much of their income if the money is salted away in what's known as a Registered Home Ownership Plan (RHOP). This scheme is particularly generous to higher-income families who can afford to save, and who may avoid taxes of 40 per cent or 45 per cent on that $1,000.

The effect of all these subsidies and changes in regulations depends to a certain extent on the state of the housing market. In cities where there are plenty of houses available for families who can afford to spend $55,000, $60,000 or $65,000, the effect of these measures is to include more people among those who can afford to pay these prices. Without the subsidies and the rule changes, fewer houses would have been sold and developers' sales — and profits — would have been smaller.

In cities where there is already more than one ready buyer for every house built, in Calgary and Thunder Bay, for example, subsidies don't increase the number of houses being sold. But they do make it possible for those willing buyers to afford even higher prices than they could have paid before. A buyer who gets a homeowner's grant of $1,000 can afford $1,000 more than he would otherwise be able to pay for his house. The money ends up in the land developer's pocket, although this is certainly not the intention of governments giving the grant.

In this situation, it's no surprise to find a spokesman for the Housing and Urban Development Association of Canada, a national organization of builders and developers, claiming the credit for persuading the federal government to give outright grants to first-time home buyers.

The third method of making houses more affordable is public land banking. The theory is that governments would buy up land at the same low prices paid by developers, service it and sell it at cost. To compete, the developers would have to cut their prices so drastically that only modest profits would be made on land.

Federal financing has been available for land banking since 1949. According to a report prepared by the CMHC, there were 1,771 lots plus 21,197 acres in federally financed land bank inventories in the summer of 1973. With some exceptions, most of the public land banks have been used to provide lots which are sold not at cost but at the going market price. In Hamilton, for example, CMHC researcher Peter Spurr found that public land banks were producing land for nearly one in three housing starts every year, yet lot prices there were among the highest in Canada, and so was the rate of price increase.

Many city halls across Canada are also in the business of competing with local developers by developing and selling house lots. Their policies vary; sometimes the purpose is strictly to make a profit, which can be used to keep taxes down, and sometimes it is partly to make a profit and partly to give lucky families who buy the lots something of a bargain.

One typical example is in Thunder Bay, where the municipality is one of the largest owners of vacant undeveloped land within the city limits and could become a vigorous competitor for Headway Corporation, Thunder Bay's largest developer. Since 1972, the municipality has developed 250 lots in a subdivision called River Terrace. The city sells the lots by auction, first setting a floor price which covers all costs plus a margin of $10 per frontage foot for the land. Individuals who buy the lots always pay considerably more than the minimum price, but they pay less than Thunder Bay's developers would charge for the same lot. One instance is a 75-foot lot in River Terrace, sold last summer. A developer would have charged $18,750. The city's floor price was $11,650. The buyer paid $15,615. He ended up with something of a bargain (a saving of about $3,000), and the city made a profit ($4,000). But this operation does little to reduce the general price level of other house lots in Thunder Bay.

In the Vancouver suburb of Port Moody, the municipality has developed 138 lots on the side of a mountain, with a southern exposure looking out over the harbour. The total cost of planning, servicing and selling the lots was $14,244 each. They're being sold to eager buyers for an average price of $27,000. This is no bargain, though nearby private developers early last year were charging $30,000 for similar lots. The real benefit goes to Port Moody and its taxpayers, who are making a profit of about $13,000 per lot.

There are one or two examples of municipalities with large land banks, large enough to supply a hefty percentage of the local requirement for new lots, where a policy of keeping land prices (and municipal land bank profits) low has been followed. Peter Spurr points to Red Deer, Alberta, where most lots come from the public land bank. From 1958 to 1973 the municipality made a profit of $4 million on sales totalling $9 million, but prices were, in late 1975, just $6,100 for a 50-foot lot.

When public land is sold for less than the market price, it is usually done in a way which does not "disrupt" the rest of the local land market — which means that prices are not pushed downward. Some lucky moderate-income families are able to buy a lot for less than the market price. Other families still have to pay the prices local land developers have set, and the land bank is not used to keep the overall market prices for land down.

With remarkably few exceptions, then, these three main methods to reduce the price of housing haven't worked. Frequently they had added to the already high profits of developers; sometimes (as with many land banks) they have diverted high profits to the local municipality; on occasion (in higher suburban densities, for instance) they have combined the possibility of somewhat lower house prices with even higher developers' profits; in rare cases (where land bank lots are sold at cost) they have offered a few lucky families housing at a reasonable price but without necessarily affecting the rest of the housing market.

HOUSE PRICE POLICIES THAT WILL WORK

Does this mean that nothing can be done about the high price of housing? That high land prices — and enormous speculative profits — are a fact of life?

Of course not. But to be successful, government housing measures must come to terms with the power of the large development firms. Government policies have been vital to the rapid expansion of the corporate land developers and to permitting enormous profits on new house lots. Changes in these policies could slow the move toward a monopolistic development industry, and could lead to drastic reductions in house prices.

One way of slowing down the process of corporate concentration in the development industry could be for Ottawa and the provinces to rule out foreign ownership of developable land and development firms. Large foreign companies like Genstar Limited, B.P. Properties Ltd., Richard Costain (Canada) Limited, and Wimpey Developments Ltd., Canada, have played a major role in Canada in hastening the emergence of massive land assemblies and of vertically integrated development and construction companies. Their foreign parentage gives them easy access to large amounts of capital, often from Canadian sources. Making foreign ownership in the industry illegal even now would slow the trend toward greater concentration.

Other government measures could bring down the price of housing substantially by eliminating the speculative profit element in the prices people pay for new suburban homes. To do this, politicians must face head-on the market power of the developers' large land assemblies.

The usual proposal for dealing with the large land banks is for governments to establish their own public land banks. Public land banking is a slow, expensive and complicated approach. Often it has involved government expropriation, at bargain-basement prices, of the farms or residential properties of unwilling sellers and, as already demonstrated, has done little to lower market prices.

A simpler, faster, more direct and fair approach would be to use those very same expropriation powers, but to use them selectively against a few existing large land banks owned by developers. Development firms carry their land banks in their financial statements at cost. Cost includes the acquisition price, all carrying costs, and land taxes. If provincial governments amended their expropriation acts to permit the acquisition of large land bank assemblies at cost plus a reasonable profit — say 10 per cent — these corporations would still make money.

Lots from these large land banks could be serviced and sold by a municipal corporation for a half or even a third of present lot prices. If this measure were combined with the proposals often made by developers for higher densities and lower servicing requirements in the suburbs, house lots could be sold for $3,000 or $4,000 each in every Canadian city. Because these large land assemblies are often already in the process of development, the impact of a non-profit operation could be felt very quickly. New houses at $30,000 to $35,000 each could be on the market in Toronto, Thunder Bay, Calgary, Vancouver and many other Canadian cities within months.

Is this idea practical? Is it reasonable to suggest that provinces and city councils should take over the land banks the large developers have assembled?

Some people think it isn't. They argue that Daon, Genstar, McLaughlin, Cadillac-Fairview and the 20 or so other large corporations which control those land banks are powerful enough to prevent this from happening. But citizens of Canadian cities have faced similar situations in the past where large corporations, whose operations depended on municipal powers and city government services, have taken advantage of a monopolistic situation to earn enormous and unjustified profits.

Private companies have supplied water services, electricity, telephone and public transportation services with a monopoly franchise granted by municipal or provincial governments in various parts of Canada. Particularly powerful and profitable ventures were the private street railway companies during the time when streetcars were the only alternative to foot travel for most people. The street railway companies often had friends in office at city hall, insurance against any change in the status quo. Local government candidates ran on platforms which denounced the high prices and high profits that the companies often earned, and called for municipal ownership of public transit.

In some cities, the private transportation companies kept their monopolies until the business was no longer profitable. In others, the fight for municipal ownership was successful and the private interests involved were every bit as powerful, as well connected and as anxious to maintain the status quo as the large land development corporations are today. Public transportation provides a precedent for municipal ownership on a large scale which could be applied to land banks.

Until such a step is taken, federal and provincial housing policies are not likely to stop the price of housing from going even higher. People are going to have to pay $54,000 or more for a house, while knowing that $10,000 to $20,000 of the price is speculative profit for the developer. The development corporations are going to continue to make hundreds of millions of dollars in speculative profit on land, in addition to the profits they make on construction. And all those profits, it should be remembered, are virtually untouched by corporate income tax laws.

How long can this situation last? No one knows, but at least one developer is worried. R.D. Keenan, of Thunder Bay's Headway Corporation, told me he doesn't approve of the enormous profits developers in cities like Toronto are making in their land development operations. He thinks the public won't stand for it.

"The developers," he said, "are going to kill the goose that laid the golden egg."

Are they?

An earlier version of this article was published in Weekend Magazine, 22 and 29 May 1976. For assistance in subsequent research in this area, I acknowledge the assistance of the Explorations Program of the Canada Council.

II Demolition– A way of city life

999 Queen:
A case study of government demolition

George Baird
research by Robert Hill

During November and December of last year, controversy raged around the Ontario government's proposal to demolish the oldest portion of the Queen Street Mental Health Centre, originally known as the the Provincial Asylum, and colloquially known as 999 Queen. Notwithstanding the controversy, the government's intention to demolish was eventually confirmed, and today the 1846 masterwork of one of Ontario's most important early architects, John G. Howard, has been razed for a parking lot.

The controversy is important in several respects. In the first place, the Howard building is one of the most prominent historic buildings to have suffered such a fate in recent years. It might have been thought that in these more enlightened times such a building could not conceivably be demolished: surely the new awareness on the part of both governments and the public would preclude such an outcome. Yet the building came down. Its numer-

A general view from the north-west of the entire complex at 999 Queen Street West (circa 1887), showing the Howard building completed in 1850, together with the Kivas Tully wings, the construction of which began in 1869. Photo: Ontario Archives

ous, articulate, and prominent defenders didn't even succeed in mobilizing public opinion behind them. The popular press generally applauded the government's decision to demolish. What Toronto Alderman John Sewell labelled the building's "image problem", as a public locus of unhappy memories, finally did it in.

The "image problem" alone would make 999 Queen an interesting case study in historic building preservation in Canada, but there is much more to the situation than just that.

The politics of the controversy split along unusual lines. While ministry fought ministry, and Tory fought Tory, the provincial NDP rejected the plea of Toronto city council's left wing for help in the legislature.

More important, the two-month dispute focussed and polarized public discussion on the alternative approaches to historic buildings and "restoration" and "recycling." In the legislature, the Minister of Government Services, Margaret Scrivener — who will emerge as the key figure in the dispute — attacked A.J. Diamond, the consultant, for a feasibility study aimed at retaining and renovating the Howard building:

If the Diamond report were to be implemented, we would not have the 1846 building as designed by John G. Howard. It would be the Howard building remodelled according to Diamond – a desecration not a restoration. ... In other words, the Howard building would have lost its architectural integrity, and would no longer be worthy of the designation historic site. It would just be a recycled relic.[1]

Moreover, the architectural principles involved in the design of the original asylum, and of the alternative proposals put forward in the dispute, were adroitly collated, by government public relations agents, into propaganda designed to steamroller opposition.

Lying behind all this is the matter of conflicting opinion among a wide range of professional consultants, and of the interpretation and use of those consultants' opinions by the civic service professionals advising the responsible politicians.

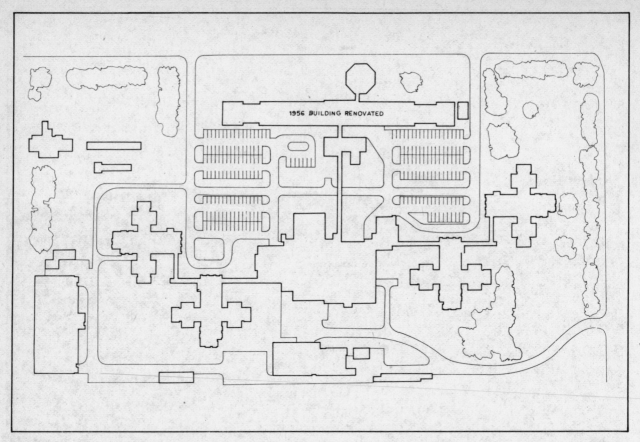

Site Plan 1, Approved Master Plan prepared by Somerville, McMurrich and Oxley. Illustration: Somerville, McMurrich and Oxley

All these important issues are thrown into sharp relief in the 999 Queen controversy, and all of them affect the future of historic buildings across Canada. A detailed account of each of them follows a brief chronology of events.

CHRONOLOGY OF EVENTS

Early in 1975, the Ontario Heritage Foundation learned of the intention of the Ontario Ministry of Government Services to proceed with demolition of the 1846 Provincial Asylum. This demolition was to form part of an on-going program of reorganization of the whole site of what is now called the Queen Street Mental Health Centre. That program had commenced in 1967, with a new master plan for the site prepared by the architectural firm of Somerville, McMurrich and Oxley. Their proposal (see illustration) called for the construction of four new "treatment units," and of a series of on-site community facilities. The first two of these units were to sit in the side gardens of the old asylum building. The second two were to replace

wings added to the original building in 1866. Following that, a 1956 building which had been erected in front of the 1846 building was to be renovated, and then, as the last stage of the reorganization, the 1846 building was to be demolished to make room for a large central parking lot to serve the whole complex. In 1968, this general proposal was adopted, and implementation began. By 1975, the four new treatment units, together with a new community centre were all in place, and the Ministry of Government Services proposed to commence phase III of the master plan — renovation of the 1956 building, and the demolition of the original main building of 1846.

Between 1968 and 1975, however, the climate of opinion in Canada in respect to historical buildings had dramatically changed. During the same period in which the first two phases of the master plan had been implemented, the Ontario Government had responded to this changed climate by passing the Heritage Act, a new piece of legislation which empowered municipalities to list, and to designate buildings of architectural or historical significance. At the same time, the Government reorganized the Ontario Heritage Foundation, a provincially funded body responsible for a broad range of heritage matters, in addition to the acquis-

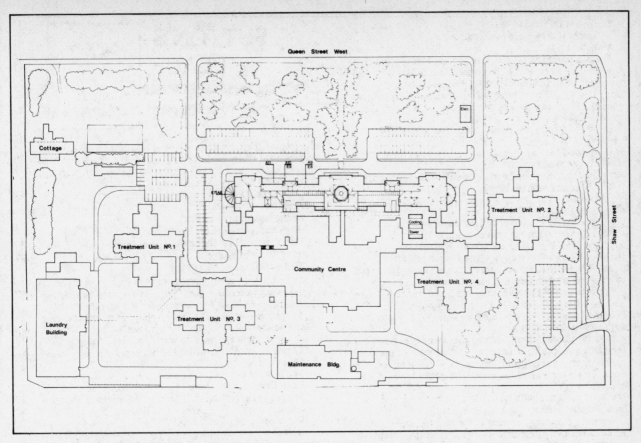

Site Plan 2, alternative showing preservation of 1846 building, as proposed by A.J. Diamond Associates. Illustration: A.J. Diamond Associates

ition and maintenance of certain heritage properties in the province. At this time, the Foundation became an agency of the newly-created Ministry of Culture and Recreation.

Early in 1975, as part of its comprehensive program of listing and designation, the Toronto Historical Board advised city council to designate John Howard's building of 1846 as an historic site. On February 19, the council adopted a report urging the provincial government to retain the building. Following this, the Historical Board approached the government to suggest that consideration be given to the possibility of renovating the building, a possibility which the government had not previously explored.

In April 1975, the Ministry of Government Services released its in-house study, which concluded that retaining and renovating the 1846 building would cost $34-million as opposed to $12.5-million for renovating the 1956 building. That is to say, it projected a construction cost of $170 per square foot for the earlier building, as opposed to $84 for the later one.

This discrepancy was so large that many observers doubted the credibility of the ministry's study. On the face of it, the comparison seemed ridiculous. One architect familiar with the high cost of renovation work for demanding private clients, remarked that he had "built some palaces in his day." but nothing had ever approached $170 per square foot. The Ontario Heritage Foundation and the Toronto Historical Board therefore decided jointly to seek an independent study, and they commissioned the firm of A.J. Diamond Associates to undertake it.

In November 1975, the Diamond report was released. It concluded that the 1846 building could accommodate the functions proposed for the 1956 building, and that the cost of the necessary renovations would be $18-million, rather than $34-million, as the Ministry of Government Services had claimed (as compared with $12.5-million for the alternative of renovating the 1956 building). The report concluded that renovation of the Howard building would "retain a fine example of Toronto's physical, cultural and institutional heritage, while providing first-class modern facilities for its users, and pride to its sponsors and the community."[2]

The Diamond report was welcomed by the Heritage Foundation, the Toronto Historical Board and the city council, but not by the Ministry of Government Services. That agency reviewed the Diamond report and announced that the feasibil-

So they want to save 999.

I wonder if they were ever in it.

I was once.

I was a volunteer, but it was soon evident to me that the line between those who could leave at night and those who had to stay behind locked doors was a vague one. It was a line composed of chance, genes, luck, money, love, family support. Some of us had those things. Others didn't.

Once a group of male and female volunteers organized a dance. A male volunteer approached a woman and asked her to dance. While they were dancing, he made small talk.

"How long have you been a patient?" he crooned.

The woman reeled in shock.

"A patient? I'm not a patient. I'm the president of a service club..."

No, you couldn't always tell the difference.

Sometimes, of course, you could.

There was the ward on the fifth floor, where you thanked God each time you visited for the difference.

999: I will never forget those haunted faces, haunted eyes, neglected bodies, and forgotten spirits.

999: rows of old people, plopped there because there was no where else to go, no one who wanted them, the debris of a society that values only youth, a world that neglects to nourish its roots.

999: a place where, from the vantage point of freedom you could, if you were open, gain some perspective on yourself and the world — so long as you knew you were one of the ones who could leave at the end of the day.

999: it was not without humor — grim humor, but humor nonetheless.

We were standing, waiting in the hall for an elevator, when I noticed the clock. It registered 10:30 and we were supposed to be out by nine.

"Good heavens," I said. "Is that clock right?"

One of the patients who was waiting with us cracked: "Lady, if that clock was right, it wouldn't be in here."

999: My emotions straddled a spectrum of highs and lows in my experiences within its walls.

There was sadness, and frustration, and pain, and anxiety, and fear.

But most of all, there was the marvellous heady

SUTTON'S PLACE

Joan Sutton

feeling of the importance of being a human being, the power that there is in eye contact, in the the warmth of the human hand, in the softness of the spoken word, in the healing quality of laughter.

For there was often response.

And that was rewarding.

So they want to save 999.

They can't have ever been there.

For if you were there once, you would not need to preserve the building.

You would never forget it.

I can sit here now, surrounded by light and warmth and companionship and recreate that monstrous building, even though it is years since I was there.

There are sounds. The heavy clang of doors shutting some in and some out: the rattle of keys that in turning brought the outside world in then closed it off.

There is laughter, often out of control; and tears, without a stopping.

Those were the sounds of 999.

I will never forget them.

There were sights: barbaric reminders of human indignity, human indifference, callousness.

But mostly, 999 was a smell.

If you were never there, I hope you never smell that smell. But if you were, it will never leave your nostrils.

Saving 999.

Why? I wonder.

As a reminder of how inhuman we can be perhaps?

But then we have other such reminders in the world and they haven't put an end to indifference, intolerance, lack of vision.

No, I don't want them to save 999.

Let's take the money and save some people.

Sutton's Place: Column by Joan Sutton, the *Toronto Sun*, December 17, 1975. Illustration: Joan Sutton and the *Toronto Sun*

ity of renovation for the required purposes had not been demonstrated. Moreover it claimed that the estimated costs of the renovations as proposed in the Diamond report were inaccurate, arguing that $23-million was a more realistic figure rather than Diamond's claim of $18-million. At the same time however, the ministry also revised the figures for its own feasibility study done in April (which had presupposed a different approach to renovation than that proposed by Diamond) from $34-million down to $30-million.

On the basis of this, the government confirmed its intention to demolish. Toronto City Council made last-minute efforts to persuade the province to delay demolition at least, pending a review of the discrepancies between the various professional experts' opinions. But this appeal was rejected.

It is an ironic footnote to this whole chronology that early in 1976 the Ministry of Government Services announced that implementation of the renovations to the 1956 building would be delayed,

since the tenders received for the work were considerably higher than their estimates.

THE "IMAGE PROBLEM"

In recent years, the Toronto public had grown increasingly conscious of the significance of historical buildings, and was sufficiently appalled by the alarming numbers of the most important of these that were being destroyed, to attempt to slow, if not actually to halt the process of their unquestioned destruction. Beginning perhaps with the 1960s campaign to protect Old Fort York from the traffic engineers who proposed a routing for the Gardiner Expressway that would have cut right across it, this public awareness reached a new plateau, politically, economically and architecturally, in the battle first for the retention of the Old

City Hall and then Union Station.[3]

Given these successes, one might have thought that such a major monument as Howard's Provincial Asylum could also have been rescued. Its architectural importance was certainly the equal of the others. But Howard's building was not a tourist attraction like Old Fort York. It did not evoke the manifold array of public and private memories which the Old City Hall does. Nor could one reminisce nostalgically and affectionately, as Pierre Berton does, when writing on the Great Hall of Union Station:

"How many kisses have been exchanged in that vast concourse? Ten million? Twenty million? More than we know for there was a time when impecunious young Torontonians, lacking a front parlour or a secluded doorstep, mingled with the swirling crowds of well-wishers and, quite unremarked, smooched shamelessly in public, moving from platform to platform to make their spurious goodbyes.[4]

As opposed to this kind of sentimental response, the Provincial Asylum elicited largely hostile public feelings. The column of *Toronto Sun* writer Joan Sutton (illustrated here) may serve as a typical example of public opinion as it was expressed during the controversy.

But this attitude was not confined to the lay public. In a paper published in the *Canadian Architect* in September 1975, sociologist Merrijoy J. Kelner quoted from an interview with a staff member: "When we pull the old building down, we will pull the old mythology with it."[5]

On December 16, 1975, Dr. Frederick H. Lowy, the chairman of the Department of Psychiatry at the University of Toronto, entered the fray with letters to the editors of the *Toronto Star*, and the *Globe and Mail*. Noting that the Howard building's forbidding "presence is a highly visible reminder of a previous era of treatment of the mentally ill from which, thankfully, we have emerged", he called for demolition.[6]

In short, a broad spectrum of lay and professional opinion revealed an inability to see past the powerful associations the building evoked, of a profoundly disturbing past. Evidently, the Howard building, like the Van Horne mansion in Montreal discussed in *City Magazine* (Vol. 2 No. 1), aroused such complex emotions as to prejudice its future, given the current inability of Canadians to come to terms with the darker aspects of their cultural heritage.

POLITICAL SPLITS

Neither the Toronto City Council nor the Provincial Legislature split ideologically over the question of preserving 999 Queen. Throughout the controversy, the city council offered virtually unanimous support to the Toronto Historical Board, in its efforts to save the building. As for the legislature, although it wasn't quite unanimous in its objections to saving the building, it is true to say that neither the NDP nor the Liberals offered any official opposition to the Conservative Government's intention to demolish. In short, the city council, broadly speaking, supported preservation, while the legislature more-or-less unanimously opposed it. Instead, the battle to save the building crossed all party lines, and conventional ideological distinctions; the bitterest disputes occurred within the various parties, ministries, and ideological groups.

For example, the principal governmental thrust towards saving the building came from the Heritage Foundation, within the newly created Ministry of Culture and Recreation; and the principal opponent of the Foundation, in its efforts, was the Design Services Branch of Culture and Recreation's fellow ministry, Government Services. Throughout the dispute, the Design Services Branch maintained the position that the Heritage Foundation lacked a grasp of the practicalities and economics of the situation; in its turn, the Heritage Foundation remained to the end unconvinced of Government Services' ability to come to grips with the cultural significance of the Howard building. This inter-ministry dispute was further complicated by the fact that the city council proposed to list, and then to designate the Howard building an historic site, under powers recently given to it by an act of the same government which proposed to demolish the building! This rather paradoxical situation was eventually resolved by a legal determination by the provincial government, that the power to list and designate, granted to municipalities under the Heritage Act, did not extend to provincially owned properties! Thus the newly re-organized Foundation, within the newly created ministry, had largely to fall back on moral persuasion, rather than on any substantial legal powers, in its precedent-setting challenge to its fellow ministry. Even though it failed to preserve the Howard Asylum, the Ministry of Culture and Recreation can at least hope that it has impressed upon the rather philistine Ministry of Government Services, the cultural significance of that part of Ontario's heritage of which Government Services is *de facto* custodian.

Within the higher echelons of the Conservative Party, the battle to save the building was led by Anthony Adamson, Ontario Conservative of long standing, pioneer of historical building preservation in the province, former chairman of the Ontario Arts Council, and chairman of the Heritage Foundation's Architectural Conservation Committee. Like his allies in the Ministry of Culture and Recreation, Adamson failed, despite vigorous efforts, to persuade his opposite numbers to reconsider. Indeed, in the end he was sufficiently dis-

The place of
999 Queen Street
in the history of
Canadian psychiatry

One of the most curious features about the public discussion of the fate of 999 Queen Street West was its revelation of how deep-seated primitive man's superstitious fear of insanity remains. Above all, this was evident in the confusion between the building itself and what was alleged to have taken place within it. A minister of the Crown referred to its "horrid connotations," while, for some members of the psychiatric profession, the very bricks and mortar of the structure seemed to possess an inherent maleficence. Another and more enlightened generation may be left the task of probing this form of irrationality: what is of course disturbing is that neither politicians nor psychiatrists were able to break free from the folk-image of the old asylum and visualize it not only as, with renovation, it might be, but also as it once was. For the Howard building was one of the first Canadian examples of a reform movement in the treatment of the mentally ill that had been sweeping the Western world. Whatever it may have become, through maladministration or the press of circumstance, it began as a fresh and innovative experiment in "moral treatment."

Two pictures may be taken to represent the old and the new in attitudes towards the insane in the eighteenth century: the first is the eighth scene of Hogarth's *Rake's Progress*, in which two idle and fashionable ladies, having paid their tuppence, have been admitted to the incurable ward of Bethlem Hospital to ogle its inmates, sunk deep in madness and beastliness. The second is of Philippe Pinel removing the chains from the mad women of the Saltpetriere in 1795, heralding the end of millenia of misery and torture and the commencement of moral treatment.

Enlightened eighteenth century opinion had rejected the ancient notion that insanity was caused by demonic possession; instead, most educated people believed that it arose from some physical cause. Perhaps it stemmed from an excess of blood, phlegm, black bile or yellow bile, or more specifically, from heredity, disease, climate, excessive emotion or even "self-pollution". If cure there was (and most people were pessimistic) it could only come through heroic methods which shocked the system and brought a physical crisis. The medical superintendent of Bethlem testified in 1815 that "patients are ordered to be bled about the latter end of May, or the beginning of June, according to the weather, and after they have been bled they take vomits once a week for a certain number of weeks; after that we purge the patients. That has been the practice invariably for years, long before my time; it was handed down to me by my father, and I do not know any better practice." The prime purpose of madhouses, however, was not treatment but incarceration in which the use of "mechanical restraints" was normal. Most of the insane in England were held not at Bethlem but in poorhouses, Bridewells and common jails, in conditions of indescribable filth and inhumanity.

At almost the same historical moment, in England and France, two men revolutionized the care of the mentally ill. Philippe Pinel, a doctor, sought to rescue this branch of medicine from its medieval state through the application of clinical observation. Since bleeding and corporal punishment seemed ineffectual in practice, he experimented with a

---

mayed by the behaviour of the Minister of Government Services, Mrs. Scrivener, that he attacked her indignantly in the letters column of the *Globe and Mail*.

The Asylum's defenders on the left fared no better than Adamson. For example, Toronto City Council's Reform Caucus looked to the NDP Caucus in the legislature for assistance, as they have done on many other municipal/ provincial issues, but they got no help. Like Margaret Campbell of the Liberals, NDP member Michael Cassidy individually challenged Mrs. Scrivener on the floor of the house, but NDP health critic Dr. Jan Dukszta remained silent throughout the dispute. Worst of all, left-wing observers had the dismaying experience of hearing NDP house leader Stephen Lewis cheer the government decision to confirm demolition, when it was finally announced.

In short, the politics of the battle can be summed up in two different ways. Optimistically, one can say that historic building preservation is a non-partisan political issue; pessimistically one has to conclude that — in the crunch — no party in Ontario can be relied upon in this important area of public policy.

RESTORATION VERSUS RECYCLING

The most apt comment on the question of "restoration" versus "recycling" was made by Anthony Adamson. At the last-minute meeting with cabinet ministers Margaret Scrivener (Government Services), Robert Welch (Culture and Recreation), and John Miller (Health), organized to attempt to delay demolition, Adamson challenged the December 10 statement to the house (quoted above), in which Mrs. Scrivener contrasted "desecration" of

therapy that was essentially psychological. Through understanding, kindness and a sustaining environment he hoped to restore in the patient his lost hope and dignity. In England, a Quaker tea merchant named William Tuke, revolted by disclosures of mistreatment in a private asylum in York, founded the York Retreat. There, physical shocks and restraints were abandoned in favour of the encouragement of self-restraint and self-control through the benevolent, and somewhat authoritarian, application of Christian principles.

Through their example and their writings, the "moral treatment" pioneered by Pinel and Tuke spread rapidly. It was the principle behind the establishment of reformed mental institutions in Britain, France and the United States in the first quarter of the nineteenth century. In North America, the first public mental hospital, the Massachusetts State Lunatic Hospital at Worcester, opened its doors in 1833, the outcome of a campaign waged by Horace Mann. As these institutions were founded in other states, the older composite institutions housing the criminal, the pauper and the lunatic began to disappear. By 1844 the Association of Medical Superintendents of American Institutions for the Insane (now the American Psychiatric Association) had been founded, with its own journal, the *American Journal of Insanity*. Both these and comparable developments in Britain began to influence Canadian thinking in the 1830s.

In British North America, then, the notion that insanity was curable, and that the mentally ill required special care at the hands of public authority, came late. In Nova Scotia, legislation of 1774 gave magistrates the power to "safely lock up in some secure place" the "furiously mad and dangerous," and the other colonies followed suit later. When, in the 1830s, Dr. George Peters was revolted by the condition of chained lunatics in the Saint John jail, "some of them perfectly naked and in a state of filth," he was drawing attention to a situation which existed in all the colonies.

It was New Brunswick which established the first public institution for the care of the mentally ill, in 1847; Toronto's provincial asylum opened shortly after. As early as 1836, the New Brunswick legislature had struck a committee to look into the whole question of the institutionalized treatment of the insane, and that committee's report, issued by the chairman, Charles Simonds, on December 2, 1836, is a landmark in Canadian medical history. Based on expert opinion obtained from the United States and Britain, the report recommended the building of an asylum dedicated to humane and moral treatment. Both it and similar reports made to other colonial legislatures in the period paid careful attention to the setting of the institution. Mental hospitals should be surrounded by varied scenery, in full view of public roads "thronged with the evidences of life and business," to encourage in patients the belief that they were "in a world of hope, and among beings who are engaged in the everyday business of life." The structure itself should exert a moral influence, a Nova Scotian report held; "good taste and a regard for comfort should characterize all the arrangements, both internal and external, as calculated to induce self-respect and a disposition for self-control."

Canada's early psychiatrists still held some peculiar notions about the cause of insanity. Though British North America was relatively tranquil — "it is a soil in which spiritualism and all other isms, so prolific of insanity, do not flourish" — yet it was not altogether free from stress. There was a danger that railroads might "overstimulate the energies of the people;" and Canadians should not become too caught up in the race for riches — in it, "the mental powers are subject to sudden and heavy strains and the brain gives way." But on one point all were agreed. Institutionalized care and humane treatment were vastly preferable to the cruelty and degradation that had preceded them, and held high promise in the cure of insanity itself. It was upon a floodtide of such humane optimism that the Provincial Asylum was launched.

Sydney Wise

Howard's masterpiece, if Diamond's adaptive policy were to be implemented, with some sort of hypothetical "restoration" of it, apparently the only treatment she deemed "worthy of the designation historic site." "It would," Adamson drily observed, "be difficult, in 1975, to find lunatics to house in a lunatic asylum."[7]

If "restoration" didn't require a new clientele of lunatics, then presumably the other obvious functional alternative would have been a "museum" use of the old asylum building. There have, of course, recently been several "museum" type restorations accomplished by preservationists in Canada, but this approach is only occasionally appropriate. It is now generally recognized that for most buildings, the alternative of "recycling" is usually more appropriate.[8] Indeed, A.J. Diamond Associates, who prepared the feasibility study of the Howard building, has (with Diamond's former partner, Barton Myers [see *City Magazine*, Vol. 1, No. 5&6]) made a significant professional reputation with schemes for "recycling" of older buildings, amongst the most notable of which are the office building at 322 King Street West, and York Square, both in Toronto. This was precisely the approach the Diamond report recommended for the Howard building. The exterior masonry shell, the dome and most of the roof were proposed to be retained and "restored", but a considerable portion of the interior was proposed to be gutted and rebuilt. What is more, a substantial infill addition was proposed to be inserted into a series of vacant bays along the rear elevation of the building, rising above the roofline to form a sort of clerestorey, visible from Queen Street.

When the Diamond report was submitted to the Ministry of Government Services for their review, it was severely criticized for, among other things, "recycling" rather than "restoring" the building. Lorne Oxley, architect for the original master plan, when asked for his comments, deplored the fact that the Diamond scheme "demolishes and re-

A history of the Provincial Lunatic Asylum

A "Temporary Provincial Asylum" had been operating in Toronto from the early 1840s, before John Howard drew up plans for a magnificent permanent structure that would embody the latest thinking on the treatment of mental disorders. Its cornerstone was laid in August 1846, with much ceremony and popular acclaim. The band of the 81st Regiment was there, the fire companies and national societies, the city and home district councils, and the provincial judges. Construction proceeded slowly, however, in the bad times that began the next year, and the building was not finally ready for occupancy until January of 1850. Even then, only the big central block with its crowning dome had been constructed. The long wings planned by Howard were not proceeded with. And while this might have seemed due economy at the time, it not only drastically interfered with the original design but also brought a looming problem of accommodation, as the inmates from the temporary asylum were transferred and many new patients added. The grand new institution would be notably full from the start.

Nevertheless, at its opening in 1850, public enthusiasm and hopes were high, as reflected in the Toronto press of the day. Reporters noted the well-planned layout of each spacious corridor, with sleeping and day-rooms, a dining room and a visiting room, and cold, hot, and shower baths. They remarked on the special ventilation arrangements (lunatics being specially susceptible to "deleterious gases"), the advanced hot-water heating system to ensure comfortable warmth, the fifty acres of grounds that would provide attractive gardens "healthily to affect the minds of the insane." The whole, according to the Toronto *Globe*, was "exceeding handsome, commodious, healthful and safe . . . a monu-ment to the Christian liberality of the people."

That widely-followed journal went further, however, to express the spirit of moral reform and humane care that had produced the new institution. Its superintendent should be both a first-rate medical man and a wise, outgoing, warm-hearted person "who would bring patients into his family." The staff "ought not to be keepers so much as companions . . . intelligent, conversational, tender, patient, to draw their people into employment and reading." There should be healthy amusements, music, socializing, productive labours indoors and out, "sustained not by mere authority or strength of will, but by perfected plans and self-operating inducements." In sum, it urged, "let the establishment be an Asylum — not a mere hospital or a prison — an asylum where disturbing influences are absent . . . where every good part of human nature is brought into play. We hope that the institution for which so much has been done will be pointed to as a sample of what Canadians can do."

Whatever the vision and the hope, the fact was that without its wings the new structure had not much more than half the room that had originally been planned — for about 300 instead of over 500 patients. Besides, there was insufficent space for their classification and separation, held to be so vital. Instead of the twelve classes provided for by the original design, there could only be three. Conse-

---

builds in different form over 40 per cent of the historical monument supposed to be worthy of preservation." Oxley went on to lament the fact that the new clerestorey wings proposed "will obscure the silhouette of the old building, reduce the legibility of its rhythmical architectural concept," and "diminish the dominance of the dome as a terminal feature of the vista down Ossington Avenue".[9] Be reminded that the building Oxley is discussing here is the building his own firm's master plan recommended be demolished. The premise here appears to be: either restore, or demolish; no more supple, let alone subtle, intermediate possibility of recycling was considered.[10]

CONSULTANT DISPUTES AND THE CIVIL SERVICE POSITION

Although it proved to be the decisive issue, the "restoration" versus "recycling" argument was only one of several which split the consultants advising their respective clients. The other issues may be summarized as follows:

Programming and Maintenance — To accommodate the Ministry of Health program, the Diamond scheme produced a final building size of 195,000 square feet, while the Oxley scheme produced one of 151,000. According to the Diamond report, this was basically due to the fact that the original 1846 building, and the various additions with which they started was 201,000 square feet while the 1956 one which Oxley's firm started with was only 113,000. The Diamond report argued that this differential should not be regarded as wasted, since it allowed for "additional space for program functions of unassigned space for departmental growth."[11] Oxley replied that the "surplus is fairly evenly distributed so that no blocks of space are left available for new uses that may develop in the future." Oxley also argued that the excess square

Lithograph showing the entire complex at 999 Queen Street West from the rear, from the "Report of the Commissioner of Public Works of the Province of Ontario for 1869." Photo: Ontario Archives

quently, as the asylum's very first report indicated in 1851, in one ward "the violent, the idiotic, the epileptic, the filthy and the mischievous" were inescapably mixed with the "quiet and harmless." There were better things also: the rule that "no cruelty or even threatening can be tolerated"; the fact that isolation, usually for short periods, had replaced the strait-jacket, used only to prevent self-destruction; and the fact that the grounds were fast being landscaped to provide agreeable walks and work for the inmates, as well as contact with the world outside.

Still, the province did not help, by loading the criminally insane from county jails on the asylum; nor municipalities which were glad to transfer to it the mentally deficient element of their local poor and not have to pay for their support. Even by 1852, it appeared that the Provincial

footage in the Diamond scheme would involve "attendant continuing added costs for operation maintenance and repairs."[12] Diamond replied that it should be remembered that 40,000 of the 195,000 square feet involved in the Diamond scheme consisted of existing masonry wall thickness, "for which no premium in construction or maintenance is paid."

Oxley argued that inconvenience to staff would result from the adoption of the Diamond scheme, since it involved 2,650 feet of corridor, rather than the 1,874 feet in the Oxley scheme. On the contrary, Diamond replied, inconvenience to staff would be reduced, despite this differential in total length, since the Diamond scheme provided two elevator cores, resulting in typical horizontal distances of 175 feet, while the Oxley scheme provided only one, resulting in comparable distances of 280 feet.

Numerous, more minor programming issues were also in dispute, but none of them appear to be as central as these.

Structure — A dispute which made a major difference between the final cost figures respectively for the Diamond scheme and the ministry scheme for renovating the 1846 building arose over the question of adequate internal floor structure. Diamond's structural engineering consultant, M.S. Yolles Associates, concluded that retention of the existing wooden floor structure of the building was acceptable, with certain improvements being made to its bearing points at the supporting masonry walls, and to its fire rating. The ministry, and its consultants, C.D. Carruthers and Wallace, refused to consider this ingenious technical proposal, arguing instead that renovation, if it were to be considered, would require the replacement of the entire existing interior floor structure of the building.

Mechanical Equipment — Diamond's mechanical consultants, Rybka, Smith and Ginsler, recommended use of a heating, ventilating and air conditioning system which the Ministry of Government

Asylum would either have to get increased grants or close to all but paying patients, thereby "casting out one hundred paupers." Yet the government, facing inflation, refused to increase the funds — while the institution, facing inflation, saw its costs per patient mounting steadily.

Underlying the whole problem was the rapid growth of the province's population, largely produced by heavy immigration around the close of the forties, which put unenvisaged pressure on its central mental institution. Moreover, the very process of immigration, with its accompanying culture shock, social alienation and plain economic failures, again helped expand mental illness to an unanticipated degree. In short, the hopefully conceived new asylum suffered sharply from the lack of public understanding that however large, carefully equipped, and costly was the handsome pile on Queen Street, it was still not adequate to cope with the results of misery and strain in a fast-changing Canada.

It still did its best, under an energetic and forthright superintendent, Dr. Joseph Workman. He improved sanitation, increased the rates of recovery, and dealt successfully with his host of problems, except the perennial one of overcrowding. Year by year he returned to the attack in his reports to the provincial legislature, urging the building of the wings and the completion of the original Howard design. The government did re-move the criminally insane to Kingston in 1855. Financial stringencies were also eased. But Workman had to go on stressing that he had only "half a house", in spite of its other merits. "Visitors to the asylum seldom fail," he noted, "to admire its architectural beauty and the amplitude of its dimensions." In external design, workmanship, and "suitability of internal arrangements" it had no superior in North America. But (as he wrote in 1858): "Why are 397 now crowded into this half-erected house?"

For years more a dilatory and insufficiently concerned government left Workman's cry unanswered. The wings were not finally built, to the design of Kivas Tully, until 1869. By then, however, the continual overcrowding, the make-do, the necessary piecemeal shifts that damaged both the integrity of the design and the spirit of the institution, had set an unfortunate pattern. Even the new wings could not then alter a tradition of too little and too late. The gardens of 999 Queen Street might be a Toronto showplace by the 1870s, frequented by citizens and visitors, who regularly admired the stately building at their centre. Yet behind its walls there seemed forbidding shadows. The failure of the edifice to live up to the original visions of space, openness and kindly comfort — through no fault of its own — had only enabled all the old irrational popular fears and prejudices concerning "lunacy" to become the more confirmed.

Who was to blame? In a most direct sense, provincial governments who had constrained the institution from the start, who had indeed created more problems of crowding in its most critical early years, and who had not listened to the plea even to complete the building on the level intended back in 1846. Their modern-day descendants have only acted true to form in turning an incomplete embarrassment of 130 years into a parking lot. Yet behind the responsible governments and the elected politicians there were always the people on whose votes they rested. And the people then did not understand: once again they have been consistent. Concern with externals, and tax rates, led them evidently to think that they had done enough. There was the splendid asylum. Now there were better things to worry about. Conceivably, it might have gone otherwise in the 1850s, if the public had been more aware that all that had been done was half-done, that the fine hopes for mental care could not be adequately sustained. Conceivably, too, had they been better informed in the 1970s that the Howard building was a monumental public achievement at its inception, and a bright promise of humanitarian, constructive care of the mentally ill, that building would not now be destroyed.

J.M.S. Careless

Services and its consultant, Engineering Interface, found "unacceptable." According to D. Dastur of the ministry's Design Services Branch, the proposed system "does not provide for adequate mechanical ventilation, which is very essential for the type of usage; is based on a proprietary American concept with no Canadian content; has life expectancy of only five to seven years; and requires fuel cost penalties to be paid."[13]

In an abrasive reply, Lionel Ginsler argued that the standards of the ministry were in many cases unnecessarily high, especially given the fact of an impending energy crisis; that his unusual proposals for the project had in fact been tested in other applications; and that the claim about an American proprietary concept was simply erroneous.

Costing — Diamond's cost consultant, A.J. Vermeulen, had concluded that the cost of implementing the Diamond scheme would be approximately $18-million, but the ministry's consultants, Hanscomb Roy Associates, costed the Diamond scheme and arrived at a figure of $21.5-million. The ministry in turn modified that figure to $23-million. Upon examining the ministry and Hanscomb Roy figures, Vermeulen revised his from $18-million up to nearly $19-million, but denied the possibility of costs higher than that. Indeed he noted that the major part of the discrepancy between his calculations and those of Hanscomb Roy lay not in the basic cost elements, but the various contingency allowances. "It will be seen," he noted, "that the suggested contingencies represent 43 per cent of the cost of the work contained in the (basic) elements 1-10, and this is excessive."[14]

All of these disputes are evidently interesting and significant. In his last-minute appeal to the premier and the cabinet, Alderman Sewell argued that "the Ministry of Government Services and the staff of A.J. Diamond Associates had not had a full opportunity to review the (differences of opinion) together."[15] The Diamond group's rebuttal was an important document, replying to ministry claims

The original building and its architect

Watercolour on paper, showing John G. Howard's original design for the Provincial Asylum. Illustration: City of Toronto Archives

What is bigger than an elephant? But this also is become man's plaything, and a spectacle at public solemnities; and it learns to skip, dance, and kneel.
                    Plutarch, *Of Fortune*

Size alone is not to be equated with grandeur, but the large scale of the old Provincial Lunatic Asylum was one measure of the government's extraordinarily grand vision in 1844, and John Howard's architectural achievement was correspondingly ambitious. Howard won the commission in a competition that year, when the population of Toronto was less than 19,000. The vast building at 999 Queen Street West was begun in 1846 and completed in 1850.

A draft statement in the architect's hand (among the Howard papers in the Toronto Public Library) outlines both the terms of reference for the commission and a claim to architectural significance for the "Building" (for it should be noted that Howard avoids referring to it as an asylum):

... the present Building was intended to accomodate [sic] 264 Patients only and the whole Building when complete would accomodate about 500 or 550, that supposing they were judiciously classified, as in the best arranged Institutions which I visited in the United States.

The instructions I received from the Building Committee were to design a Building for the care (not incarceration) of about 500 of the Insane of Upper Canada, and I made a tour of the United States in serch [sic] of the best information upon that subject. The present building was designed and [when] the Plans were submitted to the Medical Men at their annual meeting at the Aster [sic] House [in]New York, after examining them the said

Gentlemen expressed themselves highly pleased with the arrangements and pronounced them the best for the purpose on the Continent of America.

In other words, it was conceived as a commodious hospital, not a crowded prison, to be built in stages, with provision for the classification and separation of patients, according to their condition, in the recently approved fashion. Howard was justly proud of the testimonial of the "Medical Men"; he omits to mention that his asylum was to be as advanced structurally, mechanically, and stylistically as it was medically.

Then, as now, commissions for large public buildings were often awarded on the basis of competitions (with just as much controversy — more, in fact — over the conditions

---

the group considered unfounded, or worse, based on misconstrued material, but the rebuttal was not evaluated by the ministry or cabinet. There was no opportunity. The cabinet proceeded immediately to confirm its decision to demolish.

ARCHITECTURAL PRINCIPLES AND PUBLIC RELATIONS

The architectural issues involved in this controversy were quite complex. The protagonists in the dispute often not only took different sides on particular issues; they also disagreed on what the crucial issues really were. Naturally enough, all this meant that the dispute was very difficult for the public to understand. In such circumstances, it might be thought that the principal actors in the debate would make special efforts to render the

complex issues comprehensible. But as the controversy proceeded, this rarely happened. In fact, the gross manner in which the Minister of Government Services, Margaret Scrivener, dealt with the issues in her statement — to the legislature, to the public at large, and to her own constituents — eventually disillusioned many observers profoundly.

The first of two examples is the "restoration" versus "recycling" question. The Diamond report had concluded that the asylum offered "a unique opportunity to at once retain a fine example of Toronto's physical, cultural and institutional heritage while providing first class modern facilities for its users and pride to its sponsors and the community." And in response, Lorne Oxley objected to the fact the Diamond proposal "demolishes and rebuilds in different form over 40 per cent of the historical monument supposed to be worthy of preservation."[16]

In turn, Oxley's comments were passed on to the

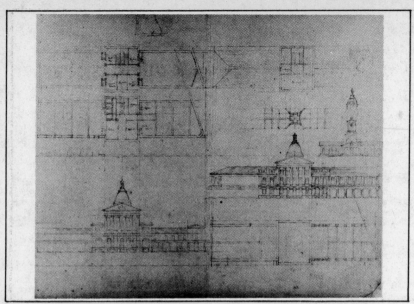

Sheet of drawings by John G. Howard, showing designs for Kingston City Hall, from Howard's private papers. Illustration: Toronto Public Library Archives

and results of the competitions). Howard was a great "competition man." In the decade before 1844, when he won the premium of 30 pounds for the Asylum, Howard carried off prizes (but not necessarily the commissions) in five major concourses. The autobiographic *Incidents in the Life of John G. Howard, Esq. ...* (1885) lists market halls in Toronto (1834) and Kingston (1841); gaols and courthouses in Toronto (1836) and London (1837); and Queen's College, Kingston (1842). We know of other competitions he entered, such as Brock's monument at Queenston in 1843, and those which he helped organize, such as St. James' Cathedral at Toronto in 1849.

Like his contemporaries, Howard seems to have found the allure of large public buildings irresistible. The challenge of such work in terms of organization, the artistic problem of big scale, the promise of fame, and the likelihood of riches, all attracted the hopefuls to possible commissions. Howard seems to have been more than usually susceptible to the temptation of creating such designs on speculation. On numerous occasions he was even the designer of *impossible* commissions, grandiloquent public buildings with no hope of execution, in the age-old tradition of "paper architects." The asylum was clearly an opportunity to seize. It was the greatest opportunity that ever came his way.

In the Canadas in the 1840s there were few precedents for monumental commissions of any sort. Only the Kingston City Hall of 1842-3, by George Browne, and Bonsecours Market in Montreal of 1845-52, by William Footner, bore comparison. Indeed, nothing would surpass the Provincial Asylum that Howard actually built until the Parliament Buildings were erected in Ottawa — a staggering undertaking of 1859-66.

Until the Howard Building was constructed the Province's mentally ill occupied a variety of makeshift homes. *Gleason's* magazine thought the conversion, for example, of Toronto's old Parliament Building into a "mad-house" had been an "easy transformation" (according to the issue of 17 July, 1852).

The monumentality of the new asylum was indicative of the magnitude of the problem facing the province after years of inaction, but it was also the generous response of an age that saw itself as enlightened — in spite of its Dickensian shortcomings. The building was the focus of civic pride. When the cornerstone was laid by the Chief Justice in August 1846, a splendid procession

---

Design Services Branch of the Ministry of Government Services. The branch then summarized the issue as follows:

The (Diamond) report proposes not only extensive changes to the interior to meet the program requirements but also a large percentage of changes to exterior walls and roof line, so that the original appearance of the building has been considerably altered. This obviously defeats the aim of the Ontario Heritage Foundation to preserve the building. The proposal merely becomes a "recycling" of an old building for a new function. A valid approach, but quite different from the preservation of a historical landmark. [17] & [18]

But in her turn, when she made the final statement to the legislature, Mrs. Scrivener summed up the whole issue by calling Diamond's proposal "a desecration not a restoration." So much for measured public exposition of complex architectural issues. In the circumstances, no wonder the fact that the Toronto Historical Board and the Ontario Heritage Foundation both found the Diamond scheme "very

commendable" was buried.

A second example is the subtle architectural question of "the reciprocal relationship between spaces and people," which was discussed in the Kelner paper on the old and new buildings of the Queen Street Mental Health Centre. Kelner and her associates had spent time at the Mental Health Centre during the summer of 1970, when staff and patients moved from the Howard building into the first of the four new treatment units to be erected. To quote her, "We had the unique opportunity of being present at the hospital before, during and after the move to the new quarters." [19]

In her paper Kelner noted various changes of behaviour and attitudes on the part of patients and staff of the hospital, and endeavoured circumspectly to relate these changes both to the differences of forms between the old and the new buildings, and to the particular configurations of spaces which characterized the design of the new buildings themselves.

made its way from Government House to this suburban site — in spite of threatening weather. *Smith's Canadian Gazetteer* for the same year featured a view of the building as its frontispiece.

The fact that Howard designed the building after making a tour of American institutions illuminates the peculiar isolation and rapidly changing character of Canadian architecture generally and of this architect particularly, toward mid-century. John G. Howard had been born near London, England, in 1803, and trained in various minor architects' offices in the metropolitan region. That training would serve him well by exposing him to a broad range of small commissions in architecture and engineering (comparable to the limited opportunities that would be the stock-in-trade of a colonial architect) while acquainting him with the usual pattern books and other basic literature in the field. When he arrived in Canada in 1832, he was one of only a handful of trained professionals in this field in British North America. By 1844 the more gifted George Browne (who had emigrated from Belfast two years before Howard) had left Kingston to return to Montreal; in Toronto, Howard's rivals were J.G. Chewett (who had trained locally with his father, the Deputy Surveyor), and Thomas Young, the City Engineer. He may have feared competition from Canada East, or some unexpected quarter. In any case, he under-

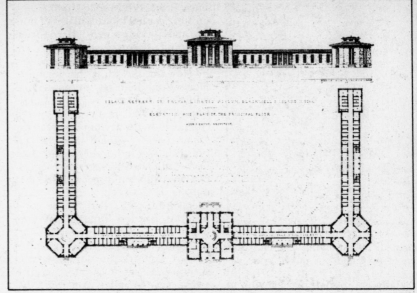

Plan and elevation of Town and Davis's Pauper Lunatic Asylum, Blackwell's Island, New York, from J.G. Howard's private papers. Illustration: Toronto Public Library Archives

took a tour of the United States in preparation for the design, which suggests at least three things: his loss of touch with major developments in architecture after a dozen years in the province; his professional inclination to review the best examples of related recent work; and his preparedness to profit from American experience (although it should be noted that American influence would not generally challenge British in importance until a quarter of a century later).

Among Howard's papers are prints that he evidently collected of plans for earlier mental institutions, including the Pauper Lunatic Asylum at Blackwell's Island, New York, designed by Town & Davis in 1834 (see illustration). It was intended to be U-shaped in design with four corner pavilions, and a nearly cubical centre block. Long windows were grouped together on either side of colossal pilasters that ran through two or three floors. Bold Greek Revival designs of this sort were fashionable and the Montreal architect William Footner considered such work par-

---

Not surprisingly, Kelner discovered that the move from the "old" to "new" facilities boosted morale significantly. At a more sophisticated level, she also noted how the somewhat dispersed and decentralized form of the new complex (four separate treatment units instead of one) favourably influenced the behaviour and attitudes of patients and staff in subtle ways. But she was cautious in her conclusions, given the complex nature of the general relationship between "spaces and people.". She noted three different factors which qualify her observations:

1. "The process of breaking down long-standing stigma is painfully slow and probably cannot be accomplished simply by the erection of a new building."
2. The design principles on which the scheme was based were only partially adopted in the built project.
3. The final buildings were used in certain respects in ways which "changed the original intentions

of the planners."[20]

Now it would not seem that this sort of scholarly discussion would play a significant role in the public resolution of the question whether or not to demolish, but it is a fact that the Kelner paper became almost the entire basis of a December 3 Scrivener news release which announced the government decision to demolish, and which offered a public justification for the decision. Dr. Kelner's cautious observations were sensationally collaged to vindicate the ministry position.

A sample paragraph reads:

The new facilities are colourful. The carpets and walls feature bright primary shades of blue, red, yellow and white. This scheme extends to the patients' rooms, which are small and private. All furnishings are modern; large windows overlook the grounds. This is certainly a change from the time – one year ago – when patients and staff worked in an environment that was noisy, stuffy, drab and confining. I believe this new Centre is a great improvement over the days when – in the old building – people were "rehabilitated" in tiny rooms with small, barred windows; thick age-encrusted

View of a corridor of the Tully wing (circa 1919), showing the civilized use of the generous public spaces.

ticularly appropriate for Canada. In his successful submission for the Bonsecours Market in 1844, he maintained that "the character of Architectural Design in Canada must necessarily be simple and masculine, aiming only at imposing grandeur, united to pleasing simplicity and harmony of proportion." Howard's design would resemble Town & Davis's somewhat in plan, with the unaffected quality that Footner advocated. But being more conservative than Town & Davis, Howard avoided their austerity of form — quite properly in an asylum.

In contrast to the heroic but unbending, overbearing image of Davis's design, Howard followed an ingratiating classical convention of unexpected origin. The high dome on a big central block with giant portico and flanking wings is a well-tried grouping of forms. And there are other unbuilt designs of the same sort by Howard, including the sheet (see illustration) that can be associated with the Kingston City Hall competition of 1841-42. In terms of overall composition the asylum has been associated with William Wilkins' National Gallery in London, which had been completed as recently as 1838. But Howard's building can be related equally to the genre that Virginia Woolf ironically called "those comfortably padded lunatic asylums which are known, euphemistically, as the stately homes of England." Like a country house, Howard's asylum was set in a park (of fifty acres), several miles from the city, overlooking the lake.

This four-storey building, extending 584 feet (according to the *Report of the Commissioner of Public Works for the Province of Ontario* in 1869), was more massive than most country houses, yet its long walls skipped, with elephantine grace, in and out — as only those of a big building that stands free in a large space could. Counting the window bays across the main front in Howard's beautiful watercolour rendering of the building, the rhythmic sequence could be expressed graphically as follows:

	5	5			5	5	
		3			3		
1	1		2	2		1	1
	3			5			3

The walls themselves were relatively plain: two storeys of white limestone (from Thorold) and then two storeys of nearly matching white brick with pilasters on the projecting pavilions. It is worth noting that the brick was laid in English bond — hence the nonsense at the time of demolition about the building being constructed of English brick — and that Howard claimed a house he had built two years earlier, in 1842, was fashioned with "the first white brick used in this city," made with clay "off Mr. Sheriff Jarvis's lot at Rosedale." Combined with stone, it was a straight-forward, inexpensive but highly effective idiom favoured at the mid-century in many important public buildings — of which this must have been the first. Though the colossal, semicircular verandahs (with three-storey columns) at the ends of the building were executed, the gigantic portico intended to adorn the centre was not built and the wings that Howard projected, at right angles to the main block, would only be erected two decades later.

This irregular plan (and the resulting broken profile) imparted a three-dimensional and picturesque quality, a sense of movement, and a congenial scale to the building that were not merely exercises in facadism. They were the outward expression of Howard's very practical (and characteristically Victorian) concern with lighting, ventilation, circulation, and fire control. The building was conceived more or less

---

supporting walls; and a series of heavy metal doors that were always locked.[21]

No mention is made anywhere in the news release of the substance of the Diamond report — either the total transformation of the building interior which the Diamond scheme entailed, or the fact that the building was in any event not primarily meant to house patients, but only to serve as an administrative centre for the whole centre.

Instead, the news release leaves the vague unstated impression that the alternative the government had rejected involved a $30-million expenditure to preserve a building for patient accommodation chiefly characterized by "barred windows," "age encrusted supporting walls," and "heavy metal doors that were always locked," as if the painful memories of "999" adhered to the 1846 building, and would adhere no matter what was done to modify it; but renovations to the 1956 building on the other hand, would blank out all unpleasant associations.[22]

THE ARCHITECTURE OF EXTREME SITUATIONS

Reflecting on the complex web of issues, personalities and attitudes which have influenced the outcome of the 999 Queen controversy, one is stunned to discover, as Alderman Janet Howard did, that architect Howard prepared his designs for the Provincial Asylum in the poignant expectation that the great edifice, once erected, might well number among its inhabitants, his own wife.

It seems to me that such a personal revelation places the whole controversy in a stark new light. For it shows that the tragic circumstances of his personal life placed Howard in a professional position in which he was forced to confront the hard questions of "man's consciously lived fragility"

as a series of staggered blocks pierced on each level by a wide corridor and with frequent wide stairhalls. The corridor was fourteen feet wide, and the ceilings generally eleven and a half feet high. Large dormitories, with fireplaces, projected at intervals from the rear of the corridor; smaller, generously scaled single rooms (ten feet by more than twelve) were ranged across the front of the building. Nearly half of the south wall of the corridors which served as day wards, was punctuated by windows. Eric Hounsom commented (in the *Journal of the Royal Architectural Institute of Canada* in June 1965): "It is indicative of [Howard's] understanding of the problem of mental illness that he provided normal size windows for his building, although in his new jail . . . the windows were very small." Even the twelve-foot corridors in Kivas Tully's later wings, which departed from Howard's proposed design and were lit only indirectly by deep "recesses" (i.e. day wards) with bay windows, appear to have been congenial spaces to judge from early views like the one illustrated. Moreover, Howard's late-Georgian style staircases, panelled doors, and folding interior window shutters with handsome mouldings were valuable not only for their elegant design and sturdy craftsmanship, but also for the sense of measurable human scale they imparted to a vast building — in striking contrast to most present-day public buildings.

In short, the plan was so contrived that every room was well lit, cross ventilation and easy circulation were ensured, yet the risk of extensive fire damage was minimized.

Howard introduced a number of important technological innovations into 999 as well (described by Peter John Stokes in *Acorn*, the Architectural Conservancy of Ontario newsletter, Vol. 1, No. 1 [Spring 1976]). The building was reputedly one of the first on the continent with hot and cold running water. The dome was no empty skyline gesture: it housed a twelve thousand-gallon tank for this gravity-fed water system. Winding around the tank, and then suspended over it, was a hanging spiral staircase — in Peter Stokes' words, "a magnificent example of the joiner's art", which originally led "to the lantern at the top serving . . . as a beacon to navigators on Lake Ontario." (Incidentally, it must also have been the CN Tower of its day for the views it afforded of the city before the erection of taller church spires and still later office blocks.) In connection with the innovative water supply, the building also featured sinks and cisterns, and even ten water closets (supplemented by privies on the grounds) and eight baths. It also had an ingenious but imperfect ventilation system. Most interesting of all, perhaps, was the heating system: the specifications (which are preserved in the Toronto Pubic Library) describe the "warming apparatus" that was used in con-

nection with a system of radiating baseboard heating — pipes set into a plastered groove in the brick of the outer walls — a novelty in the period.

Pathetically little remains of the work of one of this province's earliest and most important architects. His own house, Colborne Lodge, built in 1836, and its magnificent grounds, High Park, were left by Howard to the city and have been carefully preserved. Though little-known, the house is an extraordinarily fine (and, characteristically for Howard, very English) example of a small, asymmetrical, picturesque villa — the earliest example of this important genre known to survive (and, it seems, the earliest erected) in North America. Little else survives that is not mutilated beyond recognition, or seriously threatened, with the exception of monuments that are unrecognized, or those whose Howard connections are overlooked (such as the Lanark County Courthouse in Perth or the Leeds County Courthouse in Brockville) and erroneously assumed to be by local talents. It seems likely that little will remain apart from the magnificent cache of the architect's drawings that survives in the Toronto Public Library, the City of Toronto Archives, Colborne Lodge, and private collections.

Douglas Richardson

(Ivan Illich), of institutions and institutionalization and of the public and the private significance of architectural symbolism; a set of hard questions which, when all is said and done, has inexorably determined the history of the asylum from its creation until its destruction 125 years later.

Evidently, these questions lurked in the back of everyone's minds as the controversy raged. For the most part, however, the various disputants endeavored to suppress them, rather than confront them directly. For Lowy, the building was "a reminder of a previous era of treatment"; as the outcome of the controversy shows, it is possible to avoid being reminded. For Scrivener, following Kelner, it is almost as though "bright primary shades of blue, red, yellow and white" can some how be expected to cheer us up for good.

In short, it becomes clear that in seeking to save Howard's building, the Heritage Foundation not only faced a philistine Ministry of Government Services. It was also up against a whole intellectual

attitude to building programs for "mental health" facilities which was quite saturated with an a-historical complacency.

A.J. Diamond Associates evidently sensed this danger, for they chose to extend the terms of reference they received from the Foundation, terms which primarily emphasized the practical task "to examine the feasibility of renovating the building in a manner consistent with the requirements of the Ministry of Health."[23]

Regarding this extension of their mandate, the Diamond group consulted Robert Pos, a psychiatrist formerly on staff at the Queen Street Mental Health Centre, who set the question in context:

We are living in an era with an intense and progressively developing historical orientation. For example, to understand an idea one now must include the historical development of it. The Soviet Union went to extreme efforts to reconstruct the Czarist structures of Leningrad which had been damaged or destroyed during the German siege of World

The architects' proposal for renovation

To accommodate the requirements of a modern hospital facility in a building over a century old required an adaptive plan, one that worked with the original building but that at the same time transformed it rather than restored it. Necessary too, however, and operating quite independently from the more objective considerations of condition, function and cost, was the elusive question of associations, for in the case of the Howard building the love and sentiment that had of themselves been responsible for the preservation of many other landmarks was lacking in the general public. What took its place was a stream of associations related primarily to administrative circumstance, a policy of neglect and grim memories all symbolized by the presence of the black dome on Queen Street. As a consequence, an aspect to the study of renovation feasibility had to aim at dispelling these associations or, as proved more feasible, countering with others more positive. Part of the report was thus reserved from the outset for a discussion of the merits of renovation and consideration of the issue whether or not the Queen Street Mental Health Centre could benefit from salvaging this piece of its past and, in fact, the past of all Canadian psychiatry.

The Survey — The main focus of the survey was the architectural and structural investigation. It was generally agreed that all mechanical and electrical systems were completely outdated and inefficient and would therefore require replacement. But since this was also the case in the 1956 building, it was not a major point of argument of the futility of renovation on key architectural and structural concerns:

1. Rot in the wood joist floor construction is extensive, they claimed, and would require replacement of all floor slabs.
2. In spite of the fact that the Howard building area exceeds program area requirements, its brick-bearing wall limits the availability of large spaces and requires additional new construction for special function spaces such as the auditorium.
3. The length of the building creates unacceptably long walking distances, especially on the patient care floors.
4. Level changes in two of the floors within the central block severely restrict horizontal movement.
5. A new ground floor datum has been established throughout the complex and the first floor of the Howard building is three feet below this datum.
6. There is no basement in the Howard building which poses particular difficulties since the hospital's automated delivery vehicles are intended to operate throughout the complex at this level.
7. Certain hospital departments require blocks of contiguous space with supervised access, unlike the planning of the Howard building with its files of rooms flanking a central corridor.

The Program — Despite the severity of the concerns surrounding the condition of the building itself, it was the technical nature of the program that made the renovation proposal particularly challenging. The Howard building was not to be restored to its original condition for which there would be, of course, no application; nor was it to be turned into a museum or general purpose space. Rather it was required for use as a modern hospital facility presenting a unique opportunity to demonstrate the potential for adaptive re-use of sound old structures.

The program divided into three aspects, each requiring about a third of the total space: research and clinical functions, administration and the constraints of an existing building would have resulted no doubt in

War II. To witness the renovation and reoccupation of old structures is now a part of life. The initiative of the Toronto Historical Board and the Ontario Heritage Foundation to protect, renovate and re-use the Howard building at Queen Street should be viewed in this light.

In fact, psychiatry itself is a typical expression of this general cultural, historical orientation now expressed in terms of the individual; in order to understand the human being one begins tracing his history from the moment he is born till the here and now. In doing so one becomes quickly aware that significant parts of the past may be repressed, suppressed or denied, while others are selectively focused on with the omission of the incongruent. One role the psychiatrist may play is to help overcoming such incompleteness of the past while aiding in changing the attitudes toward it. It might be helpful if psychiatry will take this same approach to its own history. The history of Queen Street Mental Health Centre is an unalienable part of the history of Canadian psychiatry.[24]

In effect then, the Diamond group set two tasks for itself. The first, following explicitly from their terms of reference, was to demonstrate the feasibility of accommodating the Ministry program, inside the shell of the Howard building. The second, only implicit in their mandate, was to go beyond that, as Wilfrid Worland puts it, "to consideration of the issue whether or not the Queen Street Mental Health Centre could benefit from salvaging this piece of its past, and in fact, the past of all Canadian psychiatry."

Their success in accomplishing their first task was literally complete. As for the second, the results are harder to evaluate: all the appropriate issues are raised, but the resolution of them is finally, only partially successful. It is this combination of complete success on one front, and only

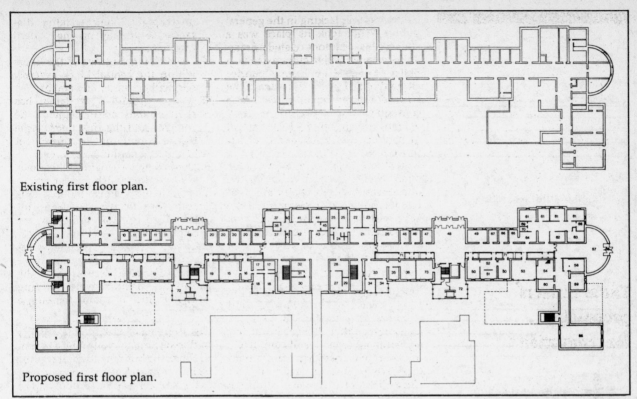

Existing first floor plan.

Proposed first floor plan.

something quite distinct from the proud Georgian shell within which the plan was to be executed. However, the plan we had to match or better was itself not a plan for new construction but for renovation of the 1956 building, and this established a precedent that guided our approach and created a criterion by which it could be evaluated.

The Renovation Proposal — The problems created by the combination of the existing building condition and the technical nature of the program, problems willingly surrendered

to in the MGS report, required a solution based not on generalized assumptions but a thorough and specific design. Viewed in isolation each of the conditions placed on the design seemed to be yet another considerable justification for demolishing the old and starting afresh. Yet viewed together, with the understanding that it was not a restoration but an adaptive re-use that was needed, the constraints of the building and the program began to sort themselves out and the solution to one problem aided in the solution to the next.

Dealing first with the major concerns expressed by MGS and the hospital architects, M.S. Yolles & Partners, Structural Engineers, opened the floor sandwich at more than 60 locations to inspect not only for evidence of rot but for clues as to its causes. In all cases, rot was found to be related to actual water penetration or condensation in the exterior masonry; there was no evidence of so-called dry-rot. Joists framing into exterior walls were rotting in their seats yet the majority of floor construction was not only sound but sufficiently over capacity to carry a top-

partial success on the other, which makes the Diamond report such an important document.

Let us consider the two issues in turn. Regarding the first, the key to their success is Worland's statement:

Viewed together, with the understanding that it was not a restoration but an adaptive re-use that was needed, the constraints of the building and the program began to sort themselves out, and the solution to one problem aided in the solution to the next.

The most striking instance of this sorting out is the proposal to insert the primary new vertical circulation elements in the recessed bays of the old south facade, thus transforming through one design idea *both* the whole internal organization of the building *and* the extent of its external periphery. But this is only one example. Raising

the first floor to create a service space below *and* to establish a new relationship of floor level to existing first floor windows is another. Manipulating the fourth floor level, *both* to clarify circulation routes *and* to articulate zones of seating in the dining room is another again. The Diamond proposal is full of such ingenious, complementary responses to the form the shell of the old building took. And these responses add up to an overall proposal which imaginatively makes use of almost all the old buildings volumetric potentials, while eliminating its many functional deficiencies. It was on this basis that the Diamond group could happily conclude that the circumstances of the study offered an opportunity to retain a fine example of Toronto's heritage, while providing first-class facilities for its users.

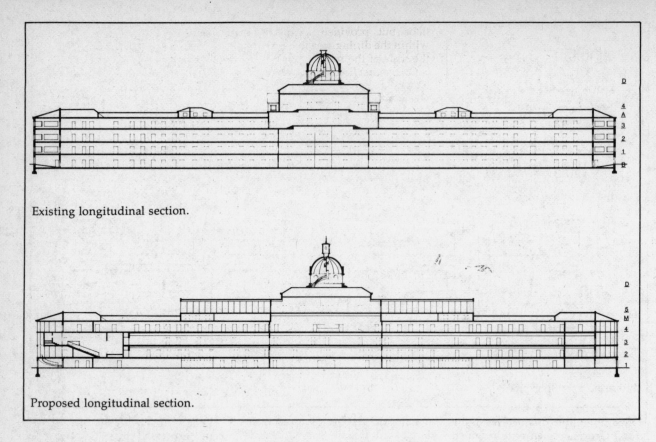

Existing longitudinal section.

Proposed longitudinal section.

ping slab of medium lightweight concrete. With drywall ceilings and new shelf-angles for the joists, the wooden structure could thereby meet the two-hour fire resistance rating required by the Ontario Fire Marshal. The installation of precast floor slabs and removal of the joist structure as proposed by MGS would not be necessary. In addition, with the topping slab, all floor finish standards could equal those proposed for the 1956 building.

The lack of large spaces was solved

in a variety of ways. First, a number of larger spaces already did exist in the central block of the building. Rather than locating the elevators and lobbies in the middle of the building and losing valuable floor area, it was decided to locate the elevators in the wings which would also reduce the horizontal walking distances. On the ward floors, supply deliveries, soiled linen storage and return would be central, directly opposite the nursing stations, a functional relationship not possible in the

1956 building. A second source of large spaces was to infill the series of recesses along the south side of the corridor. These spaces, provided in the original plans to allow natural light and ventilation to reach the corridor, are pleasant and afford views to the outside from the corridor but are less necessary with modern lighting and ventilation methods. In addition, they considerably increase the exterior wall surface of the building with consequent energy loss. Infilling these spaces, therefore, has a

Now for the second, self-imposed task; to address, architecturally, the task of salvaging the past of Canadian psychiatry. It seems to me that the complete accomplishment of this task necessitated not only an address to the question, but also the creation and presentation of an architectural image of such salvaging. The Diamond report certainly addresses the issues, but the architectural image presented remains symbolically obscure. Perhaps the beginning of the difficulty may be seen in Pos' own comments. For having definitely raised the question of period for historical orientation (quoted above), Pos goes on to say:

To identify the Howard building at Queen Street, now surrounded by four modern new buildings, solely with the "insane asylum business" and the "bad old days," meaning

painful memories of the past inadequacies for the mentally ill, the medical profession and the community at large, is short-sighted, grossly incomplete and historically unjust. It means confusing a painful phase of North American psychiatry as related to provincial and state institutions with a historical building. *(my emphasis)*[25]

It may have seemed prudent to Pos to attempt to dissociate the building from its connotations, in order to save it, but this, it seems to me subtly, but critically, evades the issue. Like it or not, the building and its painful associations are inseparable. In fact, it may be said that as good a case can be made for saving the building *because of* its associations, as can be made for doing so *despite* them.

One couldn't look to the *Toronto Sun* for much enlightenment during the controversy, but on this one point, the *Sun's* eager philistinism struck closer

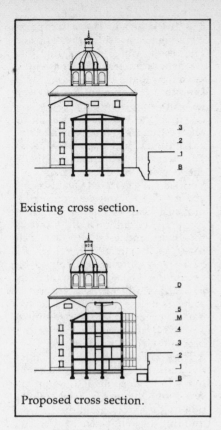

Existing cross section.

Proposed cross section.

two-fold advantage. Additional large spaces were also provided by removing for the full height of the building certain bearing walls and replacing them with steel beams, permitting the original floor structure to remain in place.

Level changes were eliminated on the fourth floor by dropping a portion of the corridor and the servery to the level of the wing corridors but retaining the existing floor level at the exterior wall. This not only kept the windows in proper relation to the

floor but provided a raised area within the dining area to help reduce the scale of the room.

On the first floor the opposite problem existed in the relationship between the floor level and the window heights. The sills were six feet above the floor, but since there was more than twelve feet of ceiling height, the solution was to raise the floor three feet, with the consequence that piping and ducting could be run, concealed, beneath the floor slab. Also, windows could then bear a proper relation to the floor. Also, brick vaulting in certain rooms could be left exposed and the new floor level would be at grade, the level one datum for the other buildings in the hospital complex. Once again, the solution to one problem became the key to solving a series of others.

By providing the new elevator cores flanking the building but actually outside its original perimeter in recesses, it would be possible to bring the automated delivery system to the building elevators at basement level, in spite of the fact that the building itself has no basement. The 15-foot space between the north face of the community centre and the south face of the Howard building would allow the service tunnel to connect directly between the elevator cores.

The fifth floor of the Howard building existed in the central block only. In placing the elevators in the wings it became both necessary and reasonable to extend this floor to the elevators in new construction above the roof, set back on the existing ridge so as to maintain the original eave line. This new space could be built of steel and glass and provide a

magnificent environment to serve the needs of the occupational therapy and vocational rehabilitation department.

Since the area of the Howard building, as proposed, exceeded program requirements, it was desirable to locate the auditorium within the building rather than provide an addition, as proposed in the Phase III plan. The dayrooms with their timber construction in need of rebuilding provided an appropriate form and, by gutting the west pavilion, it was possible to accommodate a full auditorium and stage with direct side stage connection to the dressing rooms and workshop. On the fourth floor rebuilt dayrooms at both ends of the building would serve the wards and the remaining dayrooms on the east end of the building would serve as lounges and lecture rooms.

Despite anticipation of its removal, the location of the Howard building in many ways provided site plan advantages for the Hospital Complex, even with the first two phases completed. With the 1956 building, landscaped grounds could provide a community park which would be compatible with the hospital objectives of integrating the community into the social activities of the Hospital Complex. Under the existing plan, this objective has not been met despite the inclusion of sports facilities in the new community centre. But out in the open, with such facilities as playgrounds, benches and perhaps even a skating rink, the intense and crowded neighbourhood north of the hospital would find welcome open space.

Parking could be amply accommodated in smaller areas than proposed

to the mark than Pos' injudicious defense. In fact, so sarcastic was its editorial stance, that its remarks may even, reversibly, be read as a defense.

There's a certain cautionary value to preserving places like Auschwitz and Dachau, as reminders of the depths to which human beings can plunge. And places like Alcatraz have a morbid fascination as tourist spots and as relics of the bad old days or for movie locations. Even London's Bloody Tower has a fascination for the murder and cruelty perpetrated there in the name of England.

With a certain amount of distortion, poetic licence, and exaggeration, such a rationale can be employed for the preservation of 999 Queen Street, as an historic site. ...[26]

What to make of an existing symbolic image, which is so intensely challenging that it precipitates such reversible rhetoric? And how, architecturally, to respond to the challenge of formulating a

counter-image, which challenges the existing one?

It goes almost without saying that the Diamond group quite properly chose — stylistically and symbolically — to *contrast* the form of their new additions with the form of the shell of the old building. However, the contrast, and the dialectic of old and new, is only the *beginning* of the formulation of a counter-image. To be sure, the full development of such an image cannot be expected of a feasibility study. It can only reasonably be expected in the development of a full-fledged design.

But it would have been interesting — indeed challenging in the extreme — had the Diamond group pressed on, in one or two particular aspects of the dialectic of old and new, and had given us a glimpse of what such a counter-image might look like.

in the master plan, close to the entrances of the respective buildings. Most users of the parking areas are staff or repeat visitors who are seeking a particular entrance and wish to park as close to it as possible, making a single large parking lot unnecessary. The configuration of the building with its high exterior wall to floor area ratio suggested that a perimeter heating/cooling system with its efficiency in distribution was far superior to a bulkier air system. Rybka, Smith & Ginsler Ltd., Mechanical Engineers, proposed a system based on heat pump units that would not only provide individual room control, but fit flush with the wall in recesses beneath the windows; and distribution piping could run in the thickness of the proposed topping for convenient accessibility. With heating and cooling thus accommodated, the air quantities actually required for proper ventilation could be reduced, and provided by means of a local system concealed above the corridor on each floor. Additional air quantities for the ward floor could be accommodated in larger ducts running the attic space, and the entire mechanical system would, following this plan, require minimal floor area and cost less than half what an air system would cost.

Plumbing systems could be accommodated for the most·part in the especially wide corridor. This corridor, nearly 15-feet wide, is sufficient for both ample corridor width and a service bank of washrooms, janitor facilities, storage and mechanical risers, while at the same time providing efficient organization of plumbing risers and stacks.

Thus the design fell into order, each of the pieces responding to an odd and seemingly comfortable union of modern requirement and existing circumstances. Each additional restriction brought with it a clue to solution, demonstrating that a well-ordered and handsomely proportioned building can provide the point of departure for many programmatic options, technical aspects of the program and a century of change notwithstanding.

The Costs — The detailed survey, program and design allowed pricing to be in considerable detail. From demolition and underpinning for the new service tunnel to the last enlarged door frame, the plans and proposed finishes were measured in detail. All areas of structural renovation and new construction were taken off as were mechanical and electrical systems. Quotations on the expanded automated delivery system were obtained from the manufacturer as were elevator and reglazing prices for the aluminium framed solid double-glazed windows with safety glass in patient areas. Allowances were included for rebuilding the lantern on top of the dome and re-roofing the dome in lead-coated copper, and for chemical cleaning to reveal the building's original colour and brick detail. The assumptions were itemized and the details listed. The results were encouraging: government estimates of the Phase III renovations to the 1956 building, escalated to a February 1976 start, were just under $16-million. This was taken as the base reference. Initial MGS estimates to renovate the Howard building had been $37-million. This was the figure that was being challenged. Priced in detail by A.J. Vermeulen, Chartered Quantity Surveyor, the Diamond renovation proposal was estimated conservatively at $19-million including contingencies and escalation to a February 1977 start. Pro-rated on the basis of area, the cost differential between the Phase III plan and the Howard building was therefore somewhat less than 5 per cent, a modest premium for the retention of a proud landmark with a significant past and elegant proportions.

Thus on November 6, 1975, an enthusiastic letter of transmittal covering a fully-documented report assured the Ontario Heritage Foundation that not only could the Howard building be renovated to meet the program objectives of the Phase III plan, but this could be accomplished at costs far below government projections.

Wilfrid Worland

For my own part, I am fascinated to suppose what the implications of such an investigation might have been for two of the more controversial parts of their proposal — their treatment of the building's silhouette and of its entrances.

The silhouette is not only the most potent bearer of the building's *present* symbolic image; it is also complicated by three distinct layers of historical perception. The form the massing of the original building makes against the sky was a principal part of Howard's compositional scheme for the building. But even Howard's vision (as illustrated in the water colour) does not conform with the reality of the building as erected. As one older photograph makes clear, the actual (but conceptually unanticipated) chimneys which liberally grace the asylum's roof top give it a far more lively and picturesque silhouette than that implied by Howard's reposeful rendering (see illustrations). In the circumstances, it seems to me that the necessity of a counter-image for the building amply justifies the Diamond group's decision to alter the historic silhouette by adding a new and modern clerestorey above the existing roof. (Thus is established the third layer of historical perception of the silhouette.) However, the same circumstances suggest the possibility of an even bolder alteration to the silhouette, by means of which an *inescapably* dialectical counter-image might have been intimated. It isn't possible to conceive exactly what sort of bolder gesture might have been appropriate, but analogies which spring to my mind are Robert Venturi's proposed "miniature" of H.H. Richardson's Holy Trinity Church, designed to sit in Copley Square in Boston, in front of the full-size, historic church. Or James Stirling's re-use as a band-shell of the facade of a burnt-out, eighteenth century assembly hall as part of his submission to the Derby Town Centre competition (see illustrations). Neither of these analogies fits precisely the circumstances of the Howard building's silhouette, but both do illustrate a deliberately dialectical design stance vis-a-

Above: Detail of watercolour on paper, showing the original design of the Provincial Asylum by John G. Howard. Illustration: City of Toronto Archives

Left: Detail view (undated) by William Notman, showing front facade of building as constructed. Photo: Ontario Archives

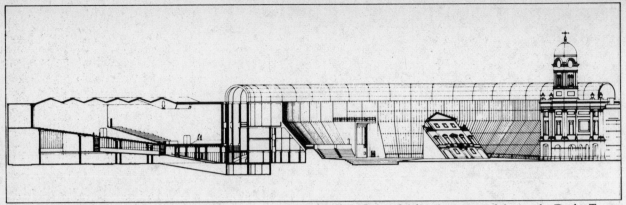

Illustration showing the re-used, eighteenth - century facade in James Stirling's proposed design for Derby Town Centre. Illustration: *James Stirling: Buildings & Projects 1950-1974*, Thames and Hudson, London, 1975.

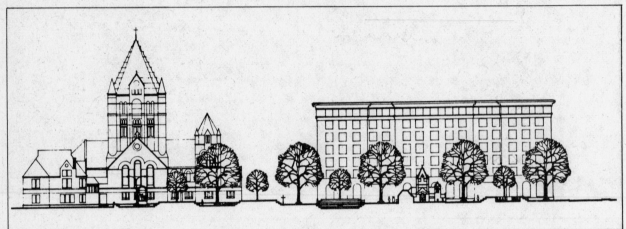

Drawing showing Robert Venturi's design for Copley Square, Boston, including the existing full-size church by H.H. Richardson, and the proposed miniature by Venturi. Illustration: Robert Venturi

vis the stylistic character of a monument undergoing calculated architectural transformations.

As for the building's entrances, their symbolic significance goes far beyond the matter of stylistic references, right to the heart of the building program itself, and to its place in the history of Canadian psychiatry. As with the question of the silhouette, the Diamond group appropriately and explicitly addressed the question, in proposing a major change to the number and the position of the entrances to the building. They proposed "to reduce the building's formality,"[27] by closing its central entrance and creating four new ones. But, of course, the formality of the building is indissolubly bound up with its historic image as an institution; any reduction of that formality must be seen to lead eventually; straight to an architectural re-examination of the role of the institution in the society it serves. This may seem a large claim to make for the mere matter of entry to a building, but anyone who doubts the directness of the connection should look at the work of the two most important psycho-analytically oriented architects of our era, Aldo van Eyck and Herman Hertzberger.

Van Eyck, has taken the concept of entrance, and transformed it, poetically, into that of "doorstep" a highly nuanced architectural conception which evokes a whole "in between" realm, neither quite inside nor quite out, neither quite public nor quite private. And this becomes the basic spatial metaphor informing his whole corpus of work.[28]

For his part, Hertzberger has attempted a complementary theoretical strategy, which is almost the reverse. In a variety of projects, culminating in the recently constructed Central Beheer office building in Apeldoorn, Holland, he has created an architecture involving the complete dematerialization of the phenomenon of "entrances" to buildings, in the name of a radically libertarian redefinition of the relationship of public and private space.[29] Naturally enough, this attempt is related, in Hertzberger's theory, to the current intellectual tendency towards de-institutionalization associated with such figures as Ivan Illich and Michel Foucault.[30]

To be sure, these are extended connections to be making in a discussion of the possible symbolic transformations which might conceivably have

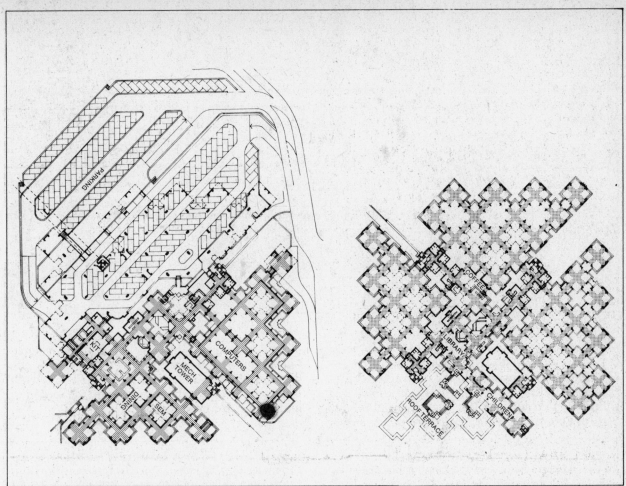

First and second floor plans of Herman Hertzberger's Central Beheer project, Apeldoorn, Holland, showing the dematerialized "mesh" circulation system. Illustration: Herman Hertzberger and *Architecture Plus*

been effected on Howard's Provincial Asylum. However, no fully developed discussion of the putative significance of "reducing the formality" of Howard's *own* conception of the building can be maintained without pursuing the relationship of that formality to Howard's poignant vision of the building as an institution, or for that matter, to the radical critique being made of institutions in our own time, a critique which may well, eventually, place even the present Ministry of Health program inside its own, evolving, historical continuum.

The Diamond report most ingeniously succeeds in fulfilling the terms of reference established by the Heritage Foundation. In addition, it goes on to address itself to the challenging question of the architectural symbolism of historic institutions which evoke complex public emotions. If it does not fully succeed in resolving this latter question, it nevertheless puts the status of the architecture of extreme situations in the clearest light in which it has stood in Canada to date.

This is no trivial accomplishment, for upon it, in many ways, will rest the fate of numerous other such historic institutions in the country. In On-

tario, for instance, the government may well choose to continue to place its own heritage properties beyond the scope of the Heritage Act it reluctantly passed to protect them. If it does, then other, smaller, but perhaps even more important buildings than Howard's asylum, such as William Thomas' notorious Don Jail in Toronto, may well soon face the same complex threat.

It is of the utmost importance that the small but growing band of Canadians who are prepared to face the darker aspects of our heritage learn all they can from the destruction of 999 Queen, both tactically and philosophically. Tactically they must understand that technical and functional demonstrations of feasibility are not enough; they must realize that the conventional media, civil servants, and political parties cannot yet be expected to grasp the serious issues at stake, let alone deal with them conscientiously. Philosophically, they must come to grips with the widespread inability of Canadians to come to terms with their past; they must attempt the prodigious feats of imagination which will provoke the collective reflection necessary for our past to survive, in all its manifold aspects, and

View showing typical room interior just before demolition. Photo: Ellen Tolmie

for Canadians to truly understand it.

For it is evident that the collective failure of imagination which resulted in the destruction of 999 Queen is ultimately a failure of self-knowledge. Culturally and historically, it shows that we citizens of Ontario, Cabinet Ministers, psychiatrists, architects and all, possess an under-developed knowledge of ourselves. We really don't know who we are. What is worse, we have demonstrated that as yet, we even lack the maturity and the courage to endeavour to find out.

1. Hansard, Legislature of Ontario, December 10, 1975.
2. A.J. Diamond Associates, *Howard Building Feasibility Study*, November 1975.
3. I am including in this listing only major public monuments threatened with demolition or relocation in the name of "progress." This excludes such important cases as St. Lawrence Hall, which was rescued more from neglect than from threatened demolition.
4. Pierre Berton, "A Feeling, an Echo" from *The Open Gate*, edited by Richard Bebout, Peter Martin Associates, Toronto, 1972.
5. Merrijoy J. Kelner, "Spaces and People" in the *Canadian Architect*, September 1975.
6. Dr. Frederick H. Lowy, letter to the editor, *Globe and Mail*, December 16, 1975.
7. Anthony Adamson, quoted in a letter from Alderman John Sewell to Premier W.G. Davis, December 12, 1975.
8. An interesting comparison of the two approaches can be made in Quebec City where two parallel projects are now proceeding. The first is the "restoration" of an historic section of the Lower Town surrounding the Place Royale. In this case, the buildings are being "restored" to a pre-conquest date, and the implications of the process are disconcerting. For one thing the "restoration" entails the obliteration of a host of interesting modifications which had been made in the eighteenth, nineteenth and early twentieth centuries, to the original seventeenth-century buildings. For another, this technique has limited the re-use of the buildings to "museum" and other primarily tourist-oriented functions. Then too, I am informed by Yves Laliberte of Laval University that the ongoing restoration now threatens one of the handsomest late nineteenth-century dock warehouses, whose demolition is called for as part of the general precinct "restoration." This all lends sad credence to the rumours around Quebec, that having once completed the whole "restoration," the government may well just lease the whole precinct to an American hotel chain to run as a sort of Disneyland north.

   In contrast to this stands the now begun "recycling" of Artillery Park, a complex of military buildings from three centuries in the Upper Town, just inside the north-east ramparts. In this case, some of the heterogeneous buildings and fortifications are being restored, but the majority of them are being recycled to serve as recreational, commercial and residential facilities. Eventually, Artillery Park will comprise a newly apparent historical precinct in the city, but it will be a precinct which will nevertheless remain a vital, normal part of the ongoing daily life of the city.
9. Quotations taken from L.A. Oxley, *Comments on A.J. Diamond Associates' Howard Building Feasibility Study*.
10. It is interesting to note, in the context of this discussion, that there are at least two significant European precedents for preservation of "asylums" from even earlier periods than Howard's in Toronto. The earlier, the Paris Saltpetriere, originally from 1670, remains to this day in use. The second, London's Bethlem Hospital of 1815, in St. Georges Fields, Southwark, survives (in part) in a re-use, as the Imperial War Museum.
11. A.J. Diamond Associates, *op. cit.*

Photo: Ellen Tolmie

12. L.A. Oxley, *op. cit.*
13. Letter from D. Dastur, Design Services Branch M.G.S. to J.C. Thatcher, Deputy Minister M.G.S., November 17, 1975.
14. Letter from A.J. Vermeulen to A.J. Diamond Associates, December 2, 1975.
15. Alderman John Sewell, *op. cit.*
16. The conservation lobby considered Oxley's objections naive if not mischevous, for he seems to have counted both the additional construction that Diamond proposed on the roof and the incongruous red brick additions to this white brick and stone building that Diamond suggested removing (additions which Oxley must have known — and should have admitted — were unrelated to Howard's building.)
17. D. Dastur, *op. cit.*
18. It struck both the Historical Board and the Heritage Foundation as curious to say the least, that the ministry should undertake either to advise them on appropriate preservation philosophy, or to recommend, by implication, that the only suitable treatment of landmarks was to restore the original form to serve the original purpose.
19. Merrijoy J. Kelner, *op. cit.*
20. *Ibid.*
21. Margaret Scrivener, news release, *Queen Street Mental Health Centre, 999 Queen Street West,Toronto, Demolition of 1846 Building*, December 3, 1975.
22. Given the disreputable uses to which it was put, it is quite disconcerting to refer back to the Kelner paper, in the wake of the resolution of the whole controversy. For in retrospect, Kelner's criticisms of conditions in the old building are highly innocuous, architecturally speaking. Leaving aside the general question of a poor "image," the specific sorts of things she found to criticize were cosmetic. The absence of doors on bedrooms and toilets, "drab" colour schemes, "faded curtains," "noisy" (because uncarpeted) floors, and the notorious "metal doors which were always locked" (and which were, of course, expedient later additions that had nothing to do with Howard's original scheme).
23. A.B.R. Lawrence, Chairman of the Ontario Heritage Foundation, letter to A.J. Diamond Associates, June 17, 1975.
24. Robert Pos, "The Old and the New at the Queen Street Mental Health Centre," in A.J. Diamond Associates' *Howard Building Renovation Feasibility Study.*
25. *Ibid.*
26. *Toronto Sun*, editorial, December 22, 1975.
27. A.J. Diamond Associates, *op. cit.*
28. For an account of the phenomenon of "doorstep" in the work of Van Eyck, see Alison Smithson, editor, *Team Ten Primer*, Studio Vista, London, 1968.
29. For a description of Hertzberger's Apeldoorn project, see *Architecture Plus*, October, 1974.
30. See Ivan Illich, *Medical Nemesis*, Calder and Boyars, London, 1975, and Michel Foucault, "The Birth of the Asylum" in *Madness and Civilization*, Tavistock Publications, London, 1967.

The Laurentien Hotel: A case study of developer demolition

Michael Fish

In Montreal, demolition has become a way of life. Since the early fifties, new highways and office complexes, road arterialization and subways have combined with real estate speculation practices of block-busting and collection into parking lots to virtually destroy the major part of the Montreal core area. One gaping open area follows after another, asphalted and covered by cars during the day, they empty at night to leave cold, hostile, windswept areas. For some of these lots, a project is occasionally thought to be at hand, for the great majority of these blocks, their only useful purpose, beyond parking, is to serve as a safe place for someone's money, where it can rest and grow quietly, relatively free of expensive management activity.

But the worst is yet to come. A project has been put in train that entails in a single demolition the quantity of homes demolished almost every year in the last four years.

Montreal's Laurentien Hotel is now closed and it will soon be demolished. It is no slum! It is a modern building built in 1948. It is fireproof. At 23 storeys, and 364,000 square feet, it is one of the city's largest hotels. It was renovated at a cost of $2-3 million only just this year. Its color TV's, shag rugs, new furnishings, and re-decoration are amongst the nicest and newest in town. It contributed directly over two hundred permanent jobs to the economy of the city. It has 1000 rooms. The rates started at $19.00 single and finished at $28.00 double.

The Laurentien had a great tradition as the mainstay of Montreal's budget tourist industry. It was the cheapest, most comfortable, reputable hotel in a city which already has the highest hotel rates in Canada.* (See Table 3)

The Laurentien was also very profitable. It returned a recent rate of $1.8 million annually in profit to its owner, Canadian Pacific. CPR purch-

* From Lawenthal & Horvath, 1976.

The Laurentien Hotel.

The new Holiday Inn located just across Dorchester Street from the Laurentien. The construction of this hotel has been abandoned after $30 million has been spent on its more than 900 rooms. Costs completed will be over $50 million.

TABLE 1
ROOM RATES IN MONTREAL HOTELS

	Single	Double	No. of Rooms
Berkley	$24	$28	100
Holiday Downtown	$33	$43	500
Holiday Place Dupuis	$33	$43	400
Ritz	$47	$57	267
Loews La Cite	$32-48	$40-56	500
Champlain	$47-51	$57-61	614
Queen Elizabeth	$41-49	$51-59	1200
Bonaventure	$50	$60	395
Royal Roussillon	$31	$42	300
Four Seasons	$48-53	$60-65	320
Sheraton	$28-33	$35-38	1004
Laurentien	$19-22	$28	1004

ased the hotel at a reported price of only $8 million in 1969 from the Sheraton chain when I.T.T. sold Sheraton's hotels world-wide to raise cash for its

TABLE 2
THE LAURENTIEN HOTEL — SOME BARE FACTS

Annual Revenue	$5 million +
Annual profit	$1.5 million + management fee
Employees	200 to 300 (seasonal)
Age (1976)	28 years
Land coverage	35,000 sq. ft.
Area of building	364,000 gross sq. ft. + basements
No. of rooms	1004

TABLE 3
CANADIAN HOTEL COSTS/ROOM MAY 1976

	Cost	Rise in Year
Montreal	$31.94	11%
Toronto	$29.24	3%
Vancouver	$29.52	7%
Ottawa	$28.76	10%

conglomerate empire.

The replacement cost of the 1004 rooms in today's building market is at least $30 million. Holiday Inn presently estimates that its new, 900-odd room, semi-luxury hotel on Dorchester Street will cost over $50 million. And construction of this hotel is now stopped because its cost may have far outstripped its ability ever to pay back its investment. It stands abandoned like a project after a South American revolution, half finished. The Laurentien is mourned by tourists and by the people who sell Montreal as a tourist and convention centre. Its disappearance puts the average cost of staying in central Montreal right out of sight. Bid conventions, those which go to cities on a low-bid basis, are sure to pass up Montreal for the foreseeable future. One person in the Convention and Visitors' Bureau estimated the loss to be at least ten such congresses per year. This will cause an appreciable drop of volume to downtown business that cannot be replaced elsewhere. Ironically, it will *decrease* business in the other higher-priced hotels of the city which are overbuilt at over 15,000 rooms, up from 5,000 rooms only a few years ago.

But besides all this, what makes the demolition of this profitable asset so incredible is that it stands on the fringe of eighteen vacant acres of *the* prime empty development land of Montreal's core. Its owners, Canadian Pacific, have been collecting land to the west of Montreal's Dominion Square ever since CP decided to locate its rail head in Windsor Station almost a hundred years ago, setting off the development boom which built Montreal's uptown. It is one of the largest private holdings of prime, open downtown land in Canada. In comparison, Place Ville-Marie occupies

Aerial view to south of C.P.R. property and empty land in the vicinity. Peel, Stanley, Drummond, Mountain Streets, from left to right, run north and south. Dorchester Street runs along bottom of photo. Laurentien is at lower left on less than one acre of land, with Dominion Square and the Chateau Champlain to the upper left. Windsor Station's covered track fan is slowly being covered by a parking lot. Including the land one block west of Mountain Street, C.P. owns 14 acres of empty land in this photo.

seven acres. CP would have us believe that the less-than-one-acre of land which will be freed by the demolition of this hotel is vital to the success of its gigantic 18-acre development, which CP admits will take many years to develop.

In fact, CP may believe that the demolition is vital. One market analysis by a New York programming firm, Landauer & Associates, states, in part:

Dominion Square tends to act as a barrier between the CP site and the principal business district to the east (Place Ville Marie). Extreme planning care must be taken to minimize the barrier effect by making the (whole) development attractive to the east.

This would imply that CP is doing the community a favour by ridding them of an ugly building.

The Save Montreal Committee took issue with this comment of Landauer's saying:

In fact Dominion Square acts not as a barrier but as an attractant to your site from the east. And the knowledge that you will have another treed plaza within your project will attract at least as much activity as anything else which you might plan. Montreal squares, Dominion, Victoria, Philips, and Place d'Armes have always been the only real generators of economic activity that can be counted on in the long history of planning in Montreal. Windsor Station is also an attractant for you, not only out of architectural curiosity but also because it is a principal transportation node which tens of thousands use daily.

You have to "attract" very little to your project compared with other developers without that node or plazas. The Laurentien is, we assure you, no less beautiful than any other building with which you have been, or are likely to be, associated.

View of the downtown from the track fan of Windsor Station. From left to right — Holiday Inn, Canadian Imperial Bank of Commerce, Laurentien Hotel, Place Ville Marie.

Its "looks" cannot be intelligently presented as an argument for its demolition in the face of its social use.

The Laurentien was almost the last of the great buildings built in Montreal on the basis of setbacks. This was a series of rules by which so many "wedding cake"-shaped big buildings were built. It was put up by people whose primary interests were speculative and it featured some of Montreal's first economy-minded modern detailing, introduced to Canada after the Second World War. It is an interesting building with very clean lines despite a fractured symmetry. However, it is held by armchair architectural critics to be "hopelessly dated", whatever that means, and "very ugly", whatever that means.

Canadian Pacific which hasn't done a "beautiful" building since Sir William Van Horne stopped working for CP, would have us believe that what it will put up will be so superior that we will forget the injury to the city. One wonders if CP will forget the injury to itself. A loss of $1.8-million per year is hard to overlook.

Several groups have criticized the demolition. One of the original conservation groups of the city, The Friends of Windsor Station, rounded up support from the Montreal Society of Architects to criticize the demolition of the hotel as early as December 1970; but these efforts were mainly directed over the next few years at preventing the demolition of Windsor Station, perhaps Canada's finest architectural ensemble and a historic building of the first rank. This fight has been successful. In late 1974, the Save Montreal Committee, a federation of 30 citizens groups, took over the fight to conserve the Laurentien.

This latter group may have been responsible, in 1974, for the withdrawal of support for the whole project by the Bank of Montreal and a reprieve for the hotel. Long-time financiers of CP, the Bank of Montreal had wanted to build its new head office

The lobby of the Laurentien. A picture taken recently. Entire public areas of hotel were re-decorated in early 1976. New carpet on floor is blue and red. Illuminated ceiling is all new. Photos by Esmond Choueki

on the site of the Laurentien, to benefit from the green public space of historic Dominion Square, just across the street.

Save Montreal pointed out how unnecessary it was to destroy the hotel to create enough open land in the vicinity; as the committee said, in part, in a letter to Bank of Montreal president Hart on September 30, 1974:

We deplore the imminent destruction of the Laurentien Hotel to be replaced by a new head office for the Bank of Montreal, or even your negotiations with the CPR to this effect.

Not for its historic or cultural significance does such demolition worry us — nor is it a neighbourhood containing a complex web of personal human relationships. But we do protest that no public purpose exists to justify the destruction of such a large, newly-built, fully-used modern asset.

In a world where resources and energy are crisis-short, in a country ravaged by increasing costs and lessening productivity, in a city where student housing is unavailable, where old people and poor people live in disgraceful conditions, the warping of community investment priorities

to justify destruction on this scale is nothing short of obscene — like the burning of food to force prices up.

This building is in scale with the largest buildings of the city. It functions profitably at high capacity. Similar quality accommodation is unavailable and irreplaceable at anywhere near this price downtown today.

Low income non-expense-account tourism and visiting is sure to be the worse off for its loss.

That such a plan could be conceived is proof of the existence of dominant corporations, unaccountable to market conditions in our community and acting outside of socially desirable goals acceptable to it.

We urge you to build on one of the city's many parking lots or highway air rights or to recycle one of the city's many older heritage buildings and invest this money in a socially productive enterprise pending passage of planning legislation to prevent such waste.

We intend to rule out no non-violent course of action in an attempt to get you to change your plans to conserve the viable with the heritage buildings on the Windsor Station — Laurentien project site or to reverse your decision to consider locating there.

Copies of this letter were sent to large mortgage institutions which might finance the future project and to governments. At the same time a boycott of the Bank of Montreal was mentioned as a possibility and a day-long demonstration of 100 people was held to protest the demolition.

In December 1974, several days before the hotel was to close, the Bank of Montreal announced its withdrawal from the scheme and the hotel was saved — temporarily as it turned out.

Just as the Olympics closed down here, CP published a perspective of its new building plans for the site and a neighbouring block. Protests, demonstrations, and political pressure over the next three months have had no effect this time. However, there was more support for the anti-demolition position. This time the Party Quebecois denounced CP; calling the demolition "revolting"; so did Harry Blank, Liberal Deputy Speaker of the Provincial Parliament and member for the riding in which the hotel is located. He used the words, "ludicrous and stupid". Montreal's city-hall opposition, the Montreal Citizen's Movement, joined their efforts to support the retention of the building. Pierre O. Courtemanche, director of the Centre d'Etudes de Tourisme, spent 15 prime time TV minutes denouncing the effect demolition would have on Montreal tourism. A demonstration was held, leaflets were passed out, letters were written to government and to newspapers, but to no avail.

This time around, many business-oriented individuals who had previously refused to support criticism of the hotel's demolition joined in the protest. They had become convinced the hotel was a positive asset that was being needlessly wasted. Many neighbourhood and historical conservancy groups lent support to the 1976 effort to prevent the demolition.

Harry Blank pointed out that a convention centre, partly financed by the provincial government, was deliberately being located in close proximity to the hotel site, and that it was insupportable that the hotel would now disappear.

F.H. Knelman, professor of Science & Human Affairs at Concordia University, called the demolition "primitive" and "a mindless act of waste" and pointed out that Canada had the worst record of all OECD nations in conservation of energy despite many promises to reduce consumption. He pointed out that the noise and dust of destruction and reconstruction would exact a physical and environmental cost which CP would never be called upon to pay and urged that a way be found to charge these to CP.

The demolition is typical of many which have blasted central Montreal since the early fifties. A building is promised at some time in the future, demolition takes place, then the site stays empty for years. CP promises that in "about five years" a speculative office building will be put on the site. This building is just a little higher than the present hotel though it will have more bulk — probably, owing to a transfer of air rights from the adjacent St. George's Church site. This may make the ultimately used land profitable, at least on paper; but what is far more likely, in the foreseeable future, is the adoption of rules of density which will subtract from present density regulations (FAR 12) to give common sense ratios which will prevent the more greedy developers like CP from profiting from their present over-density mistakes which take place at great public cost. As well, a near certainty is that new zoning regulations will require hotel and residential space to be included in all office projects in the core of the city. This means that a building very similar to the hotel will soon have to be built as part of the future CP project. Meantime, this steady $1.8-million profit per year, going up all the time, is lost to the company and much more to the community. Amongst these losses are over a million dollars in direct income taxes on profit on the hotel and real estate taxes on the building to the city.

It is interesting to note that Mayor Drapeau and the vice-president of the Civic Executive Committee, Yvon Lamarre, both thought the building to be a real asset to the city because the building was "very beautiful." But both men felt that the "sacred" right of the private property owner "even to destroy" his property "must be maintained" or society could not continue to function in an "orderly" manner. Neither appeared to comprehend other arguments based on social or economic considerations.

Unfortunately, so many Montreal investors are only interested in investing in empty land in Montreal, that the city's downtown cannot long continue to function in any manner, because it is ceasing to be there.

Unlike other cities, Montreal's city fathers have no plans to institute major changes in planning regulations which would either protect collective rights to participate in the city design processes or protect the more fragile assets of the city. The worst feature of civic life in Montreal is the lack of regular forums which are open to citizens to be heard on development questions. Like all other city business projects, permits and planning regulation changes are sprung upon the public from behind closed doors, by which time it is "too late" to effect change.

The city executive keeps steadfast to its protection of individual property rights to plan and build without having to lay projects open to other people who presumably have no rights, even to criticize, until it really is too late.

CP has stayed absolutely mum during the whole process. It seems determined not to defend its action publicly, probably because when CP tried to defend the demolition of Windsor Station a few years ago it opened the door to increased criticism and attention which became, finally, too embarrassing.

An interesting sidelight is the complete handwash done by federal government officials. The demolition is outrageously inflationary. But because no prices are being raised, and firing workers is not covered in anti-inflation legislation, federal law does not apply. Local federal MP's have entirely ignored the matter, saying that it is a provincial affair.

One spin-off benefit to CP which is little referred to and is little understood by the public is the enormous amount of economic advantage that needless obsolescence and reconstruction will generate within the CP empire itself at the expense of the rest of the community. Increased jobs and sales within CP all the way through its integrated real estate, transportation, manufacturing, and raw materials corporate structure will return profits and power eventually, even if the real estate part of the operation doesn't add up. This is a classic case of maximizing its own economic activity at the expense of other projects which the economy would otherwise bear to the profit of others or to the benefit of the whole community.

It is probable that the early new year will see this building come down. We are too realistic to think that another delaying action can be fought with any real chance of success. But the spectacle of a 23-storey building evaporating is not one that Montreal, or indeed Canadians, are likely to forget — ever.

It is known that other cities have been similarly treated by Canadian Pacific. Perhaps a collection of all its similar sins throughout the country would prove that the rules of development in Canada must be changed to prevent powerful members of society from abusing the urban environment so badly. .

III Developers and city politics-Four examples

Winnipeg and Trizec:
Giving it all away

This article was prepared by David Walker of the Department of Political Science, University of Winnipeg, assisted by Sherryl Nathanson with the co-operation of the editors of City Magazine. Some of the interviews quoted in the articles were conducted by Winnipeg Tribune reporters Ron Kustra, Robert Matas and Tom Shillington.

The research included land and company searches on all the properties and corporations involved in the project. Participants were interviewed, but their recollections were often hazy and contradictory, and written records such as minutes and other documents proved far more reliable.

The Institute of Urban Studies at the University of Winnipeg supported the research project, and is publishing a detailed report soon. Anyone wishing to purchase a copy of the report should write to the Institute at the University of Winnipeg, Winnipeg, Manitoba.

The project model for Trizec's commercial - office redevelopment scheme at the corner of Portage and Main. A promise of 1,500,000 square feet of building.

Portage and Main. If people know one thing about the city of Winnipeg, it's that intersection. At that corner, the best address in the city, the location where it would be hardest for a new development to fail, city officials and politicians have become enmeshed in a complicated, drawn-out, delayed project for a commercial-office scheme with developers Trizec Corp. and the Bank of Nova Scotia.

Winnipeg's politicians went after Trizec in 1971, asking if they would like to put up a development on that corner. Trizec responded by asking for everything: city expropriation of the site (agreed), city leasing of the land to Trizec for 99 years (agreed), a ground rent fixed at half the *cost* of the expropriated land — not its value — for 40 years (agreed), and a parking garage in the development complex paid for by the city (agreed). In addition, Trizec asked for two rent-free years after the garage was completed (agreed). The only provision the city apparently asked for in return was that Trizec commit itself to erecting 300,000 square feet, although Trizec had repeatedly claimed it was planning to put up 1,500,000 square feet of building. Apart from that single concession, Trizec has no obligation to build anything on the site, at any time. And, much to the embarrassment of the Winnipeg politicians who have boosted the deal, four years after the agreement was concluded the

site is still vacant. The city-expropriated buildings have been demolished, but nothing has taken their place.

Asked in May this year when the project will be build, Trizec chairman James Soden said: "At the earliest possible date." Just when that date is, Soden declines to specify. He did, however, insist that the city proceed with spending an estimated $9.5-million on its parking garage on the site. And, on June 3, a majority of Winnipeg's city council agreed to do so in the last in a long series of votes which have gone Trizec's way since the project was launched in 1972.

HOW IT ALL STARTED

In the 1960s, the city of Winnipeg and its parking authority, the Winnipeg Parking Authority (WPA), were developing off-street parking lots in the central city area. As Winnipeg was anxious to keep its downtown prosperous and growing and suburban commuters preferred driving to work to public transit, the city made parking one of its priorities to support the downtown and encourage growth.

107

Four years and almost $4-million later, the site still sits empty.

Off-street parking was thought to be needed in the vicinity of Portage and Main, and Winnipeg's powerful engineering department run by influential city bureaucrat Bill Hurst, chairman of the WPA, got the job of proposing sites. Urging the process along was Winnipeg's perennial mayor, Steve Juba, who attended a meeting of the WPA in 1968, encouraging it to proceed with downtown parking garages because lack of parking was holding up investment and development.

Juba does not recall the meeting. In fact he denies attending any meetings of the Parking Authority.

The engineers started with an assumption which was crucial to the results of their search. They assumed that a driver would not walk more than 600 feet from his parked car to his destination — which meant that the proposed parking facilities had to be located close to the office buildings in the Portage and Main vicinity. This ensured that any parking facility would be in the first block north or south of Portage Avenue, since the distance to the next street is 822 feet.

The first site design suggested by the engineering department was a simple parking structure, mid-block, near Portage and Main. When the idea reached Winnipeg City Council, however, it had expanded to a larger site. Once council decided in principle, in July 1970 to proceed on this site with the expropriation, the WPA hired a firm of outside consultants, Smith Carter Parkin, to advise on how the project should be handled. City council approved their appointment as "engineering consultants" in September 1970. Within a year Smith Carter Parkin were accepted by Trizec to prepare its design work and later hired by both the city and Trizec to oversee the development of the whole block.

The consultants inevitably decided that the land was too valuable to be used for surface parking, or even for a simple parking garage. They recommended instead a project combining a 450-space parking garage with stores, offices, and perhaps an apartment or a hotel. They proposed that the city do this in association with a major private developer.

At a meeting on November 25, 1970, the consultants made a preliminary report to the WPA. They talked here for the first time of a redevelopment project encompassing the entire block from the Portage and Main intersection. Mayor Juba also attended this meeting, according to the minutes, and urged the building of parking facilities as soon as possible. He was also present on January 15, 1971, when the WPA approved the final report from the consultants proposing the full-block development.

THE APPROACH: WHO MADE IT AND WHY

Now that the Trizec project is in trouble, no one seems very anxious to take the credit for initiating it. There are three versions of how the city and Trizec got together.

From official minutes, it appears that city engineer, Bill Hurst, started things off with Trizec. The first mention comes in April 1971, when Mr. Hurst, according to the minutes of the WPA, had been in touch with Trizec president James Soden. But by that time Trizec was well into its examination of the project.

Hurst has denied that he was responsible for bringing Trizec in. He recalls Mayor Juba arrving at city hall with news about a possible City-Trizec development.

On February 3, 1971, only two weeks after the consultants made their proposal, Trizec and the Bank of Nova Scotia announced a proposal for an office building right on the corner of Portage and Main. Simultaneously, Juba announced to the public the recommendation of the WPA that there be a development on the rest of the block, in cooperation with a developer yet to be decided, but in conjunction with the corner site.

Juba's recollection of what happened on this crucial day is not very good. "The press conference was held next door, so I walked next door," he said recently in an interview. "No, I wasn't involved in the press conference. I didn't make any announcements. I saw the pictures of Trizec and thought it was a wonderful thing."

Juba's story is that Trizec had plans in early 1971 for an office building at the corner of Portage and Main. It did not know the WPA was planning to build a garage on the same block. And, says Juba, when the authority heard of Trizec's plans it decided to get together with the developer.

The third version of the story comes from Trizec president James Soden. Soden claims that in the 1971 mayoralty elections in Winnipeg the two candidates, Jack Willis and Steve Juba, both approached Trizec with schemes which they wanted the developer to support.

Willis wanted Trizec's blessing for an underground concourse connecting the various developments focussing at Portage and Main.

Juba wanted Trizec to take an interest in the "air rights" on the parking garage site — in other words, on the development potential of a site where the city was planning to provide a large parking facility.

Soden says that Trizec endorsed Willis' idea but was cautious about Juba's because no major tenant was in sight. Later, however, Trizec located "a very major tenant" and returned to the city with its offer. The first formal statement of what Trizec wanted — and eventually got, with one minor change — came in a letter dated April 1972.

Juba claims he does not know who first contacted Trizec on behalf of the city about a joint development on the Parking Authority site. "Was it Hurst?" he responded in answer to the question recently. "Hurst . . . okay. I don't know the exact details. But Trizec didn't come to the city. I'm not carrying the torch for Trizec."

Juba does seem the most likely candidate to have taken the initiative. In the first formal mention of the project in city council minutes of a meeting on February 8, 1971, council authorized the mayor and the WPA to "continue negotiations" with Trizec, the Bank of Nova Scotia, and any other developers interested in the city's site. This suggests that there were contacts before or shortly after the WPA adopted the final recommendations of their consultants on January 15, and almost certainly before Trizec's announcement of their own corner project on February 3.

THE DEVELOPER

The developer the city chose to deal with is Canada's second-largest public real estate company, involved in every aspect of land develop-

Mayor Steve Juba

ment and in a number of controversial downtown projects across Canada. Trizec's assets in 1974 were $875-million, second only to Cadillac-Fairview Corp.

The firm was set up by a group of foreign investors in 1960, and it has remained a foreign-owned corporation through the intervening period. Recently Edward and Peter Bronfman, one side of the wealthy Bronfman family in Montreal, whose two branches also hold a controlling interest in Cadillac-Fairview and several other major Canadian corporations, proposed a deal which would give them 51.54 per cent of the voting shares of Trizec. The Bronfmans have had a minority interest and seats on Trizec's board for many years. It is not clear, however, where final control of Trizec will rest under this deal since the English owners propose to continue treating Trizec as their subsidiary in their own financial reports.

Much of Trizec's rapid growth since 1960 has come through takeovers of smaller real estate companies, most of them Canadian-owned.

Trizec has not been a strong presence in Winnipeg until recently. Its purchase in the late 1960s of Central Park Lodge Ltd. gave it control of two residential buildings in Winnipeg. It also has an interest in a Winnipeg shopping mall, Unicity Fashion Square, through a two-thirds owned sub-

109

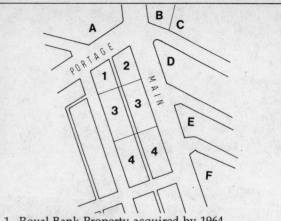

1. Royal Bank Property acquired by 1964.
2. Scotia Winnipeg Development, Joint Venture, B.N.S.-Trizec, acquired by B.N.S. 1971-1973, transferred by B.N.S. to Scotia Dev't., 1975.
3. First parking garage expropriation by-law, 1970.
4. Second development expropriation by-law, 1974.

A. Marathon Realty
B. The Richardson Building
C. The Winnipeg Inn
D. The Bank of Montreal
E. Bestlands Building
F. Federal Government Building

sidiary, Tristart Western Ltd. Trizec has 50 per cent interest in the 132-site Southgate trailer park.

THE DEAL

No one has revealed how the initial negotiations between Trizec and the city took place, or who asked whom for what. The first public document setting out what was to become the final deal is a letter from Trizec president James Soden to Mayor Juba dated April 1972. The letter asked for:

- a 99-year lease on development rights on the city's land above the parking garage;
- rent based on 7 % of the aggregate of:
  (a) the value attributed to the air rights, being fifty per cent (50%) of the city's cost of acquisition of the site
  (b) 100% of the extra costs required to provide for the structural support of the building;
- no increase in rent for the first forty years and negotiated increases after that;
- free rent on the site until two years after the city completes construction of a 1000-stall parking garage.

What Soden asked for, in effect, is expropriation by the city of his development site, provision by the city of the parking facilities necessary for his development project, a donation by the city of the land for the development for a rent which is as-

tonishingly low, and guarantees of no increases in this low rent over the first 40 years of the lease. It is hard to think of anything more Trizec could have requested, except a direct subsidy from the city towards the cost of building their project. Expropriation of property owners for the benefit of a large foreign-owned corporation, free parking garage, and almost-free land were presumably what Soden considered to be his opening position.

The proposal came in only months after Winnipeg had been reorganized into its one-level, one-government unicity structure. Soden's proposal was reviewed by the board of commissioners, headed by chief commissioner D.I. MacDonald. Representatives of the city's departments of finance, assessment, law, transportation, land surveys and planning were involved. The final conclusion of the officials was that Soden's offer was "reasonable and fair to both parties."

Within two weeks, city council moved to make the first firm commitment to Trizec. A memorandum of agreement was confirmed three weeks later. The only change from Soden's original proposal was that, in exchange for the city being committed to build its garage within two years after plans for it are approved, Trizec agreed to build a minimum of 300,000 square feet of office building on the city's land. "We only did that as a sign of good faith," Soden said recently in an interview.

The agreement refers only to the southern two-thirds of the city block which the original development proposal was to cover. Interestingly enough, although city reports repeatedly described the northern corner of the block as being owned by Trizec, this is not the case. Trizec does not have a controlling interest in the corner site right on Portage and Main. This land is owned by Scotia Winnipeg Developments Ltd., a company which is an equal partnership of Trizec and the Bank of Nova Scotia. The city's agreement is with Trizec Manitoba Ltd., a different corporate entity.

The first major vote on the Trizec deal at Winnipeg City Council came on June 7, 1972, on a motion to approve the agreement in principle. The vote was 32 to 8, with the business-oriented Independent Civic Election Committee (ICEC) majority swamping the NDP and left-leaning opposition. The detailed memorandum of agreement was approved later that month on a 30 to 5 vote.

In October 1972, another Trizec-related vote came up when the politicians had to approve a settlement with one of the major property owners the city was expropriating for Trizec. This time the split was 31 to 11. One NDP councillor, Alan Wade, voted for the settlement but some independent-minded, middle-of-the-road councillors opposed it.

When a formal lease deal came forward in January 1974, the vote was 21 to 12. But by March 5, 1975, after changes in the 1974 civic election, the vote was a narrow 22 to 19. By this time the ICEC could count on only its hard-core members to support Trizec, and even a few of them discreetly managed to avoid the vote.

THE EXPROPRIATIONS

Expropriation of land for the development came first in July 1970, when the former City of Winnipeg took eleven properties with 300 feet of frontage on Main and Fort Streets.

Land title records indicate that three of the eleven changed hands in the two years previous to the expropriation when a study was being conducted of the feasibility of a parking garage on the site.

One purchaser during that period was the Carleton Club, which bought a parking lot with 36 frontage feet on Main Street in 1968 for $19,025. The club settled with the city for its land, expropriated two years later for $55,000.

Another parking lot with 96 frontage feet on Fort Street was purchased by Oxhold Properties Ltd. in September 1969, ten months before the expropriation. Records of this sale have disappeared from the land titles office, and the companies involved in the transaction refuse to reveal the price paid by Oxhold. The city has agreed to pay $457,217 for this land, considerably more per frontage foot than was paid on the more valuable Main Street parking lot.

The original estimate of the total cost of this first expropriation was $870,000. The city has now settled on the price for nine of the eleven properties, and the total cost so far is $1.8-million, more than double the original estimate.

The southern portion of the block was expropriated by the city in February 1974. A search of land title records indicates very little change in ownership in the years preceding expropriation, and no evidence of any attempts to profit from the city's desire to take the land. The cost of this second expropriation is estimated at about $2-million, meaning that the total cost to the city of the Trizec site is now estimated to be about $4-million.

While the city was making deals with Trizec for land, only half of which it owned between 1971 and 1974, Trizec and the Bank of Nova Scotia were doing something even more extraordinary by talking about an office development at the corner of Portage and Main. When the Nova Scotia-Trizec project was announced in early February 1971, *neither corporation held title to any of the land on the proposed site*. The first acquisition came on March 21, 1971, almost two months after the announcement. The two further properties which completed the Bank-Trizec site were bought in November 1971. Even so, title to the land remained with the Bank of Nova Scotia until August 1975, when it was transferred to the 50-50 partnership with Trizec, Scotia Winnipeg Development Ltd. Total cost of buying these properties was $1,585,000.

THE AFTERMATH

Just when Trizec decided not to go ahead with its project on the original schedule is not clear, but there's no doubt the company once intended to have some office space completed by 1976. Apparently the delays arose from the soft office rental market in Winnipeg, and Trizec's inability to find a tenant willing to pay the rent levels it was seeking.

Winnipeg city politicians, heavily committed to the project, have been in the unusual role of seeking out possible tenants for Trizec. At least two official delegations have gone to Ottawa to lobby the federal government, but Ottawa has shied away because of changes in its own policy about office space and because of the controversy surrounding the project. The Department of Public Works now looks for deals in which they are equity partners or will gain future ownership of a building they rent. Ironically, if the city had not committed itself to a 99-year lease to Trizec, Ottawa might have proved a willing partner.

One tenant that Trizec did find in 1973 was Manitoba's provincial government. Manitoba signed a lease for about 50,000 square feet in the new building. Said Public Works Minister Russ Doern recently: "The papers were signed in 1973, at a time when the company was anxious for tenants. Trizec gave the provincial government a very good rental fee — somewhat below the going rents at the time." Doern said that Trizec expected to have the first tower finished by late 1975 or early 1976. Now that it is 1977, construction hasn't started and market rents have increased. And so Trizec wants to drop one of the firm tenants it does have for the project. "Trizec wants to either renegotiate or drop the deal," says Doern. "But we're not prepared to."

WHAT HAPPENS NEXT

Trizec apparently feels no embarrassment about its failure to develop the city's site. It was not specified in the contract that Trizec had to build a full-site development by any particular date. Because market conditions have not improved since 1971-72, Trizec continues to refuse to commit itself.

But the politicians who promoted the project, led by Mayor Steve Juba, have been embarrassed by Trizec's failure to build, so much so, that no one is

111

now willing to take the credit for initiating the deal. Equally damaging has been the public criticism of the incredible details of the bargain struck by the city with Trizec.

The most recent development in the project has been a debate about whether the city should proceed with building its 1,000-car, $9.5-million garage even though there is no guarantee that Trizec will put the announced development on top of it. Trizec has submitted no detailed plans of its scheme. Yet, according to the *Winnipeg Tribune*, "Trizec . . . warned as recently as last month that unless the city built a 1000-car garage with maximum supports, the project would be scrapped."

The city's Board of Commissioners and the Council Executive Policy Committee recommended in late May 1976, that the city proceed with calling tenders for construction of the garage. Critical councillors proposed that a garage much smaller than the 1000-car building be built, and that it not incorporate supports for a massive tower which no one is sure Trizec will build. But the ICEC majority managed to carry the project again with a 25 to 17 vote in favour of calling for tenders.

MEDIA BOOSTERS

The Trizec deal, when it was originally announced in 1971-72, provoked mildly positive comments from the Winnipeg media. Criticism of the terms of the deal by opposition councillors received some attention, but not enough to change the position of the powerful ICEC caucus leaders.

The results of a major research project on the Trizec project were published just before the June 1976 meeting by the *Winnipeg Tribune*. The articles took a strong line against the Trizec deal, and argued that it was highly unfavourable to the city.

But a columnist in the same newspaper, Richard Purser, responded to the information with the same approach that had been tried and had worked four and five years earlier. He argued, on no better evidence than an appeal to his anonymous "business advisers", that the city's parking garage would "pay for itself within eight years and be a net revenue producer for the city thereafter."

He trotted out the underground pedestrian walkway which, only if the project were proceeded with, would link the four corners of the Portage and Main intersection. Jack Willis, the 1971 mayoralty candidate who had gone to Trizec with this idea, must have smiled.

And he dangled the Trizec project itself before the supposedly ever-gullible reader. "A handsome glass-enclosed banking pavilion and regional headquarters for the Bank of Nova Scotia will occupy the Portage and Main corner. Farther back, down Main Street, will be a low-slung first-class hotel in an enclosed garden courtyard type of setting. A leading hotel chain — its name is a household word around the world — is ready to step in. The office towers . . . will complete the project."

And, on what must surely be the crucial question of when, he wrote: "The bank and hotel will be triggered early by approval of construction of the garage."

It was as if the clock had been rolled back to 1972. Purser's prose could have been written in Trizec's publicity department, except that Trizec isn't willing to go even as far as Purser on the question of when all these wonderful things will happen.

THE LESSONS

There are many Trizec-type stories in Canadian cities. Sometimes the details are flushed out and then taken apart by outside critics or by reform-minded politicians. At least as often, no one notices as a municipal government agrees to give a developer everything it can think of asking for.

Some of the lessons are obvious. It seems clear that no criteria other than progress for progress's sake, development for development's sake, were ever applied to the Trizec project. No city official ever did a serious analysis of the value of the concessions given to Trizec, and no one bargained with the firm. The city did not even go so far as to invite development proposals from other developers, let alone offer the land on Trizec-type terms to the federal government or some other public body. Even today, it appears that Winnipeg politicians and officials have no idea of the real value to Trizec of the concessions they made.

The incompetence of the agreement between the city and Trizec can be explained only by the anxiety of some city politicians to get the project at any price. City lawyers would have been perfectly capable of pointing out that the agreement committed Trizec to almost nothing, but tied up the city completely. However, officials refuse to comment publicly or privately on any aspect of the agreement, claiming only that it reflects the "will of the politicians."

Trizec did nothing more or less than it should have. Approached by a mayor before or after an election eager for a big development on the biggest downtown corner, who can blame James Soden and Trizec for asking for a free parking garage and free access to over three acres of land in a deal which committed them to almost nothing? Had the city proposed less favourable terms, Trizec might have walked out on the deal — but they might not have. And there is more than just one developer in

Canada capable of undertaking such a project. And, as Winnipeg has discovered, even giving a developer virtually everything he asked for is no guarantee that he will produce a development.

Exposed as the incompetent deal that it is, middle-of-the-road reformers reassure themselves by noting that it will never happen again. Hopefully, they argue, the philosophy which led Winnipeg to the Trizec deal is dead and buried. But next time, if there is a next time, city hall must let the public in, and allow full debate and discusson before making sweet deals with companies which hold all the aces.

The irony is that there have already been several next times, and the pattern is no different. Winnipeg has since built a convention centre which is likely to run at a million-dollar loss every year, while its main function is to act as a publicly-subsidized service to the city's hotel, restaurant and tourist industry. A city which wasn't looking for ways of subsidizing private developers would tax hotel rooms to pay the cost of such a facility. Their currently-proposed absurd solution is not to tax this industry but to bring in a Las Vegas-style gambling operation.

In another situation, the city entered into an agreement with another large corporate land developer, Markborough Properties Ltd. controlled by Hudson's Bay Company, for a project on a large vacant downtown lot, the former St. Paul's College site. Despite generous terms, the developer did not hold firm to construction dates, and potential income to the city is being lost. •

Now before Winnipeg's city administration is a proposal for development of the East Yards. This is the largest project to date, and there has been no evidence so far that city politicians or officials are approaching it with a spirit any different from previous development projects.

The Trizec deal, then, is no exception for Winnipeg, and no exception from what many Canadian city councils are willing to do for developers. It is a dramatic example of how anxious pro-development politicians are to facilitate the proposals of large real estate corporations. In an exhaustive investigation of every aspect of the Trizec deal, there is no reason to think that money has to change hands under the table to provide reasons for politicians and officials to be so generous. Present city development strategies lead to these deals and will continue to do so as long as parties such as the ICEC control city governments.

But, as the Trizec deal shows, it seems very unreasonable that city governments should put in so much of the money, take up most of the risk, and then have all the potential profits flow to a development corporation. Still, Winnipeg and many other Canadian cities did it for the CPR a hundred years ago. Why should things be done any differently now?

Public criticism about the City of Winnipeg's approval of the Trizec deal has been rejected by city council. In fact their recent actions confirm their dedication to support, if not subsidize, the developers.

On December 20, 1976, city council authorized the spending of $12.4-million of public funds to build a 1,000-car garage for the Trizec development and to build an underground shopping concourse below the famous corner of Portage and Main to link surrounding business to the Trizec development.

The 1,000-car garage is expected to cost $7.7-million. It is intended to serve 1.5-million feet of commercial space for the Trizec development to be built above the parking garage. However Trizec is only committed to build 300,000 square feet of commercial space as established in the previous agreement.

The underground concourse is expected to cost $6.5-million, of which the owners of property on the corner will contribute $1.45-million. These owners are the Royal, Scotia, Montreal and Toronto banks, the Richardson's and Marathon Realty (CPR). For participation in the project which serves them, the six companies received a "sweet-heart" deal from the city. In their agreement with the city, the following concessions have been made:

— the Bank of Montreal gets to name the southeast corner of the concourse First Bank Square

— the city will not "foster programs for the conservation or rehabilitation for reason of alleged architectural or historic interest, or the like, of the Toronto-Dominion Bank Building, the Child's Building or the Nanton Building"; (the latter two are already classified as buildings of historical or architectural interest by the Manitoba Historical Society)

— the city will pay for operation and maintenance of the concourse for the next 40 years

— exemption from property tax increases resulting from the concourse

— the city agrees not to lease commercial space in competition with the Bank of Montreal

— the city agrees to prevent a pedestrian crossing at the surface level of the corner of Portage and Main to "thus eliminate the possibility of short-circuiting the concourse."

In the vote approving the public expenditures and agreements, the pro-development ICEC councillors with one exception voted as a block in favor, while the NDP councillors voted as a block against. Alderman Zuken estimates that the capital and borrowing costs to the city of this project will be $40-million over the next 20 years. If Trizec only builds 300,000 square feet of commercial space, this could result in a loss of about $25-million to the city over the 20 year period.

Mississauga:
An inquiry
that never happened

Desmond Morton

To anyone with even a modestly developed interest in politics, recent events in Mississauga, the sprawling suburban community to the west of Metro Toronto, might seem puzzling. They revolve around a judicial inquiry launched by unanimous resolution of the local council to investigate municipal government in the community.

A tangle of charges, counter-charges, judicial decisions and exchanges at Ontario's Queen's Park lasted for most of 1975 and promised to affect the December 1976 municipal elections. Was the inquiry, launched on April 28th, 1975, an act of vengeance by Mayor Martin L. Dobkin? Was it a fishing expedition, despatched in vague pursuit of damning evidence? Has the provincial government, in frustrating the investigatory powers of the inquiry commissioner, acted to preserve respectable reputations or to protect political friends?

The use of the courts, whether to find an inquiry commissioner or to settle the legality of the inquiry, probably only complicates what remains an essentially political issue. In very large measure, the legal battles which have drawn Mississauga politicians and lawyers into the courts are a simple prolongation of a fight that should have been settled on October 1st, 1973.

That was the day when a minority of the voters in four new regional municipalities around Ontario's Golden Horseshoe trooped to the polls to elect officials for the new structure of government. Almost everywhere the contests were uneventful. Well-established local politicians were easily returned to their new jobs. The only excitement in most areas occurred where two or three municipal veterans were compelled to shoehorn their way into a single vacancy.

The exception was Mississauga. Composed of almost all of the old town of Mississauga, a sliver of Oakville and the two towns of Port Credit and Streetsville, the new city would form the southern tier of the new Region of Peel. An area of rapid development and population growth, Mississauga had changed dramatically even in the three and a half years after the previous local elections. One innovation was an upsurge of community organizations, half-modelled on the highly publicized groups in central Toronto. The unifying theme was resentment at the pace and direction of development. The organizing force came largely from younger professionals in the more affluent and recent subdivisions. The common target was a town council which, under the former mayor, Robert Speck, and his successor, Charles "Chic" Murray, saw its duty as providing hard services and a friendly reception for industrial and residential developers and allowing a minimum of public meddling with council affairs. In the small municipality of Port Credit, noisy allegations of mismanagement were levied against Mayor Cy Saddington and some members of his council.

Whether the criticisms were sound or foolish, the critical mood helped explain why four of the faces in Mississauga's new nine-member city council were new. Even more unexpected was the defeat of Mayor Murray by a little-known, local general practitioner and part-time coroner, Dr. Martin L. Dobkin.

While Dobkin's election campaign had been as cheap and amateurish as his opponent's was slick and expensive, it had not been entirely uneventful. On two occasions during the final weeks of campaign, Dobkin was summoned to Mississauga's police station and forcefully warned against mentioning certain allegations of municipal corruption. The mayor would later claim that this was the first he had heard of charges made by a small-time local developer named Jan Davies that he had been invited to pay $2,000 to James Murray, son of the mayor and a local realtor. The chief, Douglas Burrows, insisted that the police had investigated these and other charges and found them baseless.

Whether or not Mississauga voters knew anything of the charges or of the solicitude of the police for the mayor's reputation, they gave Dr. Dobkin a comfortable lead from the moment the first poll reported. It was a defeat that hurt more than Mr. Murray's pride; it was also an embarrassing setback for the local Progressive Conservative machine. Heavily dependent on local notables, the Peel County Tory organization had survived the trauma of regionalization of municipal government virtually intact. As a reward, Lou Parsons, a prominent local real estate agent and Mississauga councillor, had been appointed regional chairman. His ward was one of those captured by the so-called "reformers."

While partisanship was, as usual, formally suppressed during the campaign, it was a badly kept secret that Mayor Dobkin and several of the new councillors were eager Liberals. Another new councillor, former Mayor Hazel McCallion of Streetsville, was one of the few local politicians not reconciled to the government's reorganization plan. In early 1975, she publicly announced her allegiance to the Liberals.

Mayor Martin Dobkin.

TURMOIL IN COUNCIL

By then, much had happened. Even an experienced and agile politician would have been challenged by the task of reconciling antagonistic council members, building and controlling an administration for the new city and participating in the new regional council. Mayor Dobkin lacked both knowledge and flexibility. An inner-directed man with little of the bonhomie or social grace of a practised politician, he seemed to feel little obligation to conciliate enemies, co-opt potential rivals or rally potential supporters. For guidance, he turned to Dr. Gordon Watt, a practising lawyer who had been a classmate at Queen's University's medical school and a fellow intern at Montreal General Hospital. As an advisor, Watt progressively lost the mayor's confidence, particularly by urging a rapprochement with the regional chairman, Lou Parsons.

The arrival of a mayor and a number of councillors with unfamiliar ideas undoubtedly complicated the task of setting up a new administration even if it also offered a rare opportunity for starting on fresh lines. However, the inevitable turmoil was increased by an astonishing turn-over of municipal officials. As local citizens watched with concern and Toronto newspapers began keeping a contemptuous box score, a procession of city employees, including most of the senior officials, submitted their resignations. Some went to better positions in the regional hierarchy, others left because of incompatibility of temperament and alleged difficulties in working with the new mayor and his supporters. A number crossed the street to work with local developers.

Although Mayor Dobkin has confessed that there were moments when he considered calling in private contractors to keep the city's services in operation, municipal administration survived without breakdown. Despite the shifting personnel and the increasing bitterness within the council, the mayor and his allies claimed some palpable achievements. Aided by constraints in the national and provincial economy, the pace of development slowed and greater restrictions were imposed on developers. The new administration congratulated itself on greater responsiveness to community and citizen organizations, while the public could im-

The Port Credit harbour. Photo: Ron Duquette

agine itself part of the civic administration by watching general committee sessions on local cable systems. Mississauga's bus system, formerly a problem-plagued private franchise, was acquired for the city and substantially improved. With help from outside experts and a highly publicized appeal for citizen response, a review of the city's official plan was launched. Meanwhile, while some councillors worried increasingly about the city's deteriorating financial position, most could show that long-cherished dreams of libraries, recreation centres and rinks were close to fulfilment.

Probably for most citizens, the positive achievements of the Dobkin administration were overshadowed by the incessant guerilla warfare within the council. Although the changes introduced by Dobkin and even the activities of local citizen groups might seem a pale and hesitant shadow by comparison with their Toronto models, they faced tough, well-organized enemies, unaccustomed to having their power challenged. The mayor's opponents could normally muster three votes at the outset — Councillors Ron Searle, Bud Gregory and Harold Kennedy — but gradually they acquired the more dependable backing of Councillor Caye Killaby and, less reliably, of David Culham, both elected as critics of the old regime.

THE DEVELOPERS RETALIATE

Outside the council, counter-thrusts developed some ingenuity. If the reformers could organize citizen groups, so could developers. When the

council decided, 7-3, to hold up a major residential development, Rockwood Estates, to determine its impact on traffic and services, the developer counter-attacked with his citizens' group, complete with bumper stickers, letters to the editor and noisy delegations to city hall. A more generalized citizen watchdog organization, Concern Citizens of Mississauga, was organized by a former Hydro commissioner, John Leighton. Though its tactics resembled those of counterparts elsewhere, the preoccupations were different: faster industrial expansion, more economy in city management, a curb on new-fangled planning.

The toughest tactics by developers involved the courts. Alerted by Professor Wyman Harrison, an Erindale College geographer, to the hazards of developing land too close to the high banks of the Credit River flood plain, a local conservation group called Save Our Trees and Streams sent briefs to both the old and the new councils, criticizing a subdivision proposed by Riverview Heights Inc. for the old Erindale village area. When the group's cautiously-worded brief reached the city council, the developer, William Sorokolit, promptly sued both the council and the association for damages. The five executive members each found themselves liable for $100,000. An attempt to throw out the case was, itself, thrown out by the Divisional Court in January, 1975. The five nervous defendants were left with their fears and their legal expenses to await a final determination in February, 1976. Other citizen organizations went silent in panic. Even when Save Our Trees won its case, substantial legal costs remained.

Unfortunately, the legal battle between Riverview Heights Inc. and the five ordinary men and women, who had had the temerity to criticize its site plan, was not the only occasion when Mississauga's politics have sent the writs flying.

ALLEGATIONS OF MALFEASANCE

On April 28th, 1975, there was another explosion. "Over the past several months," the mayor announced to the council at its regular Monday meeting, "a number of persons have come to me and made serious and startling allegations of malfeasance in the conduct of city business, including allegations of bribery, influence peddling, obstruction of justice, assault and the unlawful acceptance of benefits." Section 210 of the Ontario Municipal Act, he pointed out, obliged him to be vigilant and to bring such allegations before the council. Since Section 240 of the Act also seemed to suggest a vehicle, he moved from his prepared statement to a lengthy resolution calling for a judicial inquiry into virtually every aspect of the business of the city, its elected officers, officials, employees and appointees to boards and commissions. The inquiry could set guidelines for the disclosure of conflict of interest, financial relationships, expenditure authority and a host of other matters. The sting was in the tail — section (f) which called on the judge to: "inquire into and report on any improper or unlawful conduct with respect to the matters touched upon in paragraphs (a) to (e) of the herein Resolution."

The statement and the resolution caught most councillors and the scattering of reporters, officials and onlookers by surprise. Of course there had been continuing rumours, suspicions and gossip. Publication of the late Mayor Robert Speck's will by a local weekly had prompted unkind gossip about how a modest but respected fruit and vegetable merchant could have become so prosperous. However, the mayor's bombshell produced a rare unanimity. "Lord knows we should have done this a year ago," claimed Councillor Gregory. "The allegations are either true or false but, more important, the people who have made them will be unveiled," he said. Ron Searle explained his support for the resolution in similar terms: "Sweeping statements reflect on every member of council, and the mayor's statements are so general and so sweeping they smack of McCarthyism." More cautious councillors could be reassured by a letter from the City Solicitor, Basil Clark Q.C. The mayor, he explained, had confided some of the allegations to him and sought his advice: "It has therefore been my advice that in view of the information that has been reposed in him, the mayor should sponsor the resolution that is before you this evening. For the mayor to do otherwise would amount to dereliction of his duty."

Within a few days, some members of the council had found reasons to reconsider their enthusiasm. Aware that he could be sued if any specific allegation was not eventually sustained, the mayor had refused to detail his charges. Now his critics and even a few allies began to wonder whether there was any substances to them all all. Newspaper headlines had proclaimed that the mayor's inquiry would put an end to rumours: now they flew with even greater velocity. The enormous majority of taxpayers who had remained oblivious of even rumoured wrongdoing were now part of the audience. Gathering after the council session of the 28th, old guard members of the group began to have second thoughts. Did Dobkin have other evidence than such episodes as the tired old Jan Davies charges, already disposed of by police investigation? Had the council authorized an unlimited fishing expedition into the past affairs of the municipality? If so, guilty or innocent, could any of them emerge with their reputations intact? When the council met in special session on April 30th, unanimity was broken: the old guard was once

A new housing development in Mississauga. Photo: Ron Duquette

again in opposition to the mayor's schemes. On May 12th, there were still further discussions and a resolution amended the inquiry's terms of reference to include all three predecessor municipal corporations, Streetsville and Port Credit, as well as the town of Mississauga. The amendment would have fateful consequences.

THE INQUIRY: A POLITICAL WITCH-HUNT?

On that day, the mayor could also announce the appointment of the inquiry commissioner. Judge Rae Stortini was a 43-year-old former lawyer from Sault Ste. Marie, called to the bench for the judicial district of York in 1971. One of the younger judges appointed by John Turner in his reforming phase as Minister of Justice, it was noted by local Progressive Conservatives that Stortini was a Liberal. With the appointment, the work of the inquiry could get underway, first in an improvised office at Mississauga's provincial court building, later at Erindale College, where the formal public sessions would be held. The counsel for the inquiry, R. Noel Bates, was a young lawyer who had worked as solicitor for the former Halton County Council and had no known political connections.

Aided by Inspector Lou Pelissaro and detectives from the Ontario Provincial Police, with the Peel Regional Police checking out details, the inquiry began by tracking down the nine allegations provided by the mayor. Most had formed the thin substance of political gossip in Mississauga for years. Part III of the Ontario Public Inquiries Act authorized an investigator to seize papers and documents on a wide-ranging warrant: on application, Judge Stortini's request for such powers was firmly rejected. If Mayor Dobkin had planned a fishing expedition, the attorney general of Ontario would not lend him a hook. On July 31st, the Mississauga Hydro Commission, already one of the apparent focuses for the investigation, announced that it refused to answer questions posed by the inquiry staff. On August 11th, the commission's lawyers demanded a judicial review to test the legal validity of the entire investigation.

With its existence challenged by the courts, the inquiry continued steadfastly, announcing that its public sessions would open on September 15th. Local Conservatives promptly noted that this would be only three days before a crucial provincial election. If explosive revelations were made in the early sessions, they could not be answered before voters had gone to the polls. The Tories could now suspect that they would not be the gainers. Fortune and the courts were on their side. On September 2nd, Mr. Justice Peter Wright announced that he accepted the Hydro Commission's arguments: the inquiry had no right to look at anything before January 1st, 1974, the day the new city of Mississauga had come into existence. The inquiry was now hopelessly stalled. Or was it? Within a week, the city solicitor announced that the decision would be appealed and the inquiry could proceed.

It was time for the Conservatives to unmask their secret weapon. Almost unnoticed by the public, Dr. Watt, the mayor's executive assistant, had resigned on April 15th, almost two weeks before the judicial inquiry was approved. His departure to resume his legal career in Ottawa appeared amicable; only a few insiders knew that he had strenuously opposed the proposal for a probe. One of the insiders was obviously the regional chairman, Lou Parsons.

If April 28th had been Mayor Dobkin's day, September 12th was Mr. Parsons's chance for a coup. A trifle unctuously, the regional chairman reminded the regional council of the circumstances of the Mississauga inquiry and its fate at the hands of Mr. Justice Wright. If the region should be involved, he suggested, it was because the financial community "might very well express concern about the stability of local government in the Peel Region" at a time when it was trying to market its debentures. All of this was routine politics: the sensation came when Parsons announced that he had an affidavit signed and sworn to by none other than Dr. Gordon Watt.

Never, according to the former executive assistant, had he heard or learned of "any incident of corruption, brutality or malfeasance" in the municipality although Dobkin had shared with him every allegation he had ever received. Instead, the real architects of the inquiry were two lawyers better known for their role as defence counsel in the sensational murder trial of Toronto developer Peter Demeter, Messrs. Joseph Pomerant and Edward Greenspan. It was they, Watt claimed, who had put the mayor up to the inquiry, arguing that even if there might not be enough evidence at the beginning, something was bound to turn up. Most de-vastating of all, if malignant motives were sought, "The said Mr. Pomerant indicated to me that he thought an inquiry would be helpful to the mayor's political future." To push the knife a little farther, Watt concluded with the suggestion that, of all the councillors, only former mayor Hazel McCallion had been busy encouraging the mayor in his actions.

The local Conservatives had been worried by the closeness of the first day of the inquiry to the Ontario election. Parsons' proposal brilliantly finessed the play. Or did it? Terry Miller, a regional councillor from Brampton and a Liberal, questioned Dirk Pepper, senior regional financial officer. Had the judicial inquiry really caused difficulties in the bond market? The official replied that he knew nothing to suggest it. Instead of accepting Parsons' proposal that the Region use the affidavit as an excuse to quash the inquiry, a majority voted instead to forward the document to the Mississauga council and turned to other business.

By now, the proceedings of the inquiry had driven most other matters from the minds of Mississauga councillors. Should the inquiry, now publicly damned as a political witch-hunt, be allowed to continue? Councillor Killaby, whose modest private land dealings years before had been revived as an issue by inquiry leaks, was furious. She had, she explained, originally supported the investigation: ". . . I have not seen or heard of any supporting evidence that warrants an inquiry — nothing from the mayor — this council — police or inquiry team." However, as Councillor Mary-Helen Spence, a reformer and Dobkin ally, pointed out, the mayor was not the only conspirator. How about the regional chairman who had busied himself so assiduously in obtaining the affidavit? "The proper forum for information relating to the subject matter of the inquiry is the inquiry itself — not in the press, not at regional council and, for that matter, not at special council meetings." The meeting on the 12th was bitter, stormy and indecisive. It ended only when the mayor's motion for adjournment passed 5-4 with Councillor Searle abstaining and proclaiming that the entire session had been illegal.

The Watt affidavit had not been allowed to end the inquiry. Instead, its substance and circumstances were added to the already almost limitless list of matters for Judge Stortini to investigate. Official inquiry sessions opened on schedule on September 15th. Erindale College's council room, a gloomy room of cast concrete and blue upholstery, was the scene. The amateur nature of the performance was suggested by Canadian and Mississauga flags of different sizes crudely suspended from an overhead ledge with the aid of a few cement blocks.

There was not much time for participants to contemplate such homely details. The inquiry had not begun when the city solicitor rose to propose an adjournment until the council could come to a conclusion about its future. The request was side-tracked in a closed session and Judge Stortini resumed within two hours. Now it was the turn of a galaxy of legal advisors summoned by former Mayor Murray, his son James, Mississauga Hydro and other interested participants.

While Murray and his son warned reporters that they might be suing Mayor Dobkin for public mischief, his counsel, Ian Outerbridge, and his fellow lawyers were demonstrating that they could tie the inquiry in knots unless it waited at least for an appeal to Mr. Justice Wright's decision to be heard. After two days of harsh wrangling, threats and counter-threats, Judge Stortini adjourned the inquiry to await the pleasure of the Divisional Court.

THE CITY'S CASE DEMOLISHED

By the time the fate of the inquiry could be settled, the provincial election was over. All three Mississauga seats had been secured by the Conservatives, one of them by Councillor Bud Gregory. Among many Conservative losses was the attorney general, John Clement. His successor, a newcomer to the legislature and a close friend and advisor of Premier William Davis, was Roy McMurtry. It was reasonable to assume that he would respect the premier's views about Mississauga affairs when Mr. Davis' own constituency is in neighbouring Brampton. However, the province had already made its views about the Mississauga inquiry public by refusing Judge Stortini the powers of search and seizure he had long since requested. It was hardly a surprise that the department of the attorney general should be powerfully represented at the Divisional Court appeal.

According to the department's brief, the Mississauga inquiry had had no right to examine the affairs of the former municipalities or of the Hydro Commission, the creation of the former Town of Mississauga which had been held over after the proclamation of regional government. Again, according to the attorney general's department, inquiries under Section 240 required specific allegations, particularly for section (f) of the original resolution and perhaps even for the general investigation into "good government." Finally, the brief insisted that the council could not delegate essentially legislative functions to a judicial inquiry but that, in asking for guidelines and other advice, it had done so.

The Divisional Court judgement, delivered on November 5th, accepted the arguments put forward by the attorney general and endorsed the positions taken by counsel for Mississauga Hydro

Mississauga's City Centre development with the "Square One" shopping centre in the foreground. Photo: Ray Erickson

(ex-mayor Murray was still one of three Hydro commissioners) and for the two Murrays.

The 32-page judgement, written by Mr. Justice R. F. Reid and unanimously agreed to, demolished the city's case on almost precisely the grounds of the attorney general's brief and left the municipal corporation bound to pay not only the expenses of its quashed inquiry but also the full legal costs of the plaintiffs, a bill promptly estimated at close to a quarter million dollars.

However well-founded this legal decision, the fact was that the issues involved in the inquiry were as much political as legal. While the mayor's enemies could rejoice at his utter defeat, echoing the judicial comments that the inquiry defied common sense, justice and the Ontario Municipal Act, there were others who noted how much effort had been made to squash the inquiry before it had had a chance to reveal its secrets. The allegations that might have come before the inquiry, presumably with some supportive evidence, had been submitted to the Divisional Court by the inquiry counsel, Noel Bates. At the end of the hearings, they were returned unopened. Did they contain matters of substance or simply old newspaper clippings? Suspicions immediately deepened when Judge Stortini, presumably in response to a request from the mayor, sent a letter to members of council on November 6th reporting the fate of the inquiry, complaining of the lack of provincial government support in conducting an investigation and concluding: "From my knowledge of the subject matters of the inquiry, which knowledge has been gained from executive session with inquiry personnel, some of the matters brought to the attention of this judicial inquiry clearly warrant *further* investigation and hearing."

For "Chic" Murray, the Judge's letter was a serious blow. His response, again with the aid of his sturdy legal advisor, was a massive law suit for a total of $900,000 against Mayor Dobkin, Councillor

McCallion, Joseph Pomerant, Jan Davies the developer, and for good measure, R. Noel Bates, the commission counsel, alleging that the entire affair was a conspiracy matured over the years against the Murrays, father and son. Plotting had allegedly begun with meetings of Dobkin and Davies in the summer of 1973 and had continued through deceiving councillors, the city solicitor and, once the inquiry had been launched, with the full collaboration of Mr. Bates.

The choice of defendants was, perhaps, a little arbitrary. At least one councillor was informed by the Murrays' lawyers that he had been left out of the suit from the goodness of their heart. On the other hand, Judge Stortini found himself involved, thanks to his letter of November 7th, and Ontario courts had the rare opportunity of deciding whether a judge had been guilty of contempt of court merely by transmitting a letter claiming that "further investigation" was in order. Not surprisingly, the claim was rejected.

Politics was certainly a factor in the Murray's $900,000 suit. Councillor Bud Gregory's election to the provincial legislature in September had left a vacancy in Mississauga's Ward 3. To general surprise and some criticism, the former mayor proclaimed himself a candidate, incidentally infuriating Councillor Searle who had picked his candidate, Frank Bean, for the vacancy. The by-election, decided on November 17th, gave Murray his seat by a margin of only 44 votes. It could hardly be called a stunning vindication of the former mayor but the lawsuits demonstrated that Murray was willing to go to court to protect his reputation. Litigation had, perhaps incidentally, served a political purpose.

A LOT OF UNANSWERED QUESTIONS

The inquiry which was to end all rumours has only spawned more and more. Only the provincial government has the powers to launch a serious investigation and the new attorney general has made it clear again and again that he would not do so. Was it simply a party battle; Mayor Dobkin and Councillor McCallion fighting Conservatives in the Region of Peel, with the backing of Liberal spokesmen Vern Singer and Robert Nixon at Queen's Park? The attorney general insisted that no evidence had been brought to his attention and that police investigations had long since disposed of all allegations. Had Judge Stortini simply acted as the creature of Mayor Dobkin in suggesting that "further investigation" was called for? Could the integrity and responsibility of a county court judge be impugned so easily by a provincial attorney general?

To some, the entire inquiry has played that destructive role. Far from resolving doubts and removing suspicions, a year of charges and countercharges, of litigation and intrigue, threatened municipal business with near paralysis. In the legal battles, the advantages lie with former mayor Murray and the political machine that traditionally dominated Peel County affairs. Condemned to silence by the threat of the $900,000 hanging over them, Mayor Dobkin and his allies will have no chance to explain the motives which led to the inquiry.

By announcing his intention to seek re-election in December 1976, Dr. Dobkin has guaranteed Mississauga voters as bitter and personal an election campaign as anyone could wish. The abortive inquiry will be an issue as local Conservatives seek vengeance for their 1973 defeat. Paradoxically, their favoured candidate may not be the faithful Ron Searle but David Culham, a Liberal whose voluble self-righteousness and self-confidence are combined with an impressive ability to see the developers' viewpoint.

The outcome of the election will depend on citizen reluctance to see development interests return to the driver's seat. It will also depend on voter perceptions of Dobkin's role in the inquiry. Will Mississaugans believe in the network of conspiracy alleged by the Murrays or the crass political motivations claimed by Dr. Gordon Watt? Or will they be persuaded that a young, inexperienced but decent mayor has been trapped by a clique of old guard politicians intent on conserving their power? An early judicial decision would settle the matter but the election date approaches more inexorably than the Murrays' day in court. Meanwhile, questions remain unanswered.

What were the mysterious matters which, according to Judge Stortini, required *"further"* investigation? Does it really matter that his opinion was sought and publicized by Mayor Dobkin while the earlier letter from the attorney general, questioning the validity of the inquiry, remained quietly filed for five months? Did Mayor Dobkin launch a cruel and irresponsible witch-hunt or was he bound, as his city solicitor apparently advised, to act or be remiss in his sworn responsibilities? What was in the sealed envelope which, according to the inquiry counsel, provided the grounds for continuing the investigation? Was a county court judge justified in his statement that further investigation was called for or was he the tool of an irresponsible elected official?

Perhaps only an open, responsible provincial investigation can now dispose of another suspicion: that the Progressive Conservative government of Ontario has combined with some of its municipal allies to choke off an investigation and humiliate its political opponents. That suspicion will give a wider significance to the contest in Mississauga

Photo: Jack Marshall

when municipal voters trudge through the snow next December.

At the outset of 1977, virtually every question raised by the 1975 inquiry was still unanswered. Locked in the vaults of the Mississauga city hall, five sealed boxes hold their secrets as securely as they did 18 months before.

Only one question has been answered. Prodded by the most expensive campaign in Mississauga history, 40 per cent of the city's voters trooped to the polls to hand power back to the old guard. In a field of five candidates, Dobkin gathered barely a quarter of the votes. The victor was Ron Searle, but the real winner was Bruce McLaughlin. Confident that Searle was a hopeless candidate, the smart money began with a Troy business executive named Gerry Townsend. An election eve survey suddenly persuaded McLaughlin that Searle could, in fact, win. The result was a deluge of money, talent and advertising that drove Dobkin's $12,000 campaign out of sight.

Perhaps Dobkin had never had a chance. As mayor, he had kept virtually all of his promises, saving green space, pushing a city plan to the edge of adoption and introducing citizen participation. As a politician, he had forgotten that it was not enough to let his accomplishments stand for themselves. What Mississauga voters read in their few local weeklies was a record of conflict, confusion and failure. Instead of pinpointing the misdeeds of the old regime, the Mississauga Inquiry became Dobkin's costly fumble. Alone, it could have caused Dobkin's downfall; as a symbol, it was probably decisive.

The stakes in Mississauga are enormously high. The multi-billion dollar prize is the chance to develop the core of a city slated to have three-quarters of a million people by 1999. With a little help from the courts and a lot from the Ontario government, the major developers have regained control of the game.

Genstar: Portrait of a conglomerate developer

Donald Gutstein

Genstar Ltd. is Canada's 25th largest corporation. Its 1974 sales were $646-million. Twenty-five years ago, it didn't even exist. How it got to be that size in such a short time is a fascinating story of the buying, selling and reorganizing of Canadian companies to suit the world-wide needs, and utilize the world-wide resources of Genstar's parent company, the Societe Generale de Belgique. Genstar, under the sponsorship and control of this Belgian company, has grown rapidly to become a vertically integrated giant in the land development, building materials, construction and other industries. At every step of the way the company has been assisted financially by the Royal Bank of Canada, legally by the bank's general counsel, the large Montreal corporate law firm of Ogilvy & Co., and politically by federal, provincial and municipal governments.

The story of Genstar's good fortune is the success story of Canada's land developers. As the housing situation for many Canadians deteriorates, land development firms have become larger, wealthier and more profitable. In the past two years, vacancy rates in many cities have dwindled to well below 1 per cent. At the same time, developers' profits have soared.

Daon Development Corporation, the largest developer in British Columbia, experienced an 86 per cent increase in profits in 1974. MEPC Canadian Properties more than doubled its profits. Genstar's growth in profitability was not as dramatic as these and other companies but was nonetheless substantial. In 1974 the company had its highest-ever profits, some $35,074,000, up a healthy 40.1 per cent over 1973. The 1973 profits had been up 39.6 per cent over 1972, and they, in turn, had shown a 42.2 per cent increase over the previous year.

Along with high profitability, two other features characterize the housing industry in Canada. Large builders now account for well over one-half of the new houses built in the country. Genstar is one of the two or three largest house builders in Canada.

Second, the supply of easily developable land on the fringes of Canadian cities has been monopolized by a few large corporations. Peter Spurr's report for Central Mortgage and Housing Corporation showed that in 1973, 24 corporations held 41,198 acres of land in the Toronto area, an amount that would supply all the land needed for housing for 11 years at current growth and density rates. In Vancouver 9 firms held 5,435 acres, a 3 year land supply; in Calgary 12 firms held a 10 year supply; in Edmonton the major firms held enough land to supply all the housing for 19 years.[1] Genstar, with over 16,000 acres in its western Canadian land bank, is the largest landowner in the country.

Besides land banking and house building, Genstar is engaged in many other activities:
— manufacturing portland cement in five plants across Canada (Genstar is the second largest manufacturer in the country);
— heavy construction in western and northern Canada;
— manufacturing chemicals and fertilizers in eastern Canada and the northeastern United States;
— marine operations in western and eastern Canada, and marine shipyards on the west coast;
— importing and exporting metal products in the U.S., Canada and other countries
— investing venture capital in the U.S.

Genstar has made its greatest corporate advances by tying together the activities of its subsidiaries in the land development, building materials and house-building industries in such a way as to consolidate its control over residential development, particularly in western Canada.

Genstar has also achieved substantial vertical integration in the heavy construction industry. BACM Industries undertakes major projects for governments and large companies, such as traffic interchanges, utility servicing, hydro-electric and water projects, mining projects and similar activities. BACM has been involved in large-scale hydro-electric projects in northern Manitoba. In many of these projects, concrete and cement from Ocean/Inland Cement and steel products from the import-export division are utilized. Ocean Cement is constructing a major new plant in British Columbia. Standard General Construction did the site preparation work; BACM Construction is the prime contractor on the $90-million project.

Genstar has been involved in the development of the Athabasca tar sands in northern Alberta. It has built over 1,000 housing units in Fort McMurray. It is involved in site preparation work for the Syncrude Canada oil recovery plant and has oppor-

Genstar subsidiaries are scattered throughout the Vancouver area.

How Genstar subsidiaries work together to consolidate the company's control over residential development — a potential scenario

BACM Development Corporation would buy and assemble the land. It has achieved significant land holdings in every major city in western Canada with its land banking. It is the largest developer in Calgary and Winnipeg.

Standard-General Construction and the other construction subsidiaries would be hired to service and subdivide the land — installing sewers, sidewalks, streets and other utilities. If the subdivision has poor accessibility, **BACM Construction Co.** would be hired to build roads and interchanges. Products from other Genstar subsidiaries would be used wherever possible. These would include ready-mix concrete and concrete block and pipe from **Consolidated Concrete** (Alberta), **Ocean Construction Supplies** (British Columbia) or **Redi-Mix** (Saskatchewan). Pre-cast concrete products for use in all western provinces would come from **Con-Force Products.** The cement would come from the **Inland/Ocean Cement Group** in western Canada or the recently acquired **Miron Co.** in eastern Canada. The company has its own pits, quarries and plants to provide the required sand, gravel and aggregates. In B.C., aggregates would be transported on the barges of subsidiary **Seaspan International.**

The serviced land would then be sold to other builders with whom the company has contracts, or to the company's own house-building subsidiaries, **Engineered Homes** and **Keith Construc-**

tion. Most of the materials used in the construction would come from other subsidiaries. Lumber, cabinets and windows would be provided for the company's own use, and **Truroc Gypsum Supplies** would provide wall board using materials from its gypsum mines.

A factory in Calgary would produce pre-assembled components for the house-building industry. The construction subsidiaries would have their own electrical, engineering, heating and plumbing divisions. Concrete products and cement would again come from **Inland/Ocean Cement** or from **Miron Co.**

Engineered Home and **Keith Construction** would then sell the houses to the public through their marketing operations. Together they make Genstar one of the largest housebuilders in Canada. Finally, one more subsidiary, **Brockville Chemical Industries,** would sell lawn and garden fertilizers to the people who have just bought the homes.

A visit to any Genstar housing subdivision — particularly in Calgary, Winnipeg or Vancouver — will show just how closely this scenario matches reality. **Ocean Cement** pipe and other materials lie scattered over the ground. Heavy machinery from **Standard-General Construction** is hard at work. **Engineered Homes** salesmen are busy selling the finished products.

Standard-General Construction Ltd. and Ocean Construction Supplies Ltd. are both Genstar subsidiaries.

tunities to undertake mining construction projects for Union Miniere Canada, another company in the Societe Generale de Belgique group.

CONSEQUENCES OF GENSTAR'S OPERATIONS

The activities of companies as large and powerful as Genstar affect Canadians in many ways. For one thing, they hamper the operations and threaten the viability of smaller, Canadian-controlled firms. This has been most clearly demonstrated in the house-building industry which, until recently, was characterized by many small companies in bitter competition with each other. With the appearance of such vertically-integrated corporations as Genstar, many of these small companies have been taken over or driven out of business.

The Spurr report presents conclusive evidence here. The data — builders receiving direct National Housing Act loans — indicates that:

Over 90 per cent of all builders are small firms but they produce less than 30 per cent of all new housing, and both of these proportions have declined during the last decade. In Fredericton, Montreal, Hull, Ottawa, Hamilton, Thunder Bay, Saskatoon and Calgary, about three-quarters of all firms are small firms, and they account for 10-20 per cent of total production. Large firms comprise 5-10 per cent of all firms in Ottawa, Hamilton, Winnipeg and Vancouver, and produce between 50 per cent and 80 per cent of all new housing . . . . This sample demonstrates then, that while the smaller builder dominates the building industry numerically, in terms of production most new housing is built at large scale by the bigger operators, and this situation is common across Canada and is increasing.[2]

Genstar is one of the largest of those house buil-

ders and one of the fastest growing. By 1973, the Calgary situation had deteriorated to the point where three major builders — of which Genstar was the largest — had gained effective control over the housing market. Alarmed by the situation, the City of Calgary commissioned a study of Genstar's activities around Calgary. This study, which was completed at the end of 1973, observed that:

. . . most small builders in the city find it difficult to match the prices established by major house builders. This could lead to smaller builders vacating the industry and a deterrent to new competitors entering the market unless they have special expertise or substantial capital.[3]

Few may mourn the passing of the small builder who, after all, was out to turn as large a profit as anyone else. But another facet of this situation directly affects the buyer or renter of housing accommodation by giving rise to an oligopolistic situation — three or four large corporations controlling an entire industry — with the attendant dangers of price leadership and excess profits. Such dangers are multiplied in the case where one of the oligopolistic corporations involved is also a major supplier for the industry and a significant customer.

In fact the two major suppliers of cement in the country, Genstar-owned Ocean Cement and Canada Cement do set the same prices for their products, at least in some cities.

Ocean Cement and Canada Cement Lafarge were charged and convicted in 1974 of indictable offenses under the Combines Investigation Act for their "conspiracy to curb competition by fixing prices and allocating jobs." When Genstar officials appeared before the Bryce Commission on Corporate Concentration in Winnipeg in November 1975 they defended the identical cement pricing set by

Genstar's Granville Island ready-mix and concrete depot.

Genstar and Canada Cement. If they weren't the same, Genstar Western president Ross J. Turner told the commissioners, "he would sell all his cement before we would sell ours."

Large land banks are another area where the price of housing can be pushed up because the companies are able to control the rate at which land is brought onto the market. The more slowly it is opened up, the greater the profit to the developer. Developers admit the fact that land is being opened up too slowly, but choose to blame local politicians who put too many stumbling blocks in their way. Genstar president, Angus A. MacNaughton, told the Bryce Commission: "We have too much land — we wish we could bring it on stream faster. But unfortunately, governments often delay things. And they are proving that they are slower than private developers when it comes to getting land on the market."

MacNaughton's ingenuous remarks ignored one critical point: the intimate connection between the land development industry and municipal government.[4]

The disclosure of such relationships is rare but several surfaced during the 1974 election campaign in Winnipeg, which saw a solid pro-developer majority returned to office. Vic Krepart, president of Metropolitan Properties, admitted having offered funds to defray expenses to councillors who were acclaimed in the election as well as donating to those candidates in contested wards who, in his words, "we as a corporation felt merited our support." The day after Krepart admitted making his offer, he told the Winnipeg *Tribune*, "I don't feel apologetic nor do I feel I have done anything improper. *It is unfortunate I put the offer in writing.*"

And Genstar, Winnipeg's largest landowner? It was around the same time that Mayor Juba announced that BACM Industries, Genstar's large subsidiary, together with the Royal Bank, Genstar's banker, would sponsor a dinner for former city councillors, reeves and mayors at the Holiday Inn at a cost of $5,000.

Given the lack of campaign disclosure laws, we will never know how much Genstar has contributed to the coffers of friendly municipal politicians. Nor will we ever know what Genstar has received in return.

WHERE DO GENSTAR'S PROFITS GO?

Although its branches have been nourished by the savings of the Canadian people, Genstar's roots lie buried in darkest colonial Africa. Genstar was incorporated as a private investment company in Canada in 1951 under the sponsorship of the Societe Generale de Belgique. In 1955 it became a public company. Until 1969 its name was Sogemines Ltd., which more accurately reflected its parentage and its purpose in coming to Canada. Genstar is 60 per cent foreign-owned.

Societe Generale de Belgique is one of the two or three largest investment concerns in Europe. It is said to control one-fifth of the Belgian economy. The company is intimately connected to the august Societe Generale de Banque, the most powerful bank in Belgium, "where attendants in black ties glide across marble floors, and the electric lights are set in gilded brackets . . ..An officer of the Belgian court, the Grand Marechal de la Cour, is always on the Societe's Board of Auditors, which usually has the odd prince and count as well."[5] Shareholders are rumoured to include members of the Belgian

Genstar's concrete products plant in Richmond, B.C.

and Dutch royal families.

The vast empire centred around the Societe Generale de Belgique and held together by an impenetrable maze of holding companies is engaged in every type of financial, resource extraction, manufacturing and commercial enterprise: banking, insurance, iron and steel production, heavy engineering, non-ferrous metals and minerals, glass, chemicals, cement, construction, oil, hydro-electric and nuclear energy, diamond and gold mining, timber and paper, frozen food products, shipping and public transport, railways and heavy equipment manufacturing, textiles, real estate and construction, in every major country of Europe, the African countries of Zaire and Rhodesia and, increasingly, on the North American continent.

The Societe was founded in the early nineteenth century, before Belgium and Holland were separate countries. For years it issued Belgium's currency; it was virtually the national bank. The company made its fortune in the Belgian Congo where it was the major shareholder in the Union Miniere du Haut-Katanga, the copper and cobalt-producing giant. In effect, Union Miniere ran the Congo for the Belgian government.

The Union Miniere achieved notoriety during the 1920s and 1930s by charging $70,000 for a gram of radium, until competition from the Canadian Eldorado company forced the price down to a mere $20,000 per gram, a price at which both companies were still able to turn a handsome profit. The Toronto *Globe and Mail*, in 1960, estimated Union Miniere profits to be about $60-million per year.

The worst thing that ever happened to the Union Miniere was independence for the Congo in 1960, even though the company tried everything in its power, including the hiring of a mercenary army, to prevent this. When the new Congo government took over, the Belgians were able to remove a substantial portion of their investment from the country. In 1966 the remaining assets of the Union Miniere were nationalized. The company howled that it was "the greatest grab in history," and claimed to have lost assets worth $800-million, but a surge in the price of copper, of which it held large stockpiles, enabled it to carry on and step up its investment in Canada and other places.

Sogemines/Genstar was just one of the vehicles for investing in Canada. Petrofina Canada, now Canada's 46th largest corporation, Miron Co., a $50-million Montreal-based cement and construction company which was merged with Genstar in 1974, and Union Miniere Canada were connected with the same Belgian interests. They also own shares in other large Canadian mining companies such as Falconbridge Nickel Mines, International Nickel Company of Canada, Brunswick Mining and Smelting Corporation, and Rio Tinto-Zinc Corporation (Rio Algom Mines).

Originally, Genstar was intended to participate directly in the Canadian mining industry, but other kinds of opportunities became evident to the Belgian investors and these were soon exploited. Inland Cement was founded in 1954, Iroquois Glass in 1958 and Brockville Chemicals in 1959, each being a kind of venture with which the Societe Generale group had long experience. Canadian capital was involved in a minority position. In 1965, Genstar amalgamated with its three subsidiaries and set up operating divisions, thus being transformed from a holding company into a large industrial corporation. In that year, the company's assets surpassed the $100-million mark.

In 1966, the year Union Miniere's assets in the Congo were nationalized, Genstar embarked on a well-planned program of major acquisitions in Canada, following a strategy of achieving vertical and horizontal integration in the building products, land development and house construction industries. With several notable exceptions, these were areas of highly fragmented competition, giving Genstar excellent possibilities for market penetration and eventual domination. This was particularly true of the house-building and land development industries which were characterized by hundreds of small operators carrying on in a secretive, highly competitive fashion. The goal for Genstar and the other large operators was to transform those industries following the model of the automobile industry — domination by three or

Genstar's Seaspan International and Vancouver Shipyards Co.

four giant firms, a highly rationalized structure and marginal competition (based, not on price, but on "extras").

As well as acquiring over one hundred smaller companies in its drive for market domination, Genstar took over three large industrial conglomerates: Winnipeg-based BACM Industries in 1968, Ocean Cement in B.C. in 1971, and the allied Montreal-based Miron Co. in 1973. Genstar's next move will probably be a major penetration of the Ontario market, by buying out a large building materials and construction firm.

HOW DID GENSTAR DO IT?

One of the first things we did after (forming a new company) was establishing relations with a Canadian bank, and I use the singular advisedly. This is because in Canada, unlike the United States, banking is a membership business. Once you are affiliated with one particular bank, that bank expects you to be loyal to it, and to bank exclusively with it, or almost so. In exchange it gives its loyalty to you and will support you in your efforts. The bank we joined was the Royal Bank of Canada which, more accurately, meant James Muir.[6]

American land developer Big Bill Zeckendorf was extremely candid about doing business in Canada and his remarks from his autobiography are germaine to the success stories of companies like Genstar. From its first entry into Canada in the early 1950s, Genstar has been allied with the Royal Bank of Canada, along with Zeckendorf and many other foreign interests.

The Royal Bank may well be the most powerful organization in Canada. With its assets of over $22-billion, its loans to hundred of thousands of Canadian companies and individuals, its substantial investments in stocks, bonds and real estate, and its mortgage loans, the Royal Bank exerts a powerful influence on the economic life of the country. It has further muscle via its intimate ties with the Power Corporation of Canada and through Power Corp. to the federal Liberal party. It showed great acumen for the Societe Generale interests to ally themselves with the Royal Bank. Not only did they thus assure themselves of adequate financing for their corporate ambitions; they also received the services of the Royal Bank's law firm, and they made the inevitable political connections. For example, when Louis St. Laurent was defeated as prime minister in 1957, he took over as chairman of Miron Co.

The Royal Bank and Genstar share concerns in four ways:
(1) They share directors and law firms;
(2) The Royal loans money to Genstar;
(3) The Royal owns shares of Genstar;
(4) They have been allied on ventures outside the country.

Succeeding presidents of the bank have been members of Genstar's executive committee and board of directors. James Muir, Zeckendorf's drinking companion, was the first. His position was inherited first by Madison M. Walter, then by W. Earle McLaughlin, current chairman and president of the bank. Edward C. Wood, a long-time director of the bank, was chairman and director of Genstar from 1964-1973.

The two are further tied together by the Ogilvy, Cope, Porteous, Hansard, Marler, Montgomery & Renault law firm, general counsel for both the Royal Bank and Genstar. W.H. Howard, a former

Genstar's gypsum products plant on Annacis Island, B.C.

senior partner in the law firm, was a vice-president of the Royal Bank and chairman of Genstar before being succeeded by Wood in 1964. (Howard was also chairman of Petrofina Canada, the other major Belgian interest in Canada.) F. Campbell Cope, another senior Ogilvy & Co. partner, has been a director of Genstar for over 15 years.

In their discussion of the big law firms, Libbie and Frank Park singled out the Ogilvy, Cope "law factory" for special attention.

Their fund of experience on what is legally possible, their technical understanding of how to manoeuvre through and around the Companies Act and Combines Investigations Act, on how to minimize tax liability and extra capital gains, are of great value . . . . Corporation lawyers often do the negotiating behind the scenes with the politicians on behalf of the monopolies . . . . Over the past 30 years, this firm has provided three vice-presidents to the Royal Bank of Canada to which it is counsel, at least three Quebec judges, one of them a Chief Justice, a senator, an ambassador, a member of parliament . . . ." [7]

Genstar's acquisition and expansion program could have been financed by the vast world-wide resources of the parent Societe Generale group. In fact, it has financed its major acquisitions through the use of Royal Bank term loans, an impossibility for almost every other competitor, considering the size of some of the acquisitions. The purchase of Ocean Cement and Supplies for a total cost of approximately $33-million in 1971 was such an undertaking.

To finance the takeover, Genstar had been planning to issue two series of convertible debentures. However, because of its close connections to the Royal Bank, it was able to negotiate a loan of up to $40-million repayable over seven years. Of that amount, $25.5-million immediately went back to the bank to pay off some short-term bank loans. That left up to $14.5-million to finance the cash portion of the Ocean Cement takeover. As it turned out, only $2.4-million was required for that purpose, since the former owners of Ocean Cement accepted a larger number of shares in Genstar as payment. But the fact remains that $2.4-million taken from the savings of ordinary Canadians was loaned to Belgian-owned Genstar for a totally non-productive purpose. By the end of 1974, Genstar had $41.5-million outstanding in Royal Bank term loans.

As part of the deal to acquire Ocean Cement, Genstar granted to the Royal Bank options to purchase 109,512 common shares of Genstar. The Royal now owns these plus other Genstar shares picked up in other deals. The Royal is Genstar's major creditor; the Royal is a substantial shareholder in Genstar; the Royal thus has a stake in Genstar's continuing profitability. Genstar will have little difficulty in arranging further financing with the bank, perhaps at the expense of Canadian-owned companies who might be able to compete with Genstar if they could only gain access to the necessary financing.

Genstar and the Royal Bank have been related in ventures outside the country as well. In 1957, the Royal was part of a syndicate that loaned $40-million to the Belgian Congo government for use in a highway building program to buy imported machinery. At the time, the international press lauded the deal as an example of Canada, a "have" country, helping out the "have-not" Belgian Congo.

Close up, it looked different. The Royal Bank was lending money to the Congolese government to build roads that would be of great benefit to the Union Miniere in its mining operations. When nationalist forces overthrew the Belgian-controlled government, Union Miniere withdrew its assets (increased in value because of the Royal Bank loan) and invested them in Canada by buying up Canadian companies. The Royal then loaned them more money to help Genstar buy up companies such as Ocean Cement, which had been engaged in price-fixing and job allocation practices which, when discovered, resulted in a relatively small fine.

Finally, Genstar, like the other large land developers in Canada, has been helped at every turn by the Canadian government. Many developers are able to defer payment of a portion of their income taxes. This loophole allows them to claim a higher rate of depreciation on their income tax return than they claim in their own financial statements. The effect of this arrangement is that many large development corporations have never and do not now pay any significant amount of corporate income tax.

During the period 1966-1971, Genstar's rate of

taxation was 18.1 per cent, higher than many other developers. But the company still had deferred tax payments of $8,199,000, which it was able to use as cash in hand for corporate purposes. The company seems to be getting better at taking advantage of this loophole. In 1974 alone, Genstar deferred payment of $5,400,000 owed to the government.

With such cooperation from the banks, law firms and federal and municipal governments, Genstar's future looks rosy indeed. A recent study of the company by the Montreal brokerage house of Nesbitt Thompson & Co. called shares of Genstar an "attractive investment because of excellent growth prospects." Genstar will probably continue to grow at its present rate of about 20 per cent per year. Its assets, having doubled since 1970, should reach the one billion dollar mark sometime in 1977. Profits which have been increasing at a rate of 40 per cent per year will continue to soar. Despite the fact that Canada's economy has been depressed, Genstar's profits for the first six months of 1975 were 28.3 per cent higher than for the same period in 1974. Genstar's dividend payments have been soaring as well. In 1972 the company paid out some $5.8-million to its shareholders. That jumped to $8.1-million in 1973 and to $12.9-million in 1974. With over 60 per cent of the shares owned outside the country, that's $16.1-million leaving the country in the last three years alone.

WHAT CAN BE DONE?

Both Peter Spurr's report to CMHC and James Lorimer's study of the Toronto land development industry show clearly the stranglehold that large developers have over the developable land around Canada's major cities. Their evidence is that the high cost of urban land is directly related to this increasing concentration of ownership. And Genstar owns the largest of these large land banks. If we are ever to achieve our goal of adequate accommodation for all Canadians, based on their real needs and at prices they can afford, action must be taken to curb foreign ownership of land and to remove the profit motive from the development of urban land.

Foreign ownership of land has only one effect — it drives up the price that Canadians must pay, since more buyers are competing for the same amount of land. If foreign ownership was prohibited, the cost of land would fall substantially. Such a measure could be instituted immediately if federal and provincial governments so desired, federally by way of its control over foreign investment, and provincially via its control over the way land may be held in the province. Given their past records little action can be expected from either source.

Genstar's gravel pit in Langley, B.C., operated by the Construction Aggregates subsidiary.

Public ownership of all land is a longer-term measure necessary to ensure the kind of housing that does get built meets community goals and not those sought by the developers of growth and profit. But public ownership must go hand in hand with local control.

Public ownership without local control would be disastrous and not much different from the present system. There is little to choose between centralized state control or centralized corporate control. Under either system people have little control over their lives.

On the other hand, local control without public ownership would be just as disasterous. The federal government could implement a policy of purchasing the land banks of Genstar and the other large developers at cost, and turn them over to the municipalities which could then service and subdivide the land and sell lots at cost or lease them. However, given the fact that most local governments are under the control of the development industry, such a policy would not work. The large developers would merely exercise their control in a modified form.

A few short term measures could be initiated immediately. The federal government could close the deferred tax loophole and collect all back taxes owing to the government of Canada. Lorimer has estimated that such a move could generate up to $200-million in government revenues. Windfall profits which accrue to land banking companies mainly as the result of rezoning land from agricultural to urban uses could be heavily taxed. A one hundred per cent tax on the increased value due to such action would seem very reasonable.

129

Genstar subsidiary Engineered Homes' subdivision in Coquitlam, B.C.

In the long term, land and corporate researchers have a central role to play. By continuing to research the activities of the large developers, they can focus public attention on the activities of such companies as Genstar and demonstrate that these companies are an essential part of the housing crisis in Canada.

Since the writing of this article in early 1976, Genstar has continued its corporate plans of growth and profits. 1975 sales soared to $721.5-million, and stated profits were up to $47.2-million, a hefty 35 per cent increase in a year that was supposed to be disastrous for the construction industry in general. Genstar also maintained its reputation for oligopoly when two of its subsidiaries, BACM of Winnipeg, and Truruc Gympsum of Edmonton, were charged in October 1976, along with two other major companies with "conspiring to lessen competition in the production, manufacture, sale or supply of gypsum wallboard," by the justice department of the federal government.

My prediction that Genstar's next move would be a major penetration of the Ontario market by buying out a large building materials and construction firm in 1976, was only partially correct. Genstar did move into the Ontario market, but it did so by acquiring Abbey Glen Property Corporation, whose assets of over $400-million made it Canada's fifth largest development corporation. Abbey Glen's treasure, as far as Genstar was concerned, was an Ontario land bank of some 2,000 acres. (This was part of a total land bank of over 10,000 acres which boosted Genstar's holdings to more than 26,000 acres and made Genstar president Angus MacNaughton's words to the Bryce Commission on Corporate Concentration a few months before the acquisition — "we have too much land" — ring a bit hollow.) That gave Genstar a good base for further expansion in the Ontario market.

In case you're wondering why foreign-controlled Genstar was allowed to take over Abbey Glen by the Foreign Investment Review Agency (FIRA), it's merely a matter of definition. Genstar officials and lawyers were able to convince their friends in Ottawa that Genstar was really a Canadian company! Don't look at the foreign ownership, Genstar told FIRA. Look instead at our board of directors. See how many Canadians are seated around that corporate table. Certainly that makes us true blue Canadians.

In fact, over the past few years, Genstar has been replacing its Belgian directors with genuine Canadians. But just who were some of these Canadians who prompted FIRA to exempt Genstar from its controls? People like Robert Rogers, president of 89 per cent American-owned Crown Zellerbach; Kelly Gibson, chairman of American-controlled Westcoast Transmission Co.; and Frank Capon, former vice-president of Du Pont of Canada, another American-owned giant. And that's how you can turn a bloated Belgian conglomerate into a friendly Canadian neighbour.

1. Peter Spurr, *Land and Urban Development*, James Lorimer and Company, Toronto, 1976, p.211.
2. *Ibid.*, p.192.
3. Burnet, Duckworth, Palmer, Tomblin & O'Donoghue, and Laventhol, Krekstein, Horwath & Horwath, *Report of the Preliminary Investigation on Activities of Genstar Limited*, Calgary, December 1973, p. IV-24.
4. These are detailed in James Lorimer's, *A Citizen's Guide to City Politics*, James Lewis & Samuel, Toronto, 1972, chap. 7.
5. Paul Ferris, *Men and Money, Financial Europe Today*, Penguin Books, London, 1970, pp.98-99.
6. William Zeckendorf, *Autobiography*, Holt Rinehart & Winston, New York, 1970, p.172.
7. Libbie and Frank Park, *Anatomy of Big Business*, James Lewis and Samuels, Toronto, 1973, p.95.

Hamilton Harbour: Politics, patronage and cover-up

Marsha Hewitt

Prime Minister Pierre Elliott Trudeau on the subject of public inquiries: They are "related to inquisitorial concepts of justice and should not be resorted to except when the rule of law cannot be relied upon to ensure that justice is done."

Hamilton Harbour used to be called "Lake Geneva" by the eighteenth century settlers who lived in the area. This beautiful land-locked harbour, ringed by the Niagara Escarpment, lies at the western end of Lake Ontario and provides excellent shelter for boats and ships. The bay was the favourite recreational area for Hamiltonians until well into the present century. Lansdowne Park was at the foot of Wentworth Street, bathing beaches went all along the shoreline, and farther east were Sherman's Inlet and Huckleberry Point, all of which were popular for fishing, swimming, and picnicking.

Many Hamiltonians still remember the steamers which left from the foot of James Street for day and night cruises around the bay and into Lake Ontario. Boathouses spotted the shoreline, providing people with rented rowboats and canoes for the day. In the winter, the frozen waters of the bay were covered with skaters and ice fishermen. Ice boating and curling were also familiar winter sports.

Hamilton Harbour is also one of the finest inland harbours in the world and by the mid-nineteenth century it was becoming an increasingly important commercial centre. This aspect of the harbour has resulted in Hamiltonians being robbed of one of their finest natural resources through the gradual destruction and isolation of the harbour. The story of Hamilton Harbour is a tale of exploitation and duplicity; the responsibility for this state of affairs rests with municipal, provincial, and federal politicians but particularly with the Hamilton Harbour Commission. As a result of the commission's selling off waterlots and miles of shoreline at astonishingly low rates to big industry and private developers, the face of Hamilton Harbour has drastically changed. The ten square miles of water surface is now reduced to seven square miles of water surface — thirty per cent less than what it used to be. The swimmers, the fishermen, the picnickers, the steamers and all but the sailing boats of the economically privileged have long gone.

Since 1929 a total of almost two thousand acres of water has been filled, almost exclusively for the benefit of industry, particularly Stelco and Do-

The Beach Strip of Hamilton Bay in the early 1900s.

fasco. The total price at which these waterlots were sold is little more than two million dollars. None of the sales was ever tendered, nor was there public notice that the lots were even available; these deals were privately arranged between the Hamilton Harbour Commission and the industries. Firms like Stelco simply asked the commission to buy lots and the sale was finalized upon the completion of the price negotiations.

One unanswered question is how prices of waterlots are determined. Stelco rarely paid more than $1500 per acre, a remarkable fact when one considers the site upon which the company rests is prime industrial land. A few years ago one harbour-based steel company sold several acres of waterlots it had acquired at prices of $1500 per acre to another company for $23,000 per acre.

All that is now left untouched by industrial development of the bay is its western end. Even this is endangered, not by industry, but by a private development scheme that has already resulted in the filling of over fifty acres of water. What has happened is a story of how the Hamilton Harbour Commission, a body formed to oversee the development of the harbour as a port facility on behalf of the city of Hamilton, has failed its trust by allowing the harbour to be plundered by industry and developers. It is also a tale of widespread corruption and scandal that has penetrated the fabric of both Hamilton's and Canada's political life.

The central issue to be resolved is the question of who has ultimate power over the fate of the harbour: the city or the commission? This issue has yet to be resolves by the courts;[1] the city has always maintained that the role of the harbour commission is to act as trustees in its behalf. As the city solicitor, Ken Rouff, wrote in 1972:

The Hamilton Harbour Commissioners are a corporation called into being primarily to act on behalf of the City of Hamilton as trustee of the city's interests. With the possible exception of the power conferred upon the commissioners to *act as delegates for the federal government with respect to the federal navigation and shipping power, it is nowhere contemplated or intended that that corporation is to become a power unto itself, free to act without reference to the wishes of the city council.*

Yet since the inception of the Hamilton Harbour Commissioners' Act in 1912 the commission has acted as a "power unto itself", allowing the city no say whatsoever as to the development of the harbour. How this came about is a complex issue, best determined by an analysis of the structure of the commission and its political context.

STRUCTURE OF THE HAMILTON HARBOUR COMMISSION

The Hamilton Harbour Commission is composed of two federal and one city appointee. As is usual with such government appointments the people chosen are prominent supporters of the party in power. The harbour commission has always been the preserve of political patronage: when the Conservatives were in power under Diefenbaker, two Hamilton Tories, Argue Martin and J. Edmund McLean were the federal commissioners. The most powerful Liberal political patron in Hamilton since 1962 has been John Munro, a fact most vividly illustrated when *Globe & Mail* reporters discovered during the 1974 federal election that out of ninety-eight federal appointments made in the Hamilton area prior to that election, fifty-two had worked for or contributed to John Munro's 1972 election campaign. In May, 1964, Munro appointed E. Delbert Hickey, a Hamilton lawyer who is both a Mason and member of the powerful Hamilton Club, and Joseph Lanza, a Hamilton tailor, and a one time alderman who was convicted in the nineteen forties on charges of bookmaking and gambling, to the Hamilton Harbour Commission.

Hickey's (former chairman of the commission) and Lanza's Liberal party connections are extensive. Both were defeated federal Liberal candidates; Hickey was an officer of the Wentworth Liberal Association for twenty-three years prior to his appointment to the commission and Lanza was Munro's first campaign manager. Munro tried to get Lanza a citizenship court judge position in 1969, but for some reason failed. According to lawyer Joe Kostyk, a loyal Munro supporter who collected over $40,000 for his 1974 campaign: "John wanted him to get it, that's for sure." The National Parole Board's refusal to pardon Lanza of his former criminal record has been reported by the Hamilton media.

Since the harbour commission was incorporated under its own act and is not under the jurisdiction of the National Harbours Board, no one seems to know to whom the commission is responsible. In February, 1972, then Minister of Transport Don Jamieson stated publicly that he could not and would not interfere with any filling of the harbour because the Hamilton Harbour Commission is an "autonomous" body and therefore out of his jurisdiction. A few days later Chairman Del Hickey contradicted his statement, saying: "Despite his statement, I feel we are responsible to Mr. Jamieson and if he told us to stop the filling we would have to." (*The Hamilton Spectator*, February 17, 1972)

From the many public statements made by Hickey between 1964 and 1973, while he was on the commission, it is clear that he exploited this ambiguity regarding the accountability of the commission to do whatever he and his fellow commissioners pleased with the harbour. In fact, the arrogant behaviour of the harbour commission in relation to the city or any group that tried to challenge its indiscriminate filling of the bay caused Tom Beckett, a fellow Liberal and former chairman of the Hamilton Regional Conservation Authority, to say that he had "nothing but condemnation" for Hickey's commission, adding that "This body appears to be responsible to no one on earth." (*The Hamilton Spectator*, December 3, 1971)

THE LAX LANDFILL PROJECT

Any government body that is responsible to no one is potentially dangerous because it is especially vulnerable to corruption and abuse of its powers. In the absence of strict controls, any harbour is a prime target for exploitation by people for their own gain. In the spring of 1957, a Philadelphia-based organization, Luria Brothers Co. Inc., approached the commission in order to buy land on the harbour bed in front of waterfront property that they already owned in the northwest end of Hamilton. This deal was for forty acres of water lots and shorefront. The site is located in the only remaining portion of the harbour which might have been suitable for recreation. Luria's plan was to erect a scrap metal processing plant on the reclaimed land. The deal was completed in November 1958 at the low price of $1500 per acre, or $60,000 for the total.

For some reason Luria's Canadian agents, Samuel and Sheridan Lax, were given this parcel of land and water lots on April 3, 1959. Not long afterwards the city began planning an urban renewal program in the north end, adjacent to the Lax site, and when Hicky, Lanza, and city appointee Kenneth Ronald Elliott came to the harbour commission a little later, they expressed a wish to co-operate with and assist in the urban renewal project by making available more property of fifty-one acres of shorefront and water lots to the Lax brothers.

By this time the scrap metal plant idea had been abandoned in favour of a new idea for development of the Lax property: a multi-million dollar residential complex of high-rise apartment blocks with marina facilities and parkland. Some fifteen

The piece of land slicing through the water in the centre of the photograph is the Lax landfill site. What the site will be used for is still the subject of controversy.

Photo: Marsha Hewitt

thousand people would occupy the development, to be known as "Bayshore Village", and in 1968, Lax began filling.

Conveniently for Lax, the city was involved at that time with tearing down a fair portion of the escarpment for the Claremont access roadway project, and what better place to dispose of the escarpment but in the bay? The Lax brothers bid for the fill from the roadway project which they won (they were the only bidders) for one cent per cubic yard. In 1973 the filling stopped due to mounting opposition from environmental and citizens' groups and the city zoned the land already filled as a "holding zone." This zoning classification means that no development can take place on the Lax site without the city's approval.

When Lax stopped filling, over fifty acres of harbour had been filled, and this reclaimed land lies vacant and ugly, slicing across the west end of the bay. The city now wants a public park with marina facilities to be made on the Lax site, but there is the problem of price, and who will pay for it — the city, the province, or the federal government? A *Spectator* article of May 17, 1974 said that the Lax's price on their land was $6.76-million. It was bought for $212,000. William Powell, chairman of the Hamilton Region Conservation Authority, commented

that the Lax water lots "should never have been sold in the first place . . . The thing was . . . a steal . . . a mistake by the harbour commissioners." (*The Hamilton Spectator*, May 17, 1974)

But, how was Luria/Lax allowed to obtain these water lots in the first place? In a CTV documentary done for W5, entitled *The Seaway: Paydirt and Patronage*, aired in the summer of 1975, Argue Martin, chairman of the harbour commission when the original transaction took place with Luria Brothers, explained that the sale occurred because the commission needed money. No other considerations entered the picture — no considerations of port planning or development.

When Hickey, Lanza and Elliott took over the harbour commission, they supported the "Bayshore Village" plan, offering Lax even more harbour property as an added encouragement to his investment. The Lax scheme was unusual because it was the only instance of a plan for private residential development at the harbour and as such, was unrelated to the development of the port of Hamilton.

The business interests of harbour commission members complicate the story of the Lax development. Ken Elliott became a vice-president and director of a cable television company, Northgate

Cable, in December 1969. This company's territory is the north and west end of Hamilton, including the Lax property. Completion of "Bayshore Village" would have added about 4,000 families to Northgate Cable's portion of Hamilton.

Del Hickey, while chairman of the harbour commission, was an executive officer of Ronark Developments, a wholly owned subsidiary of Ronyx Corporation Ltd. Sam Lax was then and still is a director of Ronyx; Del Hickey is today vice-president of Ronyx. While Hickey was on the commission, the mailing address of Ronyx Corporation Ltd. was his law firm of McBride, Hickey, Green, McCallum and Mann at 20 Hughson St. South.

ELLIOTT AND THE COMMISSION

It was in 1969 that Ken Elliott's integrity as city representative on the harbour commission was first questioned. The issue came up when Elliott's interest in Northgate Cable came to light.

The facts came out in public when Elliott applied to the CRTC for permission to buy half the company's twenty thousand shares for less than $500; his application was turned down. Up to that time Elliott had been popular at city hall because he kept the politicians well informed about harbour matters. Elliott was on the commission only two years when Hickey and Lanza began to complain about his "tendency to act independently" of the commission in reporting to council.

Elliott clashed with his fellow commissioners in January 1966, when he publicly revealed that the commission had awarded a five-year contract to the higher of two bidders. The favoured one was Hamilton Terminal Operators Ltd. (HTO), a cargo-handling firm which had worked for the commission at its overseas terminals since 1960. Because of its "proven competence" the commission decided to waive a $100,000 performance bond. On January 31, 1968, only two of the five years of the contract having been completed, HTO went out of business and the harbour commission, at the urging of John Munro,[2] took over the work, buying the necessary equipment from the defunct company. The cost to the commission for this fiasco was approximately $500,000.

Elliott's popularity with city council began to wane in 1971, the year Hamilton lawyer Herman Turkstra began his term as controller. Turkstra has a solid reputation in Hamilton as a brilliant courtroom lawyer as well as a man of high moral principles. The story of his fight to remove Ken Elliott from the commission and to probe the harbour is fascinating indeed because it very quickly became a fight with his fellow city councilmen as well. Turkstra was a key figure in uncovering corruption at the harbour through the activities of Elliott.

THE LAND SWAP

In 1971 the harbour commission was quietly negotiating a deal with Stelco and Dofasco that would allow the companies to fill the harbour by yet another 328 acres. This deal involved an exchange of land and water lots between the commission and the steel companies whereby the commission would acquire 313 acres of water lots along the Beach Strip.

The completion of this deal was announced publicly November 11, 1971, to the surprise of many people on city council as well as the Hamilton Regional Conservation Authority. Controller Turkstra was angered that the city had not been first consulted and that there was no accounting as to why the deal was necessary. He described the situation as "three men, responsible to no one, agreeing with . . . men responsible to two bodies of shareholders, to take an asset that belongs to the citizens of Hamilton and convert it to the use of the companies, without the public's being aware of it." (*Globe & Mail*, November 12, 1971)

When the commission first announced its deal with the companies it said that the total acreage to be given them was 103, a fact which was later found to be totally untrue. The commission also said that it would give the city 176 acres of its newly acquired Beach Strip holdings for a public park. According to Turkstra, a park at that location was unfeasible for two reasons: first, if the province was to carry out its plans to extend the Queen Elizabeth Highway over the Skyway Bridge it would need that site, and second, a park of that size would require 1.75-million cubic yards of fill, an amount almost impossible to acquire. Hickey certainly would have been aware of these obstacles, therefore he must have mentioned the park in order to soften the impact of the land swap. Hickey's commission had been plagued that entire summer by protesting environmental groups concerned about additional landfilling in the harbour and pressure was rising to stop further filling.

The conservation authority was upset because it had already agreed with the harbour commission to begin a joint waterfront study of the bay. Tom Beckett was outraged at the commission's duplicity in keeping the deal a secret from the authority when the former knew full well that a freeze on all further landfilling was necessary until the study was finished.

John Prentice, a member of the Conservation

Authority at the time, was concerned about the swap because the area to be filled by the steel companies was the deepest part of the bay. Thus the fill would displace the largest amounts of water in the bay, dangerously depleting the oxygen content which is already non-existent below the 30-foot water level. (*The Hamilton Spectator*, December 3, 1971) Once all the oxygen has gone from the bay, it would become septic and no longer able to dilute its pollutants. The deputy director of the Municipal Laboratories, A.V. Forde, supported this warning, adding that increased landfilling was endangering the quality of Hamilton's drinking water.

The other danger of filling in this area was that the channel connecting the bay with Lake Ontario would become too narrow for the bay to flush itself out into the lake, this being the only way the bay rejuvenates itself. If this flushing-out process stopped the bay would become a cesspool.

In spite of the warnings, the deal went ahead. Those on council who protested to the harbour commission met with an abrupt response from Hickey: "As far as we're concerned, the deal has been finalized." (*The Hamilton Spectator*, December 22, 1971) City solicitor Ken Rouff challenged the legality of the swap on the grounds that harbour lands held in trust for the city could not be disposed of without the approval and consent of council. In response, Hickey merely scoffed and allowed the companies to fill.

Hamilton City Council was far from unanimous in its opposition to the land swap, however. When some city aldermen argued against it, they were almost jeered at by Mayor Vic Copps. When confronted with the serious environmental dangers to the bay as a result of this filling, Copps retorted: "Our greatest problem in this city isn't ecology. It is unemployment. This deal will help ease that problem." (*The Hamilton Spectator*, December 1, 1971) The land swap did not result in creating more jobs for Hamiltonians. Copps was strongly supported by Controller James Campbell who did not seem to mind that the bay was being filled for various projects. Said Campbell of the Lax scheme: "If filling is taking place for that development then it's my position that the bay should be filled . . . go ahead and fill it."(*The Hamilton Spectator*, February 15, 1972)

Although four of the five people on Board of Control (the exception being Herman Turkstra) supported the land swap, city council appealed to then provincial Minister of the Environment James Auld for help in stopping landfilling in the bay. Auld regretted that he had no constitutional authority in the matter, but promised to do what he could. For a while it appeared that he was not only sympathetic to the environmentalists' concern over the condition of the harbour, but was also really willing to take action on the issue. In March, Auld

granted through provincial legislation the power to control all landfilling operations in the harbour to the Hamilton Regional Conservation Authority. Except for the Hamilton Harbour Commission, anyone desiring to fill in portions of the bay would henceforward be compelled to apply to the conservation authority for a permit.

Board of Control (except Turkstra) generally agreed with the new legislation with one reservation: that Stelco and Dofasco be exempted from the new restrictions. Along with several aldermen, Board of Control urged Auld to withhold granting the powers over filling to the authority until *after* Stelco and Dofasco had filled in their lots. Auld was not swayed by this manoeuvre, stating that he would not even discuss the matter of exemptions for anybody.

Both Stelco and Dofasco began to pressure city council. They met privately with Board of Control three days after council asked Auld to exempt the companies. Alex Fisher, vice-president of research and development for Stelco, and John G. Sheppard, executive vice-president of finance for Dofasco, presented "briefs" to Board of Control arguing for their case; these "briefs" were never made public. It was decided at this meeting that Board of Control would support Stelco and Dofasco in their bid to be exempted from the legislation.

When this decision became public, many aldermen were enraged. Alderman Dave Lawrence castigated the mayor in council, saying: "We have to have a little guts — and not say yes to every person who comes into your office." Rankled by these remarks upon his courage and integrity, Copps informed Lawrence that "the people with guts are . . . the people who are not swayed by every little mob screaming about ecology."[3] (The Hamilton Spectator, March 8, 1972)

Auld stuck by his word not to allow any exemptions to the new legislation in spite of pressure from city council. In reply to this refusal to give in, Copps called Auld a "tyrant" and accused him of maliciously trying to curtail industrial expansion in Hamilton. Copps screamed about unemployment and the fact that one in eight families in the city depend upon the economic prosperity of Stelco and Dofasco.

While this debate was raging and Auld maintained his tough stand on the exemption issue, Stelco and Dofasco were continuing to build the berms (retaining walls) required as preparation for the filling of the water lots. The harbour commission began constructing its own berms at the Beach Strip and the Lax brothers went on as before, filling in their lots. Hickey said flatly that he had no intention of following the new legislation and would never recognize the authority of the conservation authority over landfilling. He maintained that "the dumping regulations are not well thought-out or even reasonable." (*The Hamilton Spectator*, April

13, 1972) It is ironic that a lawyer would defy laws he does not agree with, but that is just what Hickey did. No one ever effectively challenged his blatant defiance of the provincial legislation.

Auld remained firm on the issue of exemptions until mid-June when he startlingly and inexplicably reversed his position: he asked the conservation authority to allow Stelco and Dofasco to fill their lots even though they had not even applied to the authority for permits. Auld directly undermined his own legislation and from then on rapidly backtracked. He said he regretted his previous stand and that he had misunderstood what the steel companies had wanted to do with the reclaimed land. According to his public statements, Auld had the notion that all the companies wanted was to fill in one hundred acres for the sole purpose of adding more pollution control equipment.

But on August 4 it was learned that both steel companies had lied about the amounts of filling to be done and its purpose: Dofasco was to get 120 acres of water lots to fill and Stelco 208, for a total of 328 acres. Of the total acreage involved, 16.2 was to be used for the installation of pollution control devices.

Meanwhile the Hamilton conservation authority was determined to exercise its newly-won powers; however, the group was willing to compromise. It offered to let Dofasco have 96 acres to fill and Stelco 86; the companies refused to budge. In early July, 1972, the HRCA gave Stelco and Dofasco an ultimatum: apply for permits within ten days or face prosecution. The companies applied for permits on the last day, but had never ceased their filling operations. On August 23 the authority met to vote on their applications. It voted twice, each vote resulting in a tie, and in each case broken by Chairman William Powell against the companies. On September 14 the Ontario Cabinet overturned the authority's decision and allowed Stelco and Dofasco to fill. The reason the province gave for its action was that the conservation authority was so evenly split on the issue the government felt it had to step in and "assume leadership." This move was fully supported by Auld and the Minister of Natural Resources, Leo Bernier, who had been as firmly against the exemptions as was Auld.

When Bernier announced the reversal of the HRCA's decision, he contacted the news media before informing the authority. William Powell angrily lashed out at the Conservative government, suggesting that Stelco and Dofasco used "high pressure tactics" in their appeal against the HRCA's decision. Said Powell: "I'll bet the lobbyists from the two steel companies were just about camping down there (at Queen's Park) . . . I can smell the whole situation from here." (The Hamilton Spectator, June 19, 1972) Powell feared that the action of the provincial cabinet would set a dangerous precedent for the Lax operation: "Who

E. Delbert Hickey

knows? The Lax brothers may make a large contribution to the (Conservative) party for the next election. Perhaps then they will have some friends in the government."[4] (The Hamilton Spectator, September 15, 1972)

Why James Auld so dramatically reversed a position to which he seemed genuinely committed has never been explained. The action of the provincial cabinet shows that Auld was acting within the party line; perhaps he was told to change his mind. Certainly there were politicians at city hall who wanted Stelco and Dofasco to have their way, and for this the municipal government must accept responsibility for what happened. The irony of this situation is that Stelco is moving to Nanticoke on Lake Erie to embark upon steel making production on a scale far exceeding its Hamilton operation. One all too obvious conclusion to be drawn from this story is that industry on the scale of Stelco and Dofasco does not often lose political battles, whatever the cost to the public interest.

It was on the issue of the land swap that Herman Turkstra tried to have Elliott removed as the city appointee to the harbour commission. At that time Elliott was in the employ of United Smelting and Refining Co., a company which sells steel to Stelco, and Turkstra felt that Elliott's support of the land swap constituted a conflict of interest situation. On November 30, 1972, Turkstra made an unsuccessful bid to have council remove Elliott; he was overwhelmingly defeated in a 19-2 vote.

At this stage Elliott still had strong support at city hall. Council already knew of Elliott's involvement in Northgate Cable and if the majority of council members were not disturbed by that, they would

Joseph Lanza

certainly not be upset by Elliott's promotion of the steel companies on the land swap. Mayor Copps even commended Elliott on his good judgement toward the steel companies, adding that Elliott had made no error in failing to inform council that the deal was taking place.

Alderman Pat Valeriano disagreed with the mayor on this last point; he even implied that a conspiracy of secrecy existed within council to keep those council members opposed to landfilling from finding out about the deal until the last minute. Elliott was invited to council in early December of 1971 to answer any questions council had about the land swap. Those aldermen who had protested against the swap were not told he was coming and were thus prevented from having the opportunity to prepare questions for Elliott. Said Valeriano: "We think the whole thing stinks because those opposed to the land swap were not informed Mr. Elliott would be at council and we would have the chance to interrogate him." (*The Hamilton Spectator*, December 4, 1971)

THE BARFNECHT AGREEMENT

The end of the Hickey-Lanza-Elliott administration began with the allegations made by a Bolton Ontario scrapdealer named Kenneth Barfnecht, who contacted Turkstra in the summer of 1972 charging corruption at the harbour. On July 21, 1972 Barfnecht made a formal statement to Turkstra, then chairman of the harbour subcommittee, which revealed that he and Elliott had agreed to enter a business partnership in breaking ships at the harbour.

A formal business agreement had been drawn up on May 31, 1972 by Brian Morison, Q.C., himself a former city controller and lawyer for the harbour commission. Within the terms of the agreement, Elliott and Barfnecht were to be partners in the new company; Elliott's role would be to procure ships for breaking, acquire sites at the harbour as well as obtain the permission needed from the commission for the operation of the business. There can be little doubt that Elliott intended to try to use his position as harbour commissioner to help him in these dealings.

A third party was to be brought into the agreement, Robert A. Henderson of Aldershot Contractors' Equipment Rentals Ltd. He wanted to receive one-third of the company profits paid to him in trust under a different name. The agreement was never signed because Barfnecht saw his company's profits shrinking as a result of various personal extravagances being demanded by Elliott. If it were not for this, the deal would have gone ahead.

While these negotiations were going on between himself and Elliott, Barfnecht had already brought three ships into the harbour and had begun dismantling them for scrap. On June 8, one week after his proposed partnership with Elliott had fallen through, Barfnecht received a letter from the harbour commissioners forbidding him to cut ships at the dock where he was located. He moved his ships to another harbour site and they were impounded in the dead of night for non-payment of a $3,000 rental fee. Barfnecht was being charged far in excess of the usual one cent per foot for docking his ships — that is, $12.00 a foot. He later received a $2500 refund from the commission as the result of a court action. It was never revealed how the commission happened to overcharge Barfnecht.

When the ships were impounded they were located on the property of Aldershot Stevedoring. Barfnecht claimed that the manager, Frank Paten, had given him permission to dock there but the company later denied this. The president of Aldershot Stevedoring is Robert A. Henderson, the same person originally involved in the aborted business agreement with Barfnecht and Elliott.

It is hardly surprising that Barfnecht became convinced Elliott was using his influence with the harbour commission to ruin his business because Barfnecht had refused to go into partnership with Elliott. He then decided to take all the damning information he had about Elliott and other harbour activities for the RCMP. His allegations included extortion, drug trafficking, smuggling and conflict of interest.

The RCMP sent Barfnecht to the OPP and the Hamilton police, on the grounds that all the charges (except drug trafficking) were out of their jurisdiction. He went to Dr. Pierre Camu, administrator of the marine transportation branch of the federal department of Transport who directed him to a St. Catharines authority who told Barfnecht: "If you don't like what's going on in Hamilton harbour, why the hell don't you get out?" He then went to the deputy minister of Transport who in turn contacted the solicitor for the marine branch of the department of Transport, John Gray. A meeting was ultimately arranged with the RCMP and it was decided that a preliminary RCMP investigation into the harbour would be launched. As it happened, the RCMP investigation did not begin until a full year later.

Barfnecht, in the course of his search for an authority who would begin an investigation into his charges saw two local Hamilton politicians, NDP MPP Norm Davidson (Hamilton Centre) and Tory MP Lincoln Alexander (Hamilton West). Although both politicians' ridings border the harbour, neither would offer him any help. According to Barfnecht, Alexander's reaction was based purely on political expediency: "Linc said it was a biggie and could go either way. If it went one way, it could destroy the Liberal Party and if it went the other, well, he wouldn't want to be on my coattails." (*The Hamilton Spectator*, March 12, 1975) Alexander, the most important federal Conservative in this area, has never spoken out strongly on the harbour.

While this was going on Turkstra began preparing evidence against Elliott. The issue he wanted to explore was Elliott's conflict of interest dealings. Turkstra saw, unlike some of his fellow council members that the involvement of Elliott in a shipbreaking operation at the harbour could easily be aided by his position on the commission. City solicitor Ken Rouff agreed with this, saying:

If this agreement places . . . the harbour commissioner, our appointee, in the position where he is operating a business, and it turns out later that for the successful operation of that business he must apply to the harbour commission, then he's wearing another hat. That sort of thing is a conflict of interest.

(August 28, 1972. Supreme Court, Ex. No. 10.)

The 1912 Harbour Commissioners' Act forbids the commissioners from having "any transactions of any pecuniary nature, either in buying or selling, with any members thereof, directly or indirectly." Yet in a strictly legal (not moral) sense it appears that this stipulation can be interpreted fairly broadly, as it was by Toronto lawyer J.J. Robinette when consulted by the former commission on the question of Earl Perkins, port director of Hamilton Harbour.

It was revealed in a *Spectator* article on December 10, 1971 that Earl Perkins was, and had been for some eleven years, part owner of a cargo-handling firm at the harbour called Direct Seaport Services. This company handles about one-fifth of all the

THE HISTORY OF THE RCMP'S HARBOUR INVESTIGATION

July, 1972: Barfnecht goes to Controller Turkstra.

August, 1972: Barfnecht contacts the RCMP.

September 12, 1972: Controller Campbell tells council that the Solicitor-General of Canada has begun an investigation into harbour. No such investigation was going on.

September 1972-February 1973: No investigation. Solicitor-General Warren Allmand claims the RCMP could not investigate due to a "jurisdictional dispute" with Hamilton city police. RCMP asked city police to investigate Barfnecht charges on November 7th and agreement was made. In December RCMP checks back and finds out no investigation going on. Hamilton police later claim no such agreement made and that according to their records no meeting about the issue ever occurred.

February 23, 1973: Allmand makes formal request to RCMP to begin investigation.

May, 1974: RCMP issues statements saying "investigation was commenced in *September 1973* by criminal investigation section."

May 3, 1975: Dr. Morton Shulman charged investigation delayed due to political interference.

The RCMP never explained the year delay in their investigation, merely insisting it began in September, 1973.

rubber imported into Canada. It employs longshoremen to unload, weigh and inspect the rubber; Perkins' job as port director is to oversee relations between the longshoremen and the harbour commission, ensuring that these relations are "harmonious." He makes recommendations to the commission as to rental rates for storage facilities on harbour property and many things that would directly involve his company. In fact, according to Del Hickey, Perkins "supervises everything" at the harbour. (*The Hamilton Spectator*, December 10, 1971)

According to former chief of Harbour Police Bob Malcolmson, Perkins supervises the law at the harbour as well. Malcolmson testified at the inquest of longshoreman Joe Hasler in 1971 that he quit his post as police chief because "I wasn't allowed to enforce the law on the docks." He was referring to the direct intervention of Perkins when Malcolmson tried to press charges against four longshoremen for drinking on harbour property. Malcolmson was told to drop the charges in order to "keep harmony between the port and the longshoremen." Malcolmson refused and while he was involved in this struggle with the port administration, he was told by Hasler that if he didn't "lay off the petty charges" his "boss's [Perkin's] rubber [would] be floating all over the bay." (*The Hamilton Spectator*, December 10, 1971)

When confronted with the fact that Perkins' involvement with Direct Seaport might be seen as a conflict of interest, Hickey replied that: "There is no conflict that I can see — Mr. Perkins devotes more than fifty hours a week to his job as port director." (*The Hamilton Spectator*, December 10, 1971) The commission then asked J.J. Robinette for his opinion and on January 20, 1972 he stated that Perkins was not in conflict of interest due to his partnership in the company. When then Minister of Transport Don Jamieson was asked his opinion of the whole affair he refused to get involved in an issue that was, in his view, "strictly the business of the Hamilton Harbour Commission." (*The Hamilton Spectator*, December 31, 1971)

The Perkins story is significant because it casts light on the way in which the harbour commission works and provides a context in which to judge Elliott's involvement in conflict of interest situations. Elliott was not the only one using his position in the harbour administration for his own benefit, but whereas Perkins was protected by legal opinions, Elliott was ultimately fired on the grounds of an intent to go into business at the harbour. The reason Elliott was fired was because there was some accountability in his case, given that he was the city appointee and thus responsible to city council which ultimately removed him. The rest of the harbour administration in Hamilton is virtually responsible to no one but itself.

Turkstra tried to probe the extensiveness of Elliott's business connections at the harbour when he invited Marvin Frank to a harbour subcommittee meeting at city hall, August 4, 1972. (Ontario Supreme Court, Ex. No. 15) Frank is president of several companies, including A.J. Frank & Son, a scrap metal company located at Hamilton harbour. Turkstra had reason to believe that Elliott might have been financially involved with Frank's company, using his position on the commission to promote Frank's business interests.

In response to Turkstra's probings, Marvin Frank vehemently denied that Elliott had ever received financial reimbursement for any work done for Frank's company. Barfnecht who was present at this meeting contradicted him, saying that Elliott used to help Frank obtain ships for breaking. Barfnecht was referring to two American ships for which he claimed Frank had sent Elliott and then Hamilton Alderman Aldo Poloniato to Europe to find markets for selling them.

Barfnecht made his statements contradicting Frank in the recorded August 4th meeting of the harbour subcommittee. (Ontario Supreme Court, Ex. No. 5) He further claimed, contrary to Frank's statements, that he and Elliott brought the American ships through the Welland Canal for Frank. When the job was done Barfnecht signed a timecard of A.J. Frank & Son; Elliott paid him $200 on behalf of the company for his help bringing in the ships.

As the meeting continued it became fairly apparent that Elliott acted as an agent for Frank while he was a commissioner. Turkstra wanted to know if Elliott was receiving any money for his work. He confronted Frank with information he had that Elliott seemed "to be operating as your employee", bidding in Frank's name for the ships and making the arrangements for their sale and transfer to Hamilton. Said Turkstra: "The question is a pretty simple one: what's Ken doing running all over the place . . . putting himself forward as your agent?" All that Frank would ever admit was that "Elliott is a friend of mine". He finally walked out of the meeting, saying: "I'm not staying any longer, gentlemen. I've got high blood pressure, I've got diabetes, I'm getting over a heart attack, I'm leaving now", and then he disappeared.

ELLIOTT FIRED AS HARBOUR COMMISSIONER

On August 28, 1972, Hamilton City Council convened to decide what to do about the revelations made at the August 4th meeting where Barfnecht's agreement with Elliott was made known. For the second time in eight months Herman Turkstra confronted city council on the issue of Elliott using his position as harbour commissioner for his personal interests. Unlike the previous occasion, Turkstra had the support of more than one alderman because the evidence against Elliott was too blatant to shrug off this time. This meeting was a bitter confrontation between pro- and anti-Elliott factions within council and turned out to be the first in a series of nasty clashes among council members.

Turkstra had the support of Ken Rouff, the city solicitor, who agreed that Elliott's agreement with Barfnecht constituted a conflict of interest. The opposition to this claim voiced by some aldermen rested upon the fact that the agreement was not actually signed, and it was felt a demonstrated intention to go into business with Barfnecht was insufficient grounds to remove Elliott from office. This was the centre of the controversy that night, and a motion was put forward to ask Elliott for his resignation. One of Elliott's supporters on council was Aldo Poloniato (the alderman who accompanied Elliott to Europe on behalf of A.J. Frank & Son) who suggested that "what we should be doing right now is rapping his knuckles and saying to Ken Elliott 'Don't get yourself involved in anything like that . . . we don't like it."[5]

This was the general tenor of the arguments against the motion to remove Elliott. Those sharing Poloniato's opinion had a difficult time wading through the basically ethical question of a public representative using his position for personal benefit. Turkstra rose in council to try to outline as clearly as possible just what was involved and why council ought to be concerned at what Elliott was willing to do. He described the commission as "three men who have an absolute monopoly and who are not elected but who are appointed", reasoning that "the obligation on those three men to administer the harbour in a scrupulously fair fashion becomes very important."

He pointed out that it could not be guaranteed that Elliott, should a conflicting situation arise involving his positions both as a harbour commissioner and businessman at the harbour, would decide necessarily in the public interest if such a decision meant a reduction in his company's profits. He finished by saying:

I think it my duty to see to it that the sole representative of 300,000 people on that harbour commission is capable of understanding the highest principles of what is good and correct for a public official in his peculiar position. It's not so much what he did, it's what he was prepared to do and couldn't see anything wrong with doing.

Controller James Campbell could not bring himself to accept such moral abstractions; perhaps he did not understand them. In any event Campbell jumped to his feet immediately after Turkstra spoke, making his own inimitable appeal to council:

Well, members of council, as far as I'm concerned, my position is this – that Mr. Elliott has not got a conflict of interest. I think that if he wants to go into the breaking of ships certainly he has the right to . . . if you want to go into any business in the city of Hamilton, to have a zoning change, you have to go to the planning board. As every member of council knows, there are real estate people on the planning board where 100 per cent of their firm is owned by them. And they go for a zoning change. Certainly these people are honest so we tolerate that in this country. And that has always been the way that it happens.

After much debate on the issue, it was decided to accept the motion that Elliott be requested to resign from the harbour commission.[6]

The matter did not end here, however: Elliott refused to resign. On September 5 he launched a libel suit against Controller Turkstra, Aldermen James Custeau, James Kern, Vince Agro, Bob Mor-

Kenneth R. Elliott

row, Pat Valeriano and businessman Ken Barfnecht. On September 12 city council met again to decide what to do about the recalcitrant Elliott, and it proved a lively meeting indeed.

It was moved by Dave Lawrence that Elliott be fired outright. This motion provoked vicious opposition from Controllers James Bethune and in particular, James Campbell. Bethune saw the issue as one of "character assasination", declaring the move by council to dismiss Elliott a "smear", an action "most unfair and corrupt."

Alderman Bill Scandlan decided it was "a vendetta by some members of council"; all this impassioned indignation moved Controller Campbell again to jump to his feet to apologize to Mr. Elliott, on behalf of council and the city of Hamilton for what council was attempting to do. Campbell's arguments against dismissing Elliott, his analogies and tortured diatribes employed for the sole purpose of defending Elliott's activites against the charge of conflict of interest are exemplative of the general line taken by pro-Elliot politicians that night. Campbell's defence of Elliott was particularly enlightening when he offered himself and his business partner, Bethune, as a shining illustration of political integrity to prove unequivocally that Elliott in no way compromised himself in his intended agreement with Barfnecht:

. . . it wasn't long ago that I discussed with Controller Bethune maybe we should build some apartments . . . and I suppose very shortly we are coming up with a situation and I think we still are that we might sign an agreement pretty soon to become partners in some construction work and I suppose

that we are going to have to go to the planning board to get some zoning changes . . . and do you know under the terms of reference set down now if we stick to a single standard that Bethune and I now, that the word is out are liable to be asked for our resignation at any moment because that's exactly . . . (sic)

At this point Campbell was drowned out by resounding booing and cheering from the spectators' gallery, where about ninety citizens frequently interrupted the evening's debate in this way. Mayor Copps was forced to demand order, threatening that he'd allow no "demonstrations" in his council chamber.

This unrestrained public outburst did not daunt the flow of Campbell's rhetoric, however. His next comment, the clinching analogy to show finally that Elliott was not in error in his deal with Barfnecht perhaps most accurately expressed the real sentiments of those pro-Elliott councilmen. "If I thought of giving Controller Turkstra a punch in the mouth, if I thought about it, you know, the fact, and I haven't done it. I mean he can't arrest me for assault." And because he knew "sincerely in [his] heart that Mr. Elliott never had a conflict of interest", Campbell, histrionics and all, "implored" council not to fire Elliott. In the end Campbell, Bethune and Copps could not prevail; Elliott was fired by a vote of 11-8.[7]

The next day, September 13, Elliott issued a writ against the City of Hamilton for unlawful dismissal. His claim was first, the city had no authority to remove him from his post as its own representative to the harbour commission, and second, that he was not guilty of a conflict of interest. He appealed to the fact that the chairman of the comission, Del Hickey, knew about his plans with Barfnecht and saw no impropriety in it. His agreement was "never signed nor put into effect and . . . the chairman of the harbour commission had full knowledge (of it) and . . . I made a complete disclosure (of it) and . . . there had been no action by the harbour commission" against his plans. (*The Hamilton Spectator*, September 14, 1972)

An effort was made to force city solicitor Ken Rouff to take on the city's defence to Elliott's court action, but in the end council voted 17-4 that night to retain a Toronto lawyer.

TRYING FOR AN INQUIRY

Coincident with the struggle in council to fire Elliott was another struggle to convince the federal government to initiate a public inquiry into the operations of Hamilton Harbour. Some council members felt that the revelations concerning Elliott alone justified an inquiry since there were several other points council wanted cleared up about the harbour. Predictably, there were those on council who were opposed to an inquiry and they tended to be, with a few exceptions, those same people who had all along supported Elliott.

Besides the motion to fire Elliott before council the night of September 12, there was another motion stating that "the Federal Government be petitioned to conduct a full-scale public inquiry into the activities of the Hamilton Harbour Commission." The motion was tabled, however, because of a curious and sudden revelation made by Controller James Campbell who stated that he had already gone to Ottawa August 31, 1972 and had placed the document containing Barfnecht's allegations against Elliott in the hands of then Solicitor-General Jean-Pierre Goyer. He said further that he had been assured that an investigation would be immediately forthcoming. Herman Turkstra proposed "on the strength of this assurance" tabling the motion for one month in order to "await a reply from Ottawa." (*The Hamilton Spectator*, September 13, 1972)

As it turned out, Campbell had not gone to Ottawa on the 31st and he had never met the solicitor-general. Amid later angry denials from Goyer that he had ever seen Campbell, it was learned that the latter had (according to *his* explanation) sent a registered letter to Goyer containing the findings of the harbour subcommittee. On the eleventh Campbell was in Ottawa, but the man he saw was the executive assistant to Goyer — John Cameron. There was a federal election going on at the time and Cameron did not tell Goyer anything about the visit from Campbell, instead sending a letter to Allan Baker, his counterpart in the Ministry of Transport, who in turn passed the letter on to the deputy minister of the department for relay to its legal advisor, John Gray.

It is not surprising that while the Barfnecht document was making its tortuous way through the labyrinthine recesses of the federal civil service, the ministers themselves heard nothing about it. Baker later said he "thought" he told Jamieson about the document, but wasn't sure. One thing is sure: Campbell's story was not accurate. That Goyer and Jamieson were busy campaigning for the election probably explains the fact that the Barfnecht document was so long kept at the level of the civil service. At any rate, this was the explanation given by the ministers and their assistants at the time.

As it happened, some Hamilton politicians were not unhappy that the inquiry was not proceeding. Alderman James MacDonald was against an inquiry because of the expense it might incur. At the September 12 meeting Controller Anne Jones objected that: "We can't have a public inquiry every time someone raises something in the paper . . .

Signs like these appear all along the shorefront of the harbour, reminding the people of Hamilton that the harbour is off limits to them.

Photo: Marsha Hewitt

the reporters have such an exciting way of putting things." (*The Hamilton Spectator*, September 13, 1972) On October 10, 1972, when the tabled resolution calling for the public inquiry from the September meeting was raised, it was defeated in an 11-7 vote.[8]

The next day Board of Control met to consider a request from Turkstra's harbour subcommittee to hire an independent firm of auditors to study the harbour commission's books in order to ascertain the amount of surplus profits owed the city by the commission.[9] Turkstra had an idea that between 1962 and 1972 the commission had accrued $2.5-million in surplus profits but auditors were required to ensure that this sum was indeed surplus profit and not something else. Mayor Copps and Controller Bethune objected to doing this, saying that the matter could easily be resolved by inviting Chairman Hickey to a Board of Control meeting to explain his interpretation of surplus profits. Hickey had on several occasions said publicly that Hamilton would never get any share of harbour profits at any time, even though the 1912 Act states specifically that all surplus profits rightfully belong to the city,.[10]

Meanwhile, yet another controversy was broiling at city hall regarding the issue of filling the post made vacant by Elliott's dismissal. A "screening committee" was set up to interview prospective candidates (twelve applied for the job) for the post as the city appointee to the harbour commission. The committee members were Mayor Copps (chairman), Controller Bethune and Aldermen Bill McCullogh, Bill Scandlan, Pat Valeriano, Ken Edge, and Aldo Poloniato. Presumably this screening committee was set up partly in order to avoid hiring another embarrassing city appointee.

This committee refused to screen candidates for a long time. According to a *Spectator* report of October 18, 1972, the mayor "bitterly fought against any screening", explaining that he knew most of the applicants and all were suitable for the job. Controller Bethune and Alderman Poloniato agreed with the mayor; some committee members such as Pat Valeriano disagreed, and when no agreement could be reached among them to begin the job they were set up to do, Mayor Copps angrily resigned from the committee.

At this point Transport Minister Don Jamieson tried to intervene by way of sending telegrams to city council urging it to quickly find a replacement for Elliott. City Solicitor Ken Rouff was urging city council to do the same, warning that if it failed to find a successor to Elliott within thirty days, the ministry in Ottawa could do so. It seemed that Jamieson did not want to do this, judging from the tenor of his telegrams. All the while, James Bethune continued to question the legal fight of city hall to remove Elliott in the first place.

One can imagine the frustration of the members of the harbour subcommittee in the face of all this opposition not only to settle the Elliott question, but also to do something about the harbour in general. The final exasperation was expressed by an angry Herman Turkstra toward the end of October when he accused Mayor Copps, Controller Bethune and Alderman Aldo Poloniato of being part of "a concerted campaign to prevent at all costs a proper examination of the role of the Hamilton Harbour Commission in the life of this city." (*The*

Hamilton Spectator, October 21, 1972)

He accused them of harassing him in his efforts as chairman of the harbour subcommittee to probe harbour activities. Turkstra circulated a letter he wrote the mayor in response to the latter's not informing him of a meeting of the three levels of government, to which all interested parties were invited, to discuss environmental issues relating to the harbour. Turkstra felt that as head of the harbour committee at city hall he should have been given the opportunity to attend this meeting by simply being told of it.

Turkstra felt a conspiracy existed within council to cover up all matters relating to a probe of the harbour. He wrote: "I have reached the point, Mr. Mayor, where I am sick to the pit of my stomach with this kind of undercover scurrying around." He further challenged Copps and the others to ask for his resignation on the basis of non-confidence in himself and his committee, and then move for the dissolution of the committee. In response Mayor Copps said that he believed the function of the harbour subcommittee "is best served if it keeps council informed on environmental matters." Controller Bethune said he'd be happy if the committee disbanded altogether. (*The Hamilton Spectator,* October 23, 1972)

On October 31, 1972, the day of the federal election, council finally passed a motion calling for a public inquiry into Hamilton Harbour. On December 15th, Justice R.E. Holland dismissed Elliott's case against the City of Hamilton, providing at last the legal ratification of Elliott's firing. On March 30, 1973, Controller James Campbell ran for the vacant position on the harbour commission. In spite of his business partner and fellow councilman James Bethune cutting short a Florida trip in order to return home to vote for him, Campbell lost the vote to B.M. Alway, the present city appointee to the commission.

THE DREDGING SCANDAL

On May 30, 1974, Kenneth R. Elliott was arrested by the RCMP, charged on eleven counts including fraud, bribery, forgery, conspiracy, and breach of trust. Charges were also laid against Reginald Leigh Fisher, a Hamilton business consultant, for conspiracy to defraud the Hamilton Harbour Commission of $365,000 as well as bribery, forgery, and conspiracy. Robert A. Henderson of Aldershot Contractors Equipment Rentals Ltd., the same man who was to be part of the Elliott-Barfnecht business agreement was also charged on a lesser offence. Two others were charged on lesser offences as well, Robert P. Henderson (no relation to the other Hen-

derson) a marine engineer and retired employee of the federal department of Public Works and Harry Atkins, a former OPP officer. They were convicted and received fines ranging from $10 to $40,000 and were put on a two year probation. Ken Elliott and Reginald Fisher were convicted and sentenced July 10, 1975, receiving prison terms of six and three years respectively.

Among several others named but not charged by the RCMP were Marvin Frank, Joseph Lanza, E. Delbert Hickey, and Ontario Minister of the Environment George Kerr. As part of the evidence it was shown that Elliott alleged his colleagues on the harbour commission accepted kickbacks on the Stratherne Street dredging project. The allegations were never proven.

Three dredging companies bid on the job, two allegedly conspiring to bid high so that the J.P. Porter Co. could receive the job. The other two companies were McNamara Corp. Ltd. and Canadian Dredge & Dock Co. Ltd.; the vice-presidents of all three companies, Horace Grant Rindress (Porter), Albin Louis Quinlan (McNamara) and Robert J. Schneider (Canadian Dredge) were named in the indictments but not charged.

Rindress told the court that Ken Elliott told him he had to pay an additional $10,000 beyond the kickbacks to the other commissioners for George Kerr, who allegedly demanded the money as a contribution to his 1971 election campaign fund as a form of compensation for his having to endure heavy pressure from environmental groups over the harbour. Kerr resigned his post temporarily in February 1975 to clear his name in court; the charges were never proven and Premier William Davis reinstated him into the Ontario Cabinet.

The significance of the Hamilton Harbour scandal cannot be properly understood unless it is perceived in its larger context of the Canadian dredging industry.

In 1970 the oil barge "Irving Whale" went down off the coast of P.E.I. It contained one million gallons of Bunker oil in its hold. At one point the federal government thought it might try to salvage the sunken barge and in October 1971 tenders were called and the contract was awarded to a consortium of three companies. Donald A.Kerr, a partner in (then called) Atlantic Salvage and Dredging Co. Ltd. put in a lower bid than the consortium, but was refused the contract because, according to federal officials, Ottawa on the advice of a consultant, felt that the consortium could better handle the job.

Prior to the closing of the tenders, Kerr was offered a $50,000 bribe to bid high on the contract by a high-ranking executive of the Foundation Co. of Canada, one of the members of the consortium. Kerr informed the federal department of transport and the contract was cancelled. Soon after this, Inspector Rod Stamler of the RCMP was called in to investigate; his official report of June 1973 recommended that a vice-president of Foundation and a vice-president of a Toronto consulting firm be charged with conspiracy. The office of the Attorney-General in Nova Scotia decided not to press those charges.

The "Irving Whale" incident precipitated RCMP investigations into the workings of the Canadian dredging industry as a whole and the Hamilton scandal was discovered during that larger investigation. What emerged from the RCMP investigation and the subsequent trial was, in the words of the prosecutor, Clayton Powell: "A long-standing conspiracy among a group of Canadian companies and executives to rig tenders, maintain artificially high prices for dredging services and share the spoils illegally."

Rindress told the court in the Hamilton case that price-fixing has been going on in the dredging industry for at least thirty to forty years. He said that the companies maintain "score cards" to keep track of whose turn it is to bid high on a given contract and how much the company awarded the contract must pay as compensation for the others bidding high. No wonder the *Toronto Star* described the Canadian dredging scandal as "one of the worst corporate scandals in Canadian history."

In March 1975 charges were laid against fourteen executives and thirteen dredging firms for conspiracy to defraud the federal and Ontario governments of $4-million through price-fixing; these charges have yet to be heard in court. Predictably there was an uproar in Ottawa from both opposition parties for public inquiries into the entire affair and demands for tighter government controls in the dredging industry. Hamilton City Hall had been asking for an inquiry since 1972. Federal Minister of Public Works Bud Drury's reply to an NDP suggestion that the industry be nationalized to prevent further public rip-offs was: "The assumption . . . that the government can do it better . . . is not an assumption I'm prepared to accept."

Drury admitted in the House that his department is still giving out contracts to companies charged before the courts with price-fixing. In fact, in March 1975, it was learned that Trade Minister Alistair Gillespie had given contracts totalling over $104-million to the Simard-controlled Marine Industries, even though at the time it was under investigation for bid-rigging and was subsequently charged. Meanwhile Drury assured the House that government controls were being implemented to prevent future defrauding of public funds; from now on, dredging companies must provide "written proof" that no "collusion" (bid-rigging) has occurred on the submission of bids for government contracts. Said Conservative James McGrath: "That's like the FBI asking Bonnie and Clyde for assurances to keep the peace."

McGrath also challenged Drury on the grounds that when he was president of the Treasury Board, he ignored reports from then Auditor General Maxwell Henderson that alleged "irregularities" existed in the dredging industry. Henderson told W5 reporters in the 1975 documentary on the seaway that millions of dollars have been wasted on dredging operations; he even once refused to approve the books of the National Harbours Board. Drury did admit in the House that no real bidding competition for dredging contracts has existed for years, especially where large operations are concerned like Vancouver Harbour or the Fraser, Mackenzie, and St. Lawrence Rivers. In fact, it was discovered during the RCMP investigation that the bid for Marchand's pet project at Ile d'Orleans was also fixed. Moreover the work was done improperly and incompletely, resulting in costs to the government of millions more than the original estimate.

Hamilton became the centre of the entire police investigation into the dredging industry because it led to the discovery of price-fixing at Ile d'Orleans and the ensuring charges against the companies. The Hamilton scandal proved to contain implications that reverberated as far as Ottawa. It also provided a microcosmic view of how price-fixing works in the dredging industry, suggested the possible involvement of provincial and federal politicians in a cover-up, and gave the opposition critics a focus whereby they could formulate questions in the hopes of constructing a total picture. Unfortunately that whole picture is as yet obscure.

JOHN MUNRO AND THE ELLIOTT TAPES

During the trial of Elliott the court heard a taped conversation between Elliott and Rindress which contained a mysterious reference to Cabinet Minister John Munro:

R: "Have you got any political clout, anything to help?"

E: "Nothing."

R: "After all you did for those guys."

E: "The way I busted my ass for all them politicians, the money I've got them over the years. Now they all go run and hide, including Munro. That's one thing that irks my ass more than anything — Munro."

R: "Well, he started this whole thing, didn't he?"

E: "You bet your ass he did."

The Globe & Mail, May 31, 1975)

The mention of John Munro in relation to the many-faceted controversy around Hamilton Harbour was not new at this point. Prior to this Munro had consistently opposed a public inquiry into Hamilton Harbour saying the city hadn't evidence

John Munro   CP wire photo

of wrongdoings from which an inquiry could justifiably proceed. It was known that Munro was responsible for the appointments of Hickey and Lanza to the harbour commission and both men were prominent Liberals. Hickey and Lanza were not, however, reappointed to their posts because, according to Jean Marchand, they were "suspect in their ethical standards." (*Toronto Star*, March 1, 1975)

With the removal of the old federal appointees Munro backed the appointment of two Hamilton Liberal Party supporters to the commission, lawyer Edward Tharen and businessman Peter Flaherty. Tharen, the chairman of the harbour commission, is a past president of the Hamilton and District Liberal Association and contributed $1000 to Munro's 1973 campaign. Flaherty is also a member of the same Liberal Association and was a campaign manager for Munro. Flaherty's appointment is particularly significant: he is part owner of a company called Flaherty Manufacturing which in 1972 received a $40,000 contract for lapel buttons from the federal department of Health and Welfare, Munro's former cabinet post. No tenders were ever called on the contract and no one knows if there was competitive bidding on it — officials in the department tend to think there wasn't. It was later discovered that a requisition for the pins went directly to Flaherty in place of the traditional tendering procedure "by mistake." And the patronage continues.

The same week that Elliott was arrested, John Munro's Hamilton East constitutency offices were raided by the RCMP. The police were interested in Munro's campaign contributors. They had a tape of a conversation between Munro and Seafarers' International Union President Roman Gralewicz in which Munro either asked for or was offered $500 for his campaign. Receiving money from the SIU put Munro in an odd position; as Minister of Labour Munro has direct jurisdiction over any disputes between the SIU and the shipping companies of the Great Lakes. Munro returned the money the following September, having had second thoughts concerning the propriety of his accepting the money and the way in which such an event might be construed. A police source in Ottawa told a Toronto newspaper that Munro had called Gralewicz soliciting the money, but this has never been proven. Solicitor-General Warren Allmand has refused to make available the Munro-Gralewicz tape or any transcript of it, saying he was satisfied that no soliciting for donations occurred on Munro's part.

Since the demands for a public inquiry into Hamilton Harbour began coming from the City of Hamilton in 1972, Munro has consistently said he could not support any such inquiry. In June, 1974, while the federal election was on, then NDP leader David Lewis came to Hamilton while campaigning and remarked that Munro was deliberately preventing an investigation into the harbour controversy. David Lewis's statements came one week after Elliott was arrested and charged in the harbour case.

Lewis's remarks provoked an angry response from Munro, who denied the allegations and challenged Lewis to a public debate. Meanwhile, in the wake of Elliott's arrest, there was much furor about the harbour including many repeated demands for an inquiry. The harbour affair and Munro's connection with it (whatever that may be) was shaping up to be a major election issue and Munro was finding himself attacked on many sides. Munro had always maintained that an RCMP investigation had begun into Hamilton Harbour in the fall of 1972; the RCMP has always insisted that their investigation began one year later, in September 1973. This discrepancy has never been explained.

None of the above incidents were reported in *The Hamilton Spectator*, the city's only newspaper. On June 6, 1974 a *Globe & Mail* reporter wrote:

The Hamilton Spectator, *circulation 113,000 and the only newspaper in the city, has on the advice of its lawyers decided not to print any stories about land use around Hamilton Harbour or the policies of the harbour commission.*

The Globe published all Lewis's charges that Munro was impeding an investigation into the harbour, the calls for a public inquiry, and the Munro television interview. No legal action was brought against the Toronto paper for doing this. Furthermore, none of the statements about the harbour from Munro's political opponents contesting his riding were ever published by *The Spectator*.

In early December, 1974, the NDP and Conservative opposition parties in Ottawa began an intensive interrogation of Munro and the Liberal government about the Hamilton Harbour issue which lasted until the end of February 1975. As the opposition pressed for a full accounting of Munro's possible connection to both the harbour and the SIU issues, the Liberal government stonewalled, always giving the same reply against an inquiry: lack of sufficient evidence of wrongdoings. At the end of February Munro — having tearfully offered his resignation to Prime Minister Trudeau, who refused it — went into hospital suffering from "nervous exhaustion." He was distressed by the "innuendo" implicit in the questions asked of him in the House.

THE COVER-UP

On July 24, 1975, John Munro, in response to mounting pressure from Hamilton City Council for an inquiry into the harbour, placed the blame for the entire scandal (as it affected Hamilton) on the city for appointing Elliott as its representative in the first place. Alderman Don Gray, present chairman of the now-called Harbour Advisory Committee described Munro's statement as a "panic reaction"; Alderman Bill McCullough said he suspected Munro had something to hide because of his steadfast opposition to an inquiry. (*The Hamilton Spectator*, July 25, 1975)

On August 6, 1975, the city sent letters to Prime Minister Pierre Trudeau and Jean Marchand requesting an inquiry; the reply was merely that the letters had been received. Munro then said there would be no inquiry unless the city could show evidence of corruption at the harbour; when the city drew up a list of charges of possible wrongdoings, many of which were mentioned at Elliott's trial, Munro dismissed them as "unsubstantial." (*The Hamilton Spectator*, August 19, 1975)

There are still many suspicions and questions to be resolved from the dredging scandal. The most pressing is, whether Elliott was the sole culprit in the piece. Certainly it was never proven in court that Hickey or Lanza accepted kickbacks for the dredging operation on which Elliott was charged. Elliott was one man on a three-member commission: it has not yet been explained how he could pursue his illegal activities at the harbour without someone in the harbour administration knowing about it.

The Hamilton Harbour scandal was a large-scale affair, leading to the discoveries of corruption in the entire dredging industry and raising suspicions about Hamilton Harbour in general, yet out of the whole case only five men were convicted, two went to jail and Elliott received the heaviest sentence.

There is also the question generated by Jean Marchand's statement that Hickey and Lanza were not reappointed due to suspicions concerning their ethical standards; he never explained that statement.

Nor has the delay in the RCMP investigation ever been explained; on May 3, 1975 then MPP Dr. Morton Shulman suggested the delay was caused by political interference. The conflicting stories between the RCMP and the Hamilton police force have been left up in the air. The RCMP insists it got an agreement from the late Chief of Police Len Lawrence on November 7, 1972 that his force would begin an investigation; when the RCMP checked back in mid-December, they discovered no such investigation was even started. The Hamilton police department says today the meeting is not recorded in their files. Conservative MP James McGrath felt "that this delay was a deliberate attempt to contain the investigation to Hamilton." (*The Hamilton Spectator*, March 10, 1975)

The other thing to be explained is the references to Munro on the Elliott tape as well as his statement about all the money he got for "politicians over the years." Elliott's words could be pure bravado, a trait to which he was certainly inclined, but Munro is closely linked to Hamilton Harbour. His supporters were appointed to be the federal representatives on the harbour commission and yet he is the very person who has consistently said he is opposed to an inquiry. However, he seems to have support from Prime Minister Trudeau who relates inquiries with "inquisitorial concepts of justice."

There are also questions concerning the surplus profit the city has never seen from the harbour commission — there is an estimated $15-million involved. The city also wants to know how the commission determines the sale of water lots and harbour lands, and who are its insurance agents and lawyers? But the commission to this day refuses this information.

In November 1975, city council made its fourth attempt in three years to persuade the federal government to hold an inquiry but Minister of Transport Otto Lang turned the request down. On October 28 of that year Munro said that "answers to questions raised by council can be answered by the harbour commission itself." (*The Hamilton Spectator*, October 29, 1975) Like the government which appointed him, present commission chairman Ed Tharen refuses to give the city any information about harbour operations.

THE STORY CONTINUES

On July 23, 1976 the City of Hamilton filed a writ in the Supreme Court of Ontario against the Hamilton

Harbour Commissioners and former commissioner Kenneth Ronald Elliott for an extensive accounting of harbour commission activities since April 1, 1948. This legal action is the city's last recourse for a public inquiry into its own harbour. A great deal depends upon the city winning its suit; it if does, harbour operations will be more open and the city will have finally established itself as the rightful overseer to the development of the harbour. If it loses, the harbour commission will continue to work as always, accountable to no one but itself, since the federal government seems reluctant to interfere in what it does.

The people of Hamilton are entitled to a full accounting of what the commission does and plans to do with this natural resource, and what the conditions were at the harbour that allowed a Ken Elliott to come along and defraud them while acting as their representative. Unless the federal government cooperates by allowing the city an inquiry, the harbour will always remain vulnerable to future abuse.

On October 4, 1976, the Hamilton Spectator announced that the harbour commission filed a counterclaim against the City of Hamilton for $600,000. The counterclaim is for the full amount the commission alleges was defrauded because of the "wilful misconduct" on the part of former Commissioner Elliott. The commission's defence against the city's writ in effect throws the responsibility for the defrauding of the commission by Elliott on the city, since Elliott was the city appointee to the commission. Thus according to the commission the people of Hamilton must pay for Elliot's crime.

---

1. In November, 1976, the city won its court case against the commission in the dispute over who has the right to control land use around the harbour.

2. In 1962, newly-elected MP John Munro wanted an inquiry into the operations of Hamilton Terminal Operators Ltd., but it never took place.

3. Stelco and Dofasco are powerful forces in the life of Hamilton, and are involved in the political scene in the city. One example of this is that in 1970 when Controller James Bethune was running for Board of Control, a Stelco public relations officer ran his campaign. Bethune strongly supported the land swap deal in council. (*The Hamilton Spectator*, March 8, 1972) It is not known who Stelco and Dofasco give campaign donations to on a municipal level.

4. Sam & Sheridan Lax, through their company Lax Iron & Steel Ltd., contributed $500 to John Munro's 1972 election campaign.

5. Minutes of September 12, 1972 meeting of city council, Ontario Supreme Court, Exhibit No. 11.

6. Those for the motion: Controllers Turkstra, Jones. Aldermen Morrow, Agro, Valeriano, Lawrence, Custeau, Wheeler, Ford, Stowe, Kern. Opposed: Mayor Copps, Controllers Campbell, Bethune. Aldermen Clinc, Poloniato, Lombardo, MacDonald, Edge.

7. The voting record on September 12 was the same as that of August 28, excepting that Aldermen Bill McCullogh and Bill Scandlan were absent from the August meeting. They voted at the September 12 meeting, for and against the motion, respectively.

8. Those opposed to an inquiry: Mayor Copps, Controllers Bethune and Campbell, Aldermen Ford, Edge, MacDonald, Scandlan, Stowe, Lombardo, Cline, Poloniato, and Custeau.

9. Between 1911 and 1966, the city of Toronto collected approximately $78,974,566 in surplus profits from its harbour commission. (*The Hamilton Spectator*, January 26, 1966).

10. In 1966, then Alderman Bill Powell said when he asked the Hamilton Harbour Commission where the surplus profits had gone, he was told "it's none of your business what happened to the money." (*The Hamilton Spectator*, January 26, 1966).

11. One of the *Hamilton Spectator*'s own reporters, Paul Kidd, challenged Munro directly on the harbour issue in a televised interview, but this was not reported.

12. The case will be heard before the courts sometime in the spring of 1977.

IV Planners and bureaucrats

The history of Canadian city planning

Kent Gerecke

City planners in Canada know little about the history of their own profession in this country. Without any historical perspective, it is very difficult to understand how planners came to have the political and administrative functions they now possess, and how they became so firmly allied with the exponents of growth, with policies like expressways and urban renewal which citizens have often resisted so fiercely, and with the property industry and land developers.[1] In the history of Canadian planning are to be found the roots of the personal and professional crises which face many planners who find that their own theories of planning are in conflict with the policies and measures resulting from their work.

There are two approaches which can be taken to the history of planning in Canada. The first involves looking at the professional history of planning, which starts in about 1910 when the first people to label themselves "planners" began to work on urban issues in Canada. This story begins with a British planner, Thomas Adams, who arrived in Canada to practise his skills in 1914.

The second approach to planning looks at planning from a broader point of view, and incorporates all the efforts, successful and unsuccessful, to make conscious decisions about how Canadian cities should be organized and should grow. There is room here for only a few particularly important examples of this broader concern which often extends beyond those people calling themselves planners. One such example is the work of early surveyors, whose decisions about how urban and rural land was laid out and used, provided the framework of the Canadian community. The surveyors may not have called themselves planners, but they made planning decisions which continue to shape our lives.

PART I
PLANNING: THE PROFESSIONAL HISTORY

There are five major stages in the professional history of Canadian planning, beginning with the Commission of Conservation of Natural Resources in 1909. The Commission was established by the Laurier government as a result of pressure on Canada from U.S. president Theodore Roosevelt who wanted a continental resources policy.

Table 1

Time Period	Stage
1909-1931	formal beginnings
1932-1943	inactivity
1944-1951	restart
1952-1964	institutionalization
1965-present	broadening and criticism

Early in the Commission's work city planning became a major concern (conservation at this time was seen to include human as well as natural resources). Two of the few, full-time experts employed by the Commission laid the foundation of Canadian city planning. Dr. Charles Hodgetts, previously Medical Health Officer for Ontario, brought an interest in urban health, and Thomas Adams, a prominent British planner, became Canada's first professional planner. In the Canadian tradition, Hodgetts and Adams did their planning by selectively borrowing from British and American experience. From Britain they followed the public health movement. They showed only slight interest in the garden city movement, even though Adams had been active in this area in Britain. From the U.S. they borrowed the legalistic approach, the technique of land-use, particularly zoning, while paying little attention to the city beautiful movement. Hodgetts commented that it was "not so much the city beautiful as the city healthy we want for Canada."

Prior to the arrival of Thomas Adams in 1914, there were only a few, scattered steps towards professional city planning in Canada: a Tenement House Bylaw in Winnipeg, a few city beautiful associations, various parks commissions, some local plans and three provincial planning acts based on the British Act of 1909. Adam's stay, from 1914 to 1921, stands in contrast as a period of tremendous accomplishment. He planted the seeds of planning across the country through talks and articles, he drafted a model planning act for Canada, which was adopted by all but two provinces, including revisions to the three existing acts (this was the origin of zoning, the master plan and the planning commission); he successfully promoted the establishment of provincial departments of municipal affairs; he established planning as a professional activity through the formation of the Town Planning Institute of Canada in 1919 (he was the first president); and he was active in consulting work. Early membership of the profession was dominated by consultant occupations as can be seen from Table 2. Only 2 of the 110 members in 1921 listed themselves as town planners.

Table 2
Town Planning Institute of Canada Membership — 1921

Occupation	Number
Land surveyors	30
Engineers	27
Architects	16
Professors	7
Landscape Architects	5
Government Officials	4
Town Planners	2
Others and Unknown	13
Total	110

In 1921, the Commission of Conservation was abolished because other government agencies were taking on its functions. Thomas Adams moved on to New York where he headed up work on a regional plan. Lewis Mumford constantly criticized his narrow approach to the New York plan and his willingness to compromise. As one historian has said of Adams, "his conservatism kept him from being a truly great planner; he was incapable of being ahead of his time." However, the selective, borrowed planning he brought to Canada carried on until the Depression.

INACTIVITY

During the Depression and World War Two, Canadian city planning ceased to exist. The nation turned to priorities other than cities. A 1943 survey of Canadian cities and towns showed that not one city or town had adopted an official community plan and few were doing any planning. Humphrey Carver has offered an explanation of this situation:

In both the U.S. and in Britain the foundation of present planning ideas and methods was laid down during the period between the two wars. In Canada this did not happen. For us the economic Depression of the Thirties was a vacuum and a complete break with the past. We had no Frederic Osbornes, Abercrombies and Clarence Steins. We had no public housing

The influence of Dr. E.G. Faludi, who led the team planning postwar Toronto, is in strong evidence today. The "Master Plan" he is discussing here, thirty years ago, is strikingly reflected in Metro Toronto. Source: *Subject to Approval: A Review of Municipal Planning in Ontario,* Ontario Economic Council, p. 40

programs and none of the adventurous social experiments of the New Deal. In the Toynbee sense, we did not react to the challenge of the Depression, perhaps our roots were not yet deep enough. We withered on the stem. So in 1946 we almost literally started from scratch with no plans or planners and we immediately hit a period of tremendous city growth. [2]

Carver's view of this period was widely shared by professional planners though it ignores some key political activities of the Thirties which are very important to Canadian planning.

RESTART

Town planning was one of six priorities of Canada's post-war recovery effort. The Curtis Report of 1944, from the federal Advisory Committee on Reconstruction, dealt specifically with Housing and Community Planning. While the emphasis was on housing for the returning veterans, the planning advice was substantial. Curtis proposed a three-level (federal, provincial, local), top-down planning mechanism, a federal program for land assembly and slum clearance, a program of public education on city planning, and assistance for planning education.

The federal response was to create a Crown corporation concerned mainly with new housing and housing finance, Central Mortgage and Housing Corporation (1946), rather than a ministry responsible for urban affairs. This reflected the priority for housing over planning and established an ad hoc federal approach to cities. As well, legislation was adopted to assist land assembly and urban renewal. Regarding public education for planning and promoting professional education, the federal philosophy preferred a popular support base for planning rather than relying on professional missionaries. CMHC promoted the establishment of a citizen-based planning organization through meetings across the country and a national conference in 1946. Out of this conference emerged the Community Planning Association of Canada (CPAC). Led by retiring military brass and related professionals, CPAC actively promoted planning through organized chapters across the country. It encouraged the establishment of local planning departments and the hiring of planners; it publicized and supported planning ideas; it held local, regional and national conferences; and it published a layman's journal on planning. Also in this restart phase, CMHC introduced scholarships for planning education in 1947 to "prime the pump," and these were accompanied by an annual cash bonus to recognized planning schools.

While the restart stage primarily laid down the ground rules and structure for later Canadian planning, some actual city planning was done. Most prominent in this regard was consultant Eugino Faludi. His firm dominated the Canadian consulting field during the post-war years and was the training ground for many planners.

INSTITUTIONALIZATION

The early 1950s marked an expansion period for Canadian city planning. In 1949 there were only 45 practicing planners in Canada. By 1967 there were about 650 and today there are about 1,500. Up to 1950 there were only six local planning departments. By 1960 there were 30 and today all cities over 10,000 in population have departments and there are numerous regional, social and special purpose planning departments. Coinciding with this growth were increases in provincial planning and the rise of planning education. The first planning school was McGill in 1947, followed by Manitoba in 1949, UBC in 1950, Toronto in 1951, Montreal in 1961, Waterloo in 1964, York in 1969, Ottawa in 1970, Calgary in 1971, Ryerson in 1973, and Nova Scotia Tech in 1975. Other planning-related programs were also begun.

The most significant aspect of this period was the institutionalization of city planning into formal departments of local government. This was not an easy task. Other municipal departments already conducting some planning functions, notably engineering departments, resisted and rebuffed the new intruders. As well, the staff planning position demanded a new relationship with separate planning commissions (or boards) enshrined in planning legislation. The planning commission structure was based on the notion that planning was, or should be, apolitical, above politics. Lay commissions, made up of influential citizens who were thought to represent the public good, prepared plans through consultants and forwarded them to city council for adoption. But their plans were rarely adopted, and Harold Spence-Sales and John Bland of McGill's planning school proposed a new structure for planning by a full time civic department. Following the work of R.A. Walker in the U.S.,[3] they pointed to deficiencies of the commission model and advantages of the departmental model. Also they prepared numerous consultant reports for cities on how to establish independent planning departments which created a whole new structure of local planning as can be seen in the diagram.

An important part of this institution-building was the formalization of a new planning function of coordination and technical planning. Again with the urging of Spence-Sales and Bland, technical planning boards were adopted in most cities. Board membership included all civic department heads concerned with physical development and representatives from library, fire, police, and school services (see diagram).

Normally, a city council was to delegate certain powers to the technical planning board so that public opinion and "politics" would not interfere with technical considerations. In this new structure, appointed planning commissions were retained as "sounding boards" of public opinion.

The establishment of planning as a regular civic department brought planning under direct political control. Previously planning commissions produced grand plans which were never implemented. Under the new arrangement planners were closer to the source of power, but their priorities were now directly set by the politicians. A 1971 survey of Canadian planning agencies, by the author, found that only 13 per cent of all important planning decisions were initiated within planning agencies. This institutionalizing stage can be characterized as legitimizing Canadian city planning; however, its apparent loss of initiative was a large price to pay.

In the 1950s and 1960s Canadian city planning was heavily involved in urban renewal. Following the United States, urban renewal was pushed by CMHC and initiated in most large Canadian cities. The failure of this program to respond to community goals and interests spurred on the citizen movement which plays a large part in the next stage.

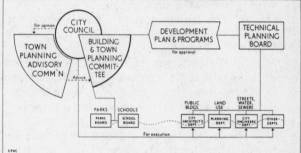

Courtesy Community Planning Association of Canada

BROADENING AND CRITICISM

The last and current stage is an extension of the former with two added dimensions: broadening of the city planning tradition into many other types of planning, and a rising criticism of planning generally.

Once city planning was in place, it began to specialize. Within local planning offices one could expect to find a variety of planners — long range, urban renewal, zoning, administrative, transportation, etc. City planning also started to move into other areas. Recognizing the larger context of cities, regional planning emerged, followed by provincial planning and in 1970,the creation of the Ministry of State for Urban Affairs. As can be seen by its proclamation, the Ministry had high aspirations. It has helped put city planning into a ubiquitous position through a tri-level planning mechanism the Ministry initiated. Most major Canadian cities now have tri-level committees composed of federal and provincial cabinet ministers and local politicians. This integrative mechanism is paralleled by administrative tri-level committees of planners and bureaucrats from all three levels.

As part of the broadening of planning, many other government agencies started to add planners. In addition, attempts were made at social planning in response to growing criticisms of bureaucratic

Proclamation — Ministry of State for Urban Affairs

His Excellency in Council is pleased to specify that the Minister of State for Urban Affairs shall formulate and develop policies for implementation through measures within fields of federal jurisdiction in respect of

(a) the most appropriate means by which the Government of Canada may have a beneficial influence on the evolution of the process of urbanization in Canada;

(b) the integration of urban policy with other policies and programs of the Government of Canada; and

(c) the fostering of co-operative relationships in respect of urban affairs with the provinces and, through them, their municipalities, and with the public and with private organizations.

His Excellency in Council is further pleased to specify that the Minister of State for Urban Affairs shall, in relation to the formulation and development of the aforementioned policies, which are policies for implementation through measures within fields of federal jurisdiction, have assigned to him the following powers, duties and functions:

(a) in respect of policy development he may
(i) initiate proposals for new policies, projects and activities,
(ii) evaluate proposals for new policies, projects and activities and seek to ensure their consistency with federal urban policies,
(iii) evaluate existing policies, projects and activities of the Government of Canada that have an influence on urban affairs and recommend changes therein where required
(iv) where appropriate, participate in projects and activities of the Government of Canada that may have an influence on urbanization in Canada, and,
(v) seek, in consultation with other authorities concerned, the co-operative development of urban policy in Canada;

(b) in respect of research, he may
(i) initiate research and policy studies relating to urbanization,
(ii) co-ordinate, in co-operation with other departments and agencies of the Government of Canada, research relating to urbanization that has been undertaken or financed by those departments or agencies, and
(iii) recommend priorities for research in ubanization; and

(c) he may perform the following co-ordination functions:
(i) he may co-ordinate, promote and recommend national policies in respect of urban affairs among departments and agencies of the Government of Canada,
(ii) he may co-ordinate the activities of the Government of Canada in establishing co-operative relationships with the provinces and their municipalities for the enhancement of the urban environment, and
(iii) he may co-ordinate the involvement of the Government of Canada with other governments and non-government organizations in urban policy matters.

Canada, *House of Commons Debates*, Ottawa, 28 June 1971, p. 7428

---

planning. Also, in the employ of land developers, planning again emerged as a major consulting activity. Whereas the first phase of consultants belonged to other professions (land surveyors, engineers, architects), the new breed of consultants in the 1960s were planners in their own right. Among the better-known ones are Murray Jones, Danny Makale, Eli Comay and Norman Pearson. However, many of the major planning consulting firms were part of larger engineering firms like Proctor and Redfern, Underwood-McClelland, and Marshall, Macklin and Monaghan. By now planning consulting was big business.

Coincident with the continued growth and broadening of city planning was rising criticism. This occurred both within the profession (see Ron Clark's article in *City Magazine*, Vol. 1, No. 8) and outside (books like *The Real World of City Politics, A Citizen's Guide to City Politics, Marlborough Marathon, The Bad Trip, Fighting Back*). Some government reports were also highly critical of planning. One such view is presented in a report done by the Ontario Economic Council.

Two things are evident. First, the senior public planners have, in effect, been doing very little planning; they have served largely as planning administrators, carrying out chiefly housekeeping functions. Second, they have offered few initiatives and innovations. Professional planners in Ontario have carried out their jobs skillfully, to greater or lesser degree. They have not, in any discernible sense, emerged as a truly innovative force in the area of public policy formulation. Nor, equally, has the profession as a profession. Its institutional apparatus (the Town Planning Institute) has similarly devoted its major energies to internal housekeeping matters and has offered its members little beyond a basic trade union service. More dishearteningly, it has lent almost none of its professional expertise and influence to matters of important public policy.[4]

One cannot but wonder about the relationship between this criticism and the broadening of planners' activities which has gone on simultaneously. It may be that the broadening of planning is mere escapism from the basic problems of cities. Always moving away from the problem, to the region, to the province, to the nation, to ecology, to growth management, the same issues remain unresolved — poverty, poor housing, inadequate public transportation.

The obvious conclusion to draw from this history of Canadian city planning is one of tremendous shortcomings. Canadian planning has chiefly carried out housekeeping functions. Planners have offered few initiatives and innovations. Planning serves the interests of the property industry and the politicians best, not the people it has so often been portrayed to serve. Planners shun citizen involvement, and concern themselves mostly with facilitating growth, usually regulating minimum requirements rather than spelling out maximum objectives. But these conclusions about planning are partial and premature without considering some major omissions to this "in-house" view of Canadian city planning history.

PART II
PLANNING WITHOUT PLANNERS

Planning the shape of settlement in Canada has a far longer history than that of professional planners in this country. In fact, planning has always been of concern to many more people than city planners claiming special knowledge and skill in this area. A comprehensive account of these activities has yet to be written, but three examples indicate that decisions and public policies about land, settlement patterns, public infrastructure and private land use have been a continual focus of political activity in Canada. This is a fact which early Canadian planners, and even some contemporary practitioners, have ignored as they have stressed their claims to a unique skill.

COLONIAL PLANNING

Colonization itself is an organized action by an external country. The relationship between a col-

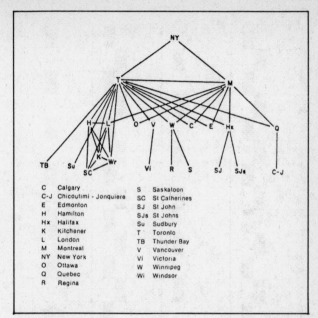

Source: Simmons, J., "Canada as an urban system: A conceptual framework," *Ekistics*, Vol. 41, No. 243, 1976

ony and mother country are governed by a set of regulations enacted into law. Those regulations established the system of government, monopolies, trading laws of tariffs and preferential treatment of goods, settlement policies, and in some cases plans for urban settlement (for instance Spain's Laws of the Indies, an early planning manual). In the context of Canadian colonial development, the rules of colonization represented a far more planned approach to land use and development than had been true in France or, later, in England.

Early Canadian cities were situated to protect colonial monopolies and to act as transportation points for the staples being exploited. Halifax, Quebec City, Montreal, Toronto and Winnipeg all owe their existence to these imperatives of colonialism. They also owe their respective places in the hierarchy of cities to these imperatives. As staples were exhausted in the East, the next westerly city became the gateway city to the West. This enhanced its competitive position and placed it in a position of dominance over the other Canadian cities.

The westward movement of the dominant Canadian city should have moved from Toronto to Winnipeg but stopped at Toronto primarily due to its linkages with New York. This established a permanent dominance by Toronto. The relationships among Canadian cities is well-explained by the concept of metropolis and hinterland. This idea has primarily been used to understand the economy of different countries by identifying their place in the global economic system. However, writes Cy Gonick,

The concept of metropolis-hinterland may also be applied

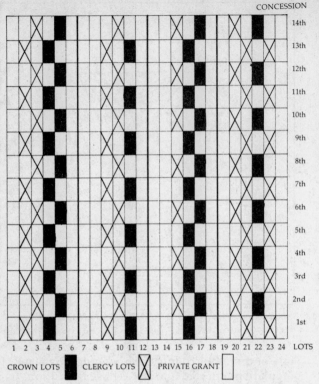

14th
13th
12th
11th
10th
9th
8th
7th
6th
5th
4th
3rd
2nd
1st

1 2 3 4 5 6 7 8 9 10 11 12 13 14 15 16 17 18 19 20 21 22 23 24 LOTS

CROWN LOTS ■   CLERGY LOTS ⊠   PRIVATE GRANT ☐

The Chequered Plan, based on the illustration of the plan accompanying D.W. Smyth's report on the reserved lands.

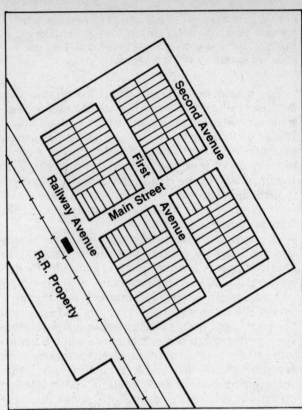

Plan of typical railroad town. Illustration: Paul Smith

within countries. *The underdevelopment of some regions is usually linked with the overdevelopment of other regions. "Probably the most interesting way to write the history of Canada," writes Mel Watkins, "is to write the history of Ontario: look up the chain and you see New York – at least if you sit in Toronto that is what you see. Then look down the chain and you see the Atlantic provinces, the Prairie provinces (and further down, the Caribbean and Brazil.)" The overdevelopment of Ontario is the other side of the coin to the underdevelopment of rural, northern and fishing communities in Canada's Prairie, Atlantic and Northern regions.*[5]

The metropolis-hinterland theory explains the size and prosperity of Canada's cities historically as well as today.

There are further aspects of Canadian colonization that involved planning. Canadian land policy is such an example.[6] One main function of colonial government in Canada was to administer policies regarding alienation of land from the Crown and the extraction of revenue from land. Under the British, land policy was seen as a means to develop a society with the right kind of social, political and religious institutions to serve British interests. For example, the practice of granting townships to individuals or companies was done explicitly in the hope of creating a feudal society of "country gentlemen" and serfs. A settler could buy a lot from the "country gentlemen" and then comply with the settlement requirements of that "country gentle-

men." Many settlers in Ontario could not meet these conditions and their land reverted to the large landowner.

The chequered plan, devised by Surveyor General D.W. Smyth in 1792, stands as an example of how land policy could mould the social structure. As can be seen on the plan, seven lots on each concession were reserved for the Crown and Clergy. This was consciously done to "tie a government, a church and a people to the land as a conservative bulwark against the liberal ideas of the American revolution."[7] The intentions regarding the desired class structure of Canadian society reflected in these land policies are clear. The sale of land in large blocks, would tend to create an economic society of large proprietors with a sharply defined class division between property owners and those without property. And there was also concern about how to ensure a large working class. Wakefield, a British statesman and expert on colonial affairs, advised:

The plentyfulness and cheapness of land in thinly populated countries enables almost everybody who wishes it to become a landowner . . . (and) . . . cheapness of land is the cause of scarcity of labour for hire. . . . Where land is very cheap and all men are free, where everyone who so pleases can obtain for himself a piece of land, not only is labour very dear, as respects the labourer's share of the product, but the difficulty is to obtain combined labour at any price.[8]

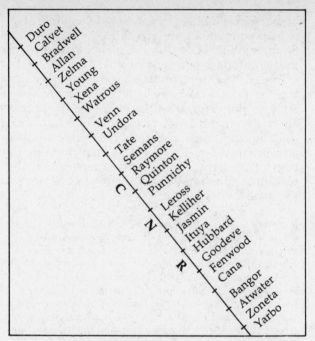

The alphabetically named towns along the CNR, formerly the Grand Trunk Railway, in Saskatchewan. (The gaps in the diagram represent subsequently established towns which do not conform to the alphabetical pattern.) Source: Rees, R., "Small towns of Saskatchewan," *Landscape,* 18, 1969, and Nader, G., *Cities of Canada,* Vol. 1, Macmillan, Toronto, 1975

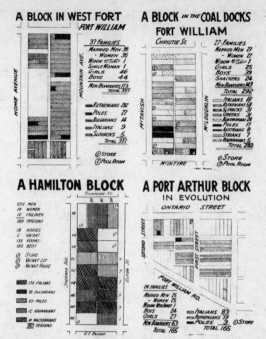

Housing density surveys done as part of the first reform movement, when evidence of overcrowding of immigrant workers called for new housing policies and better city plans. Source: *Papers and Proceedings,* Canadian Political Science Association I, 1913, as reproduced in Rutherford, Paul (ed.), *Saving the Canadian City,* University of Toronto Press, 1974, p. 147

Railroad building and prairie settlement offers another example of the colonial planning system. The railroad was part of an economic plan to bring staples to central Canada. Accompanying it was a settlement pattern with towns plopped on the landscape at regular intervals, with identical plans, and of course land ownership by the CPR. The full extent of this planning is symbolized by the naming of towns in alphabetical order as illustrated on the diagram. Along with this settlement structure is the ubiquitous rural grid of sections and quarter sections. Altogether, these actions make the prairies one of the most formally planned areas in the world.

In addition, the "gridiron plan" (rectangular blocks with straight streets and an intersection at each corner) was applied to the expansion of all Canadian cities. Its dominance is due to its preference by land speculators because it was simple to lay out and survey.

In short, colonization established the location, rate of growth, land system, and pattern of Canadian cities. This was done as a system of planning, to meet the needs of colonization, and not by chance. There was extensive government involvement from England and by the colony-based governments in order to implement colonialism in a formal way. Government worked for the interests of major economic forces. Any understanding of Canadian city planning must recognize this part of the history of Canadian development and its relevance to today.

FIRST URBAN REFORM MOVEMENT

A second major contribution by non-planners to Canadian planning came from the first urban reform movement. Between 1880 and 1920 urban reform ideas became of widespread importance in Canada.

As Paul Rutherford has said of this period:

So wide was the scope of the urban reform movement that some readers may feel it was merely a collection of assorted causes linked only by a general focus on the city and its problems. Clearly there were many different concerns sheltered under the umbrella of urban reform – the elimination of vice and crime, social justice, the creation of a healthy environment, the regulation of utility corporations, the beautification of the industrial city, town planning, tax reform, and the remodelling of the municipal government. Yet the reformer rarely limited his activities to one cause.[9]

The first prime instruments of reform were the maverick newspapers. The *Star* and *La Presse* in Montreal, the *Telegram, World,* and *News* in To-

J.S. Woodsworth. Photo: Courtesy Metropolitan Toronto Library Board

ronto, the *Journal* in Ottawa, and the *Herald* in Hamilton all were independent in their politics and sensational in tone, but they appealed to an expanding readership by writing about local affairs, and these came to rival provincial and national concerns. This effort was soon supplemented by a new breed of urban reform specialists: Mayor William Howland in Toronto, Herbert Ames of Montreal, and J.S. Woodsworth of Winnipeg, as well as Thomas Adams.

William Holmes Howland, mayor of Toronto from 1886 to 1888, was Canada's first "citizens candidate for mayor" and first urban reform mayor.[10] Contrary to the norm that mayorality candidates should have a record of business success, Howland campaigned on philanthropy, religiosity and teetotalism. To the surprise of the political veterans, he won. Generally, he represented moral purification, and his successful attack on saloons and crime resulted in the slogan "Toronto the Good." He also fought the Toronto coal ring which had established a fixed price for coal.

Herbert Ames was a Red Tory businessman from Montreal who decried social and housing conditions of a working-class district in Montreal. His statistical analysis of these conditions was published in *The City Below the Hill* (the hill, of course, being Westmount), an important contribution to reform research.

J.S. Woodsworth popularized the notion of social action. The superintendent of the All People's Mission in Winnipeg, he observed the plight of the urban poor and immigrants. *My Neighbor* and *Strangers Within Our Gates* brought a class analysis to this reform movement.

In part, the spirit of the first reform movement was borrowed from the U.S. where there was a strong calling for a return to the country. Such agrarian romanticism was expressed in Canada in the magazine *Conservation of Life*; it was essentially anti-urban. More importantly, there was, by the turn of the century, an explicit recognition that Canadian cities were not working. As Clifford Sifton said:

It seems a terrible indictment of modern civilization, but it is undoubtedly a true one that the growth of unsanitary, unhealthful conditions, the growth of slums and slum populations, are in direct ratio to what we call progress. The immense growth of the city is invariably accompanied by these undesirable conditions. . . . The growth of poverty, misery and crime accompany industrial and commercial expansion on a large scale. . . . Why is it that, as countries grow richer, the rich become richer and the poor become poorer?[11]

The founding of Canadian city planning, led by Thomas Adams, occurred as a part of this reform movement. Early Canadian planners were serious about their reform, and they criticized American planning for its liberal laissez-faire ethic. But Canadian planning did not go beyond dealing with symptoms to basic changes in the social structure. Belief in philanthropy, social engineering and the salvation of science was its ultimate weakness.

Why has contemporary planning not maintained a reform orientation? Perhaps the void in Canadian city planning between 1932 and 1946 broke the continuity of reform thought and led us to mimic American planning in the post-war start-up phase. Or the move to city hall, from the independent commission, turned planning into a bureaucratic activity under the discretionary control of city council. Or, lastly, perhaps the professionalization of planning has replaced social goals with career goals. I return to this matter in the conclusion.

THE SOCIALIST ALTERNATIVE

A third important phase in the involvement of non-planners in planning matters came in the Thirties, during the period which professional planners like Humphrey Carver term a "vacuum."

Social Planning for Canada appeared in 1935. Responding to the crisis of the depression, *Social Planning* was written by the League for Social Reform (LSR). The LSR was an association working for the establishment in Canada of a new social order in which the basic principle regulating production, distribution and service was to be the common good rather than private profit. Through their 528-page analysis of Canadian capitalism, they advocated a democratic form of socialism of the British and Scandinavian type.

Manifesto of the League for Social Reform

Eugene Forsey, J. King Gordon, Leonard Marsh, J.F. Parkinson, F.R. Scott, Graham Spry and Frank H. Underhill.

1. Public ownership and operation of the public utilities connected with transportation, communications, and electric power, and of such other industries as are already approaching conditions of monopolistic control.

2. Nationalization of banks and other financial institutions with a view to the regulation of all credit and investment operations.

3. The further development of agricultural co-operative institutions for the production and merchandising of agricultural products.

4. Social legislation to secure to the worker adequate income and leisure, freedom of association, insurance against illness, accident, old age, and unemployment, and an effective voice in the management of his industry.

5. Publicly organized health, hospital, and medical services.

6. A taxation policy emphasizing steeply graduated income and inheritance taxes.

7. The creation of a National Planning Commission.

8. The vesting in Canada of the power to amend and interpret the Canadian constitution so as to give the federal government power to control the national economic development.

9. A foreign policy designed to secure international co-operation in regulating trade, industry and finance, and to promote disarmament and world peace.

The year after its publication, an anonymous, undated, pamphlet appeared attacking *Social Planning*. Simply called "A Criticism of the Book," it was distributed to the business community from the head office of the CPR. It was later discovered that its author was the CPR's economist, P.C. Armstrong.

Social Planning for Canada, a classic of socialist thought, provides the first thorough analysis of Canadian capitalism. It documents the end of a century of progress, the nature of the Canadian economy including Canadian industry, agriculture, government intervention and the mechanism of the market. The major conclusions from this analysis are that capitalism can only make rational decisions about production and distribution — that capitalism cannot plan. Viewing planning as a solution in itself, the LSR identified five counter characteristics of state-capitalism as follows:

1. self-government in industry, which means government of industry by big business for big business;
2. state regulation of the monopolies to safeguard the public interest means nothing more than government in business;
3. state subsidies, loans and guarantees transfer money from the poor to the rich;
4. while social legislation and preserving profit may seem paradoxical, the former saves the country from revolution;
5. state-capitalism public ownership is common to fascism (capitalism stripped of its disguises).

The authors conclude that capitalism cannot plan, for however much it is regulated it remains capitalism. Nonetheless, they recognize that capitalism can plan in a special way, but "planning for the few cannot meet the mass of our people's demands. Capitalist industry in this as in much else has provided the technique for socialism, but the effective use of the technique is impossible as long as the inequality of capitalist control survives."

Social Planning proposes a scheme of national economic planning for Canada with a National Planning Commission and the socialization of industry. Within this scheme the authors discuss money, banking, investment, taxation, fiscal policy, foreign trade, a code for labour, health and welfare services, the rehabilitation of agriculture, and housing. Planning in a socialized economy emerges as not an omnipotent blueprint set out once and for all, but the bringing of technicians of every type required in a modern economic system into organized relation with the organs and aims of government. In this context, parliamentary and constitutional reforms are outlined.

What we have here is, for the first time in Canada, a complete definition of socialist planning as an alternative to capitalism. Canadian planning before and since has, of course, attempted to bring about the planning without the socialism.

Undoubtedly the major contribution of *Social Planning* to Canadian planning thought was the linking of planning and socialism. The history of city planning, in relative terms, may be seen as a token acceptance of planning. Let's plan our cities, let F.W. Taylor impose his "scientific management" on industries, but let us not apply planning to the economic system.

The League's discussion of city planning identified many urban ills resulting from capitalism: land speculation, insufficient housing, premature subdivision of land, inadequate parks and public buildings, shack towns and housing policy only for the well off. They strongly maintained that solutions were at hand — "all we need is the will to do it." Included in the available solutions were the following:

1. public housing estates for low income families
2. government housing corporations
3. socialist housing plans based on the "neighborhood unit"
4. comprehensive plans based on surveys
5. housing designs "to liberate the housewife from the monotonous servitude of domestic chores."

In addition they supported the elimination of "rake-offs" by promoters, breaking monopolies in building supplies, and compulsory purchase of inner-city lands below their "fictitious" value.

Looking back, *Social Planning for Canada* made a significant contribution to the foundation of an alternative political party. It influenced the Regina Manifesto of the Co-operative Commonwealth Federation (CCF, now NDP). For city planning, this view of planning linked to socialism was lost in the post-war period.

CONCLUSION
WHY PLANNING?

To understand the history of Canadian planning, one must turn to the context — the social, economic, and political circumstances — in which planning has developed. Two explanations have been offered for the cycles of expansion and retraction which appear in the history of formal city planning since 1909. Donald Gutstein in *Vancouver Ltd.* uses Vancouver as his example and identifies a series of real estate booms and busts in the city. During boom periods, Gutstein says, city planners are in great demand to administer and facilitate the development which the private sector is pressing forward with. This work of city planners has so dominated the profession during the last urban real estate boom period, which seems to have now come to a close, that some critics have argued that planners are nothing but servants of growth and of the development industry.

An alternative explanation of the history of Canadian city planning, and one which also sees a cyclical pattern, has been offered by Shoukry Roweis of the University of Toronto's School of Planning. Roweis has, however, rather a different definition of planning than Gutstein. For Gutstein, planning is what city planners employed by city hall (or developers) do. For Roweis, planning is deliberate collective action by a society, the activity of making collective decisions after consideration of their implications and consequences. Planning as Roweis defines it is the attempt to avoid haphazard, let the chips fall where they may, who worries about consequences kind of decision-making. It is rather deliberative collective action:

Collective action here means social activities whose consequences are objects of political decisions. (It) may, for example, be achieved by traditional/cultural consensus, by elected government through taxes, subsidies, and public spending, or by dictatorial decisions. Business decisions of real estate corporations do not constitute collective action since their aggregate consequences (total number of housing starts, etc.) are not themselves objects of political decision. The construction of a subway system in a metropolitan area, in contrast, is indeed a collective action. [12]

This kind of activity, substantive planning involving decision-making about public works and public projects, is indeed quite different from the administration of growth Gutstein is talking about.

Through the cycles in the history of twentieth-century Canadian city planning, it might appear that planning has progressed to a more influential role than it had 65 years ago. That view, however, appears overly optimistic. In fact the corporations whose business is affected by the work of urban planners have responded to the development of greater public planning activity by strengthening their own private planning capacity as corporations and as an industry. The Housing and Urban Development Association of Canada (HUDAC) has, for example, one of the most complex, sophisticated and successful political lobbying organizations in existence in Canada. HUDAC has a long-range, ten-year plan regarding the policies which they want from government, and as well as putting closed-door pressure on politicians and senior civil servants, they pay close attention to influencing public opinion. Not only is HUDAC organized to cope with any short-term crisis that might appear in the housing and development area anywhere in the country; it also has plans and the capacity to *make* crises in appropriate circumstances. Through this organization and the other national groups which bring together real estate and development interests and through the corporate activities of the large companies involved in urban development, what Galbraith terms the "planning system" of the corporate sector has become a far stronger determinant of the future of Canadian cities than planners working for the public. And indeed it is easy to identify crucial decisions about how Canadian cities should grow which have been forced on the public by the corporations with very little consideration of their real consequences, while public planners have either stood by saying very little or have acted as a cheering section for the private sector. How else would one explain corporate suburban development, the emergence of shopping centres as an alternative to local commercial centres, or sprawl based on universal automobile use?

The failure of Canadian city planning to play a major role in influencing the development of Canadian cities sets up a major tension between what planning actually is and what planners are taught to think it could and should be. In the literature of planning and in the education of planners, there is still a very strong strain of the reformist ideas conceived by early professional planning activities here. There is also still some sense of the radical possibilities of planning of the type the League for Social Reform discussed, and a notion that explicit political and social decision-making about urban matters may not produce the same outcome as allowing the corporate sector to continue running things as it wishes. Planning students encountering this planning literature first, then faced with the impossible task of reconciling it to the day-to-day practice of planners working for public agencies, often are unable to handle the contradictions. An historical perspective on Canadian planning may make it easier to be realistic about how it relates to social, economic and political reality. Planners who founded the radical, early notions of what planning is about have never been able on their own to have this approach accepted. No doubt there are many who still find this an attractive ideal, and a far cry from the administrative growth-promoting work which occupies the time of most Canadian planners. With a clearer view of the politics of planning and a notion of

where they may find allies and supporters, radical planners might find ways of promoting the cause of interventionist, socially-oriented, anti-corporate planning. That would be far better than giving up on planning altogether, or knuckling down to doing what the corporations and their friends in government want.

---

1. See articles and bibliography in *The City Book*, James Lorimer and Evelyn Ross, ed. (Toronto: James Lorimer and Company, 1976); Kent Gerecke, "Report on the Future of the Planning Profession," 1972; and Ron Clark and Henry Ropertz, "The Planning Profession and the Status Quo," 1973.
2. Humphrey Carver, "Planning in Canada," *Habitat*, Vol. III, No. 5, 1960, p.10.
3. R.A. Walker, *The Planning Function in Urban Government*, (Chicago Press, 1940 and revised 1950).
4. Ontario Economic Council, *Subject to Approval: A Review of Municipal Planning in Ontario*, 1973, p.41.
5. C. Gonick, "Metropolis/Hinterland Theme," *Canadian Dimension*, Vol.8, No.6, March-April 1972, p.25.
6. This discussion on Canadian land policy owes much to the current research of Meena Dhar of Toronto.
7. G. Teeple, "Land, Labour and Capital in Pre-Federation Canada," in *Capitalism and the National Question in Canada*, G. Teeple, ed. (Toronto: University of Toronto Press, 1972), p.47.
8. M.H. Dobb, *Studies in the Development of Capitalism* (London: Routledge and Kegan Paul, 1946), p.325.
9. P. Rutherford, *Saving the Canadian City* (Toronto: University of Toronto Press, 1974), p. xiii.
10. See Desmond Morton, *Mayor Howland: The Citizens' Candidate* (Toronto: Hakkert, 1973).
11. T. Adams, *Rural Planning and Development in Canada* (Ottawa: Commission of Conservation, 1917), p.12.
12. S.T. Roweis, *Urban Planning in Early and Late Capitalist Societies*, Paper on Planning and Design, Department of Urban and Regional Planning, University of Toronto, 1975, p.22.

William Teron vs Walter Rudnicki: Portrait of a bureaucracy

The case of William Teron and CMHC vs. Walter Rudnicki received considerable press coverage across Canada earlier this year when it was being heard in Ottawa. The issue was whether or not Teron, as CMHC president, was justified in firing Rudnicki from his job as senior policy adviser to CMHC almost three years ago.

Rudnicki's firing occurred shortly after Teron joined CMHC as its president on July 1, 1973. It came when Rudnicki and his policy planners were working on a native people's housing policy for CMHC. At the time, the firing provoked considerable criticism of Teron, CMHC, and the then Minister of Urban Affairs, Ron Basford, particularly from the native people's groups with whom Rudnicki had been working. Rudnicki's dismissal signalled the beginning of a new regime at CMHC, and was accurately seen as the first stage in a reversal of CMHC's tentative move toward social housing and away from its almost-exclusive concern with the private housing sector and with the housing and land development industry.

The judgment in this case makes fascinating reading. It is first of all a carefully-told, blow-by-blow account of how policy actually gets made in Ottawa. The situation is the classic one of federal politicians and bureaucrats faced with an outside interest group, in this case Indians and Metis. It is an outside group that government is not very comfortable with but one which has the political muscle to be able to make trouble for the government if it doesn't like government policy. Government agrees to develop policy by "consultation," but exactly what "consultation" means varies enormously from minister to senior civil servant to policy adviser to outside interest group.

Second, it throws a certain amount of light on the kind of politician that Ron Basford is. At the time of Rudnicki's firing, Basford was in the relatively minor portfolio of Urban Affairs. Since then, he has been elevated to Justice. His reported performance on the matter of consultation and policy development in this case is intriguing.

Finally, and perhaps most important, this judgment shows William Teron in action. At the time of these events, Teron was a highly-successful land developer but a very inexperienced Ottawa bureaucrat. In the ensuing three years, Teron has gone from strength to strength to reach his current position of chairman of CMHC and deputy minister of Urban Affairs. His conduct in the events surrounding Rudnicki's firing and his subsequent conduct in this court case offer outsiders a rare chance to judge his suitability for the important offices he holds.

A brief introduction to the judgment itself. On October 12, 1973, Walter Rudnicki, then head of CMHC's Policy Planning Division, was dismissed by CMHC president William Teron. On July 23, 1976, after a nine-day trial, the Ontario Supreme Court found that CMHC and Teron had no good reason to terminate Rudnicki's services, and awarded Rudnicki his full damages of $18,006.14 plus his court costs.

At the time he was fired, Rudnicki and his policy group were working on a native housing policy proposal for CMHC which had been demanded by Ron Basford, then Minister of State for Urban Affairs. CMHC had been working on a native housing policy in 1972, but after the minister returned some policy proposals the matter was dropped until the fall of 1973.

Then in September 1973, Basford found he was about to go into a meeting between himself and his officials and representatives of the Native Council of Canada. The minister was upset that he had no comprehensive policy regarding native people's housing, and ordered that CMHC produce a proposal for him within 10 days.

At the September meeting between the minister

A SOUTHAM BUSINESS PUBLICATION

JULY · AUG 1976

executive

**Direction Canada-
People and households**

William Teron of CMHC:
Facing tough facts

$1.25

and the Native Council, questions were raised concerning the consultation which would be done by CMHC policy people with representatives of the native peoples. Both Basford and Teron made commitments that full and extensive consultation would take place between CMHC and the Native Council.

What follows is a partial text of the judgment in this case, starting with the judge's account of the events leading up to Rudnicki's firing. Preliminary matter on procedural and legal questions has been omitted. The detailed calculation of the damages which CMHC was required to pay Rudnicki has also been left out. Minor changes have been made in the text in order to make it more readable, and occasional pieces of explanatory material are added in square brackets.

The decision was not appealed by CMHC, and the time for appeal has now expired.

EVENTS LEADING UP TO SEPTEMBER 12, 1973

During 1972, CMHC had a group dealing with native housing but according to the evidence of Walter Rudnicki a dozen or more drafts of policy proposals were produced; the Management Committee of CMHC reviewed one proposal during the winter of 1972 and forwarded it on to the minister. According to Rudnicki that proposal was returned after the election of 1972 with marginal notes and thereafter native housing was allowed to lapse until the late summer of 1973.

On August 24, 1973, Tony Belcourt [then president of the Native Council of Canada] and Lawrence Gladue [then vice-president of the Council] went to visit with William Teron, the new President of CMHC, in his office so that they could familiarize him with the Native Council of Canada, how they operate and also to try and arrange a meeting with the minister.

SEPTEMBER 12, 1973

On September 12, 1973, there was a half-hour briefing session of the minister, the Honourable Ronald Basford. Present at the meeting were: 1. The minister and his advisor; 2. CMHC personnel: (a) President William Teron, (b) Jean Legasse, (c) George Whitman, (d) John Michael Pine, (e) Robert Marjoribanks, (f) Lynne Smythe, (g) Lorenz Schmidt, (h) Walter Rudnicki.

The purpose of the meeting was to brief the minister prior to his going to a meeting with the Native Council of Canada.

At the minister's briefing there was a discussion of the "Winter Warmth Program" which the minister re-named "Emergency Repair Program."

According to the evidence of Rudnicki the minister was "upset and irritated" that CMHC did not have a "Native Housing Policy." The minister ordered that a policy be in his hands by September 21, 1973, some nine days hence.

The minister, his advisors, the president of CMHC and those employees of CMHC who had been at the minister's briefing then moved into a committee room of the House of Commons to meet the delegation of the Native Council of Canada.

The minster, Belcourt and Teron all sat at the head table and the minister chaired the meeting.

Belcourt presented the Native Council of Canada brief which is filed as Exhibit 43.

Belcourt testified at trial that the minister responded to the brief by saying that he was upset that he had not received a "Native Housing Policy" but that he would have one by September 21, 1973. Belcourt states that both Daniels and Spence of the Native Council of Canada said words to the effect "We thought we were going to get some input."

Belcourt testified at trial that Teron assured Daniels and Spence that they would be consulted; Belcourt asserts that he and Teron talked of a meeting the next day when they would discuss the "consulting mechanism."

Rudnicki testified that the minister assured the members of the Native Council of Canada that they would participate in the policy — be involved step-by-step and that the minister went on to say: "If a policy comes to me that I don't agree with, it will go back."

Rudnicki further testified that Teron on that occasion said that the native housing policy that would be designed "will not be something you will read about in the newspapers."

Rudnicki testified that Teron at this meeting placed him, Rudnicki, in charge of the CMHC side of the matter.

George Whitman in his evidence contended that Teron said to the Native Council of Canada personnel that "You will be consulted every step of the way."

Lawrence Gladue recalls that Teron said: "When policy is developed it will be in full consultation with the Native Council of Canada."

Gene Rheaume, the author of the brief [which is] Exhibit 43, testified that at this September 12, 1973, meeting, the minister told the CMHC people to go and consult with the Native Council of Canada and give him a policy proposal in two weeks. Rheaume asserts further that after Stan Daniels of the Alberta Metis Association protested that CMHC would produce a meaningless program, the minister said "You will be consulted — you will have a hand in preparing the program." Rheaume recalls that the minister said to Teron "I want these people plugged into the program" and the president, Rheaume recalls, replied "That is how it will be — you won't first read about it in the newspapers."

Witness Ernest McEwen [a CMHC consultant] recalls the minister saying that nothing would go forward that was not mutually acceptable.

Jean Legasse's recollection [Legasse was a CMHC policy adviser at the time] of the September 12, 1973 meeting is that the minister in answer to Daniels said that his (the minister's) record had been one of consultation and he would continue it and that Teron had also said "This will be a close consultation; people from the CMHC will work with a group assigned by the Native Council of Canada."

On the other hand Teron's recollection of the September 12, 1973 meeting with the Native Council of Canada is to the effect that when Daniels and Spence made strong representations regarding consultations, he, Teron, said that CMHC had made available millions to the natives for research and "We assured them that they would be consulted first prior to a public announcement — they would not read it first in the newspapers." Teron recalls that he and the minister told the Native Council of Canada that they were pleased with the consultation that had taken place and assured the Native Council of Canada that it would continue.

Teron pointed out in his testimony that in January of 1974, "When the government had reached a decision on native housing, a meeting was held with the Native Council of Canada and a reasonable consensus was obtained and then a public statement was made."

The witness called for CMHC, Lorenz Schmidt, [then a policy drafter in Rudnicki's division and now equivalent to an associate deputy minister in CMHC] was at the meeting on September 12, and he said in his evidence "I recall Basford talking about consultation — it wasn't clear — I did not know if it was new or different; I recall Teron saying 'You'll be involved in the process' and Daniels saying that he wanted 'full consultation'." Schmidt recalls that on September 13, 1973, Teron came to the meeting that I will refer to shortly and "affirmed the consultation process."

SEPTEMBER 13, 1973

On that date Rudnicki and other representatives of CMHC met with the Native Council of Canada and the presidents of the provincial associations. Initially at the meeting the funds for the "Winter Warmth Program" (now the Emergency Housing Program) were allocated amongst the provinces.

The Native Council of Canada had conducted an in-camera meeting amongst themselves and elected Belcourt, Gladue, and Gloria George as the committee to meet with the CMHC officers for the purposes of consultation.

Teron, the president of CMHC, came into the meeting to approve the allocation and he said that he would have to confirm it with the minister.

Teron recalls in his evidence that he was asked to go to the meeting near the end of the day; he recalls that "I was told that the Native Council of Canada had elected an executive group to work with us in developing a native policy paper — I encouraged them to work speedily."

POLICY DEVELOPMENT AT CMHC

Exhibit 74 is a document prepared by Messrs. Pine, Schmidt, and Marjoribanks; it is dated September 17, 1973, and entitled "Draft No. — Confidential; Emergency Housing Program for Designated Remote and Fringe Communities."

Rudnicki asserts that after he read Exhibit 74 he discussed it with the Native Council of Canada people who took strong objection to the title "Remote and Fringe Communities" because they wanted a "Metis policy" and not a "poverty policy." Rudnicki is the only one who testifies as to a meeting with the Native Council of Canada on September 18, 1973.

Rudnicki testified that as a result of Belcourt's objection to Exhibit 74 (Belcourt called it "garbage"), he, Rudnicki, instructed his staff to re-do the paper and they produced Exhibit 75. It is dated September 19, 1973, and is entitled "Housing for Metis and Non-Status Indians." Rudnicki testified that he and Pine and Marjoribanks and Schmidt met with representatives of the Native Council of Canada in the persons of Belcourt and Rheaume and the Native Council of Canada representatives were shown Exhibit 75 and it was pointed out to them that some of their objections to Exhibit 74 had been removed.

In my view it is significant to note the evidence of Belcourt (which was not mentioned by Teron in his evidence) that Belcourt left Ottawa the following day for Labrador but before doing so he called Teron on September 20, 1973, about 9:00 a.m. and told Teron that he had met with Rudnicki. Belcourt swore in evidence that "I told Teron of our objection to the paper" and Belcourt further asserts that Teron said that either he (Teron) or Rudnicki would get in touch with Belcourt.

Pine and Schmidt both testified that the meeting with the Native Council of Canada in fact took place on September 20, 1973, and the document that was produced and reviewed at the meeting was Exhibit 76.

For the purposes of these reasons it does not

> **At Teron's office Schmidt produced Exhibit 79 and upon perusing it Teron tore out some pages and threw them onto the rug.**

make any difference which is the correct recollection; representatives of CMHC met with the Native Council of Canada and showed the Native Council of Canada a draft proposal. A comparison of Exhibit 75 and 76 did not appear to produce much in the way of difference in content.

On September 21, 1973, there was a meeting of the president and other members of the Management Steering Committee of CMHC with Rudnicki, Legasse, Marjoribanks, Pine, and Schmidt (see Exhibit 20); the purpose of the meeting was to discuss "the draft cabinet document on Housing for Metis and Non-Status Indians."

Rudnicki testified that he took to that meeting Exhibit 21 which is a letter to him from Marjoribanks, attached to which are:
1. suggested outline for Rudnicki to follow at the meeting; and
2. a document entitled "Consultation with the Native Council of Canada" and it commences with these words: "The substance of these proposals has been discussed with the Native Council of Canada."

Pine, a witness called for CMHC, testified that at the September 21, 1973 meeting with the Management Steering Committee "management was made aware of objections of the natives — management was aware that we had discussed the contents at least with Native Council of Canada." Pine swore that Marjoribanks read the objections of Belcourt to the meeting.

The instructions of management was for the Policy Program Division to "re-read the document in the context of the concerns that had been expressed" (Exhibit 20) — that is, re-draft the document.

On September 25, 1973, the Policy Program Division met with the Management Steering Committee and did an item-by-item review of a new draft dated September 24, 1973.

The next draft was Exhibit 78, dated September 28, 1973, and prepared for an October 1, 1973 meeting between the Policy Program Division and the Management Steering Committee.

Items in the document were altered at that meeting and the Policy Program Division went on to draft Exhibit 79. But on October 2, 1973, Rudnicki, Pine, and Schmidt went to see Teron to seek clarification of management's position — in the words of Teron they were "fine-tuning" the draft.

On the morning of October 3, 1973, the plaintiff received a call from Teron who stated that the minister wanted to see something in writing on the Native Housing Policy and he wanted to see it that day; the plaintiff contacted Schmidt and told him to bring what he had which was Exhibit 79, a draft dated October 3, 1973, and he came with it to Teron's office.

At Teron's office Schmidt produced Exhibit 79 and upon perusing it Teron tore out some pages and threw them onto the rug.

Teron in his evidence said that "the document did not meet the criteria and so I tore out a sheet and Schmidt was to get it amended."

Schmidt stated in his evidence that there was "an altercation in the hallway" as he and Teron disagreed about the meaning of "aggregate program costs." Rudnicki states in his evidence that Teron accused Schmidt, "and by implication me, of trying to manipulate him (Teron)."

Teron instructed Schmidt to re-do the pages that had been ripped out of the document and to deliver the completed document to the minister's office.

Schmidt, according to the evidence of Rudnicki, threatened to resign and he (Rudnicki) tried to placate him and in order to do so called in Halliday and asked him to speak with Schmidt.

Thereafter, Rudnicki left with Teron to go to the minister's office. Rudnicki swears that en route to the minister's office he told Teron that Schmidt was tired and that Teron's criticism of Schmidt was not warranted.

Late in the afternoon of October 3, 1973, Schmidt arrived at the minister's office with a copy of Exhibit 79 [the October 3 draft] as amended and gave it to Teron. Rudnicki testified that Teron presented a copy of Exhibit 79 to the minister and said that he (Teron) was happy with the result — that it was a model the way it was produced.

Teron testified that the minister upon receiving the document pulled out a pen and said "Where do I sign?" and that he (Teron) said that "We want to make a full presentation" and that the document was not ready for his signature.

Schmidt recalls in his evidence that the minister was happy that he had received the document and that Teron dissuaded the minister from signing the document — "I think it was a little joke" Schmidt added.

Schmidt testified that Teron had told the minister that the document was one that management was happy with; Schmidt denies in his evidence that Teron said that the document was not for the minister's signature.

After the meeting in the minister's office, Teron and Schmidt left together and the next day Schmidt told Rudnicki that all was fine between him and Teron.

Exhibit 79 [the October 3 draft] was never presented to the Management Steering Committee of CMHC until, if at all, after Rudnicki had been dismissed.

On October 5, 1973 at the suggestion of Rudnicki, there was, in the words of Schmidt, a "consultative meeting with the Native Council of Canada." Schmidt was instructed by Rudnicki to scrounge around and find enough copies of Exhibit 79 [the October 3 draft] to cover the meeting; he did so and distributed them at the commencement of the meeting.

Initially present at this meeting for the Native Council of Canada were Hayes, Rheaume, and Gladue.

Initially present for CMHC were Whitman, Legasse, Pine, and Schmidt.

Belcourt and Rudnicki both arrived late.

The evidence appears uncontradicted that both Rudnicki and Legasse had told the representatives of the Native Council of Canada that the proposal was the result of a joint venture but there was still a long way to go — Management Steering Committee, the minister or Cabinet could change the proposal. There appears to be uniformity in the evidence that the representatives of the Native Council of Canada appeared to be satisfied with the proposals in the document.

Some of the members of the Native Council of Canada present at the meeting asked if they could keep a copy of Exhibit 79 and it was agreed by everyone that Rudnicki said "No," that Rudnicki asked Schmidt to collect and count the document (Exhibit 79), and that this was done.

I accept Pine's evidence that Belcourt at that meeting asked if he could write a letter to the minister regarding the policy proposal and all present said "No," that it would be unwise to do so because the policy may be changed on the way.

Pine said that Belcourt appeared to accept the reason for not writing to the minister.

I accept Belcourt's evidence that he tried to reach Teron by telephone on that day [Tuesday, October 9, four days after the Friday meeting] without success.

I accept Belcourt's evidence that between 9:30 and 10:00 a.m. on Wednesday, October 10, he reached Teron by telephone and discussed policy proposals and told Teron "We were quite happy with the policy and we are prepared to back you on this"; Belcourt told Teron "We were happy about the open way we have been consulted."

I accept Belcourt's evidence that Teron told him that it had been reviewed and that he (Teron) was going to discuss the matter with the minister that very morning.

Belcourt told Teron that the Native Council of Canada was happy and Belcourt asked Teron "Would it be helpful if I wrote to the minister" and to that, I find, Teron replied "Yes."

I further accept Belcourt's evidence that Teron told him that the matter was to be discussed at the minister's office at 11:00 o'clock in the morning and

```
                              7 1
                                    OUTLINE - DRAFT I
                                    CONFIDENTIAL
                                    September 17, 1973

TITLE:  Emergency Housing Program for Designated Remote and
                        Fringe Communities

1.  The Problem
    Large number of substandard/dilapidated houses in remote
    and fringe areas.  Difficult to deal with problem through
    current provisions of NHA.

2.  The Proposal
    This memorandum seeks Cabinet approval for CMHC to initiate,
    obtaining co-operation from provinces and other Federal agencies
    when possible, a five to eight year program to replace or
    rehabilitate at least 30,000 of the most grossly inadequate
    houses found in remote and fringe communities.

3.  The Background
    (1)  Métis and Non-Status Indians have one new house
    per year per thousand, Eskimos got ten, status Indians
    nine, and average for all Canadians is ten per thousand.

    (2)  The average income of Métis and Non-Status.

    (3)  The number of Métis and Non-Status and the number
    of units they require.

    (4)  The amount of monies allocated to them in all
    programs 1970-73.

    (5)  The organizational capability of Métis and Non-Status
    Indians.

4.  The Factors
    (1)  The limitations of the Winter Warmth program.

    (2)  The emerging capability of natives in the housing
    area.

    (3)  The requirement for their involvement; development
    of native work forces around housing projects.
```

I find that Belcourt had no knowledge of Teron's proposed meeting with the minister until he was advised of it on the morning of October 10, by Teron himself.

I accept Belcourt's evidence that he telephoned the minister's secretary and told her that he wanted a hand-delivered letter he was dispatching to be in the minister's hands before Teron saw the minister.

Belcourt then had Rheaume prepare Exhibit 42 [such a letter] which was delivered by a House of Commons messenger to the minister's office before 11:00 a.m.

Rheaume testified that he did not want to prepare the letter because "It struck me that we should not have to write to the minister and tell him that Teron had done his homework."

Exhibit 42, the letter of Belcourt to the minister of October 10, reads:

Dear Mr. Minister:

The purpose of my letter is to report on the progress we feel has been made in our dealings with the officials of Central Mortgage and Housing Corporation in matters relating to the Native Housing Policy.

> ... Teron said [to Rudnicki's secretary]: "I had no part in this — I was forced to do this by Mr. Basford. The minister is very angry — it is a resign (Teron) or firing (Rudnicki) issue — either he or I have to go over this native housing document."

After our excellent sessions with you on September 12, we subsequently met with Mr. Teron and his senior officers. While our main purpose at that time was to work out the details of an Emergency Housing Repair Program, we also had wide-ranging talks about the elements of Native Housing Policy over the long haul. With the concurrence of your officials, our Council appointed a committee to assist CMHC officers in working out the details of the proposed program. Several meetings have been held since then, culminating in a lengthy session last Friday at CMHC headquarters.

As a result of these joint sessions we have been made aware of the major elements of the proposed new Native Housing Program which would make it possible for the Metis and non-status Indian people of Canada to acquire decent housing using a variety of techniques whereby existing programs and those now available under the amended NHA can be enriched and adapted to meet our shelter needs.

We believe we have a good general understanding of the outlines of the program and we feel that we have been able to contribute substantially to its development. We have been advised that your office will now be reviewing the matter and if you approve will submit the program to Cabinet for a final decision. I thought it timely to let you know that, for our part, we believe the proposals are excellent and they have our full support. We are aware that the additional steps that must now be taken will require some time but we hope that this proposed program can be advanced quickly because housing for our people remains our number one priority in our efforts to better the conditions of the Metis and non-status Indian people of Canada.

On October 10, 1973, Teron, Rudnicki, Legasse and Schmidt went to the minister's office; Teron went into the minister's inner office while the rest waited in the outer office and after one to one-and-a-half hours Teron emerged and said that the meeting to review Exhibit 79 [the October 3 draft] was cancelled. Rudnicki, Schmidt, and Legasse returned to the CMHC offices.

On the afternoon of October 10, 1973, Teron called Schmidt into the former's office and asked if the draft policy proposal documents had been available to the Native Council of Canada people and Schmidt said "Yes," and according to the evidence of Schmidt there followed a discussion about the "concepts of consultation."

On the afternoon of October 10, 1973, Teron called Legasse into his office and asked him if he had been at the meeting where the documents had been on the table and to this Legasse answered "Yes."

Legasse testified that Teron said that it's "Either Rudnicki or me." Legasse replied that in his view it wasn't that serious and Teron further stated "You recall Mr. Walter Gordon" and Legasse replied "It was the opposition that asked for his resignation."

I accept Rudnicki's evidence that on October 11, 1973, he, Rudnicki, obtained an appointment with the president, Teron, and at that meeting:
1. Teron said that he had been speaking to the minister who was most unhappy;
2. that the minister had told Teron that he would not take any proposals to Cabinet that the Native Council of Canada had seen;
3. Teron said that the Native Council of Canada had known of Teron's October 10, 1973 meeting with the minister before it had taken place;
4. Teron said to Rudnicki that "The minister blew his stack";
5. that Teron advised Rudnicki that the minister had said that it's either Rudnicki's head or Teron's head;
6. that Teron had asked Rudnicki for his resignation.

The next day, October 12, Rudnicki was called into Teron's office and he was asked to resign and upon refusing Teron gave him a letter of dismissal which has been filed as Exhibit 24 and reads:

> I spoke to you recently concerning your indiscretion and lack of judgment in showing a Cabinet document to members of the Native Council of Canada.
>
> I consider your action in this matter constitutes serious misconduct and regret to have to tell you I have no alternative but to terminate your employment with Central Mortgage and Housing Corporation. You may therefore take this letter as notice of termination of employment as of today, October 12, 1973. You will be paid two months' salary in lieu of notice.

On the same day, October 12, 1973, Ms. Dorothee Skarzynski [Rudnicki's secretary] was called into Teron's office at a time after the plaintiff had been discharged.

I accept her evidence that the following occurred in the president's office:
1. Teron said that she was due an explanation and that he knew she was feeling badly;
2. that Teron said to her "I had no part in this — I was forced to do this by Mr. Basford. The minister is very angry — it is a resign (Teron) or firing (Rudnicki) issue — either he or I have to go over this native housing document";
3. That Teron said that while he had no control over the dismissal, he regretted it very much;

4. that Teron said "Mr. Basford forced this on me — it was either me or Rudnicki and I'm not prepared to give up my position here, all things being equal."

5. that Teron said maybe the best thing for Ms. Skarzynski to do would be to resign and that she would be offered a generous severance pay.

On October 24 [twelve days later] Rudnicki had an appointment with and saw the minister and left with him Exhibit 46 — a 13-page document prepared by Rudnicki entitled "Events Regarding the Consulting Process on Native Housing."

On October 29 Rudnicki wrote a letter (Exhibit 31) to the minister asking that the matter of his dismissal be reconsidered and he subsequently received a reply dated October 31, 1973 (Exhibit 32) advising that the whole matter was one for the president of Central Mortgage and Housing and by further letter dated November 5, 1973 (Exhibit 33), Teron advised Rudnicki that the matter had been reviewed by him but there would be no change in the dismissal.

In the minister's letter of October 31, 1973 to Rudnicki, which said letter was marked as Exhibit 32, the following appears:

> As you are undoubtedly aware, the president of CMHC is charged with the administration of the corporation. Matters relating to personnel, including appointments, discipline and dismissals, are not the responsibility of the minister or subject to his control or decision. It was accordingly the president who investigated the events that preceded your dismissal and who came to the conclusion that, in all the circumstances, they did, in fact, require the action that he took in the discharge of his responsibility for the administration of the corporation.

In these reasons when I accept the evidence of one witness in preference to the evidence of another witness, I do so on the basis enunciated by O'Halloran, J.A. in *R. v. Pressley* (1948), 94 C.C.C. 29, 34:

The Judge is not given a divine insight into the hearts and minds of the witnesses appearing before him. Justice does not descend automatically upon the best actor in the witness box. The most satisfactory judicial test of truth lies in its harmony or lack of harmony with the preponderance of probabilities disclosed by the facts and circumstances in the conditions of the particular case.

I emphasize that in these reasons when I find that Teron said to Ms. Skarzynski, for example, "Mr. Basford forced this upon me," I am simply finding that Teron said that to Ms. Skarzynski — I need not and I do not make any findings as to whether the minister said such a thing to Mr. Teron ...

CMHC (the employer) was entitled to dismiss Rudnicki (the employee) without notice and without remuneration in lieu of notice if such dismissal was for "cause."

What constitutes "cause"? The Privy Council in *Clouston & Co. Limited* v. *Corry*, [1906] A.C. 122, 129 stated:

Now the sufficiency of the justification depended upon the extent of misconduct. There is no fixed rule of law defining the degree of misconduct which will justify dismissal. Of course there may be misconduct in a servant which will not justify the determination of the contract of service by one of the parties to it against the will of the other. On the other hand, misconduct inconsistent with the fulfilment of the express or implied conditions of service will justify dismissal. Certainly when the alleged misconduct consists of drunkenness there must be considerable difficulty in determining the extent or conditions of intoxication which will establish a justification for dismissal.

Law of Torts, Linden, p. 477 "Wrongful Dismissal: Tortious Breach of Contract" by Bruce C. McDonald at p. 478:

'Cause' includes incapacity through protracted illness and, more importantly, conduct by the employee that seriously impairs the basic confidence required for a positive

---

2⁵ Confidential
Second Working Draft
September 19, 1973

MEMORANDUM TO CABINET

TITLE: Housing for Métis and Non-Status Indians

I. PROBLEM

1. Housing conditions among Métis and non-status Indians are extremely poor. Although some federal assistance has been given, existing NHA housing programmes have not been able to meet the need for rehabilitation or replacement of substandard units.

II. BACKGROUND

2. Housing among all native peoples has been a serious problem for many years. Substandard accommodation has contributed to the high infant mortality rate and the short life expectancy among this group. It has also aggravated the other social and economic problems faced by native peoples. Inadequate housing has become a particularly acute problem in isolated areas where many of the social services that might supplement family resources are not available.

3. Métis and non-status Indians have the most pressing housing problems of all native people; they are not eligible for the Department of Indian Affairs and Northern Development assistance given to Eskimos and status Indians. The discrepancy is reflected in the rates of residential construction in remote communities; Métis and non-status Indians have an annual rate of 1 unit per 1000 population, while the rate for Eskimos is 14 per 1000 and for status Indians, 9 per 1000. Associations representing Métis and non-status Indians have become very active in recent years, in part as a response to the situation where houses are being built every year for status Indians while non-status natives in the same communities receive virtually no assistance.

4. Since 1970, CMHC and various federal departments have made grants to Métis organisations to study their housing conditions and to survey the need for rehabilitation and replacement of units. For the years 1970-72, CMHC made grants totalling $3,664,168. This included funds for materials for the Winter Warmth programme, conducted jointly by CMHC and the Department of Manpower and Immigration (through), to allow Métis to make emergency repairs to their units. Although Winter Warmth did achieve upgrading of severely inadequate units, it was a relatively small programme designed only to provide temporary assistance.

However when counsel for Rudnicki asked Teron if he would put the designation "Cab. Doc." on a comic book if it had the proper face sheet attached to it, Teron demurred and said "I would want to look at the contents."

employment relationship. This latter includes a significant failure on the part of the employee to exercise due care, skill or diligence, consistent absenteeism, gross insubordination, disobedience to reasonable orders, incompetence and important types of work-connected dishonesty. Minor or non-recurring errors, even if costly to the employer, will rarely constitute cause.

In this case the "cause" of the dismissal appears; first, in the statement of defence, paragraph 5:

... The defendant states and the fact is that the plaintiff was dismissed for just and sufficient cause, and without limiting the foregoing, the plaintiff was dismissed for conduct inconsistent with the discharge of his responsibilities and prejudicial to the good management of the affairs of the defendant in disclosing or causing to be disclosed certain confidential documents relative to the affairs of the defendant and in violation of the oath of fidelity and secrecy aforesaid.

Second, it appears as stated in the letter of dismissal — Exhibit 24 signed by William Teron:

I spoke to you recently concerning your indiscretion and lack of judgment in showing a Cabinet document to members of the Native Council of Canada.

I consider your action in this matter constitutes serious misconduct and regret to have to tell you I have no alternative but to terminate your employment with Central Mortgage and Housing Corporation.

"CONSULTATION," "CABINET DOCUMENTS" AND "CONFIDENTIAL DOCUMENTS"

The Shorter Oxford English Dictionary, Vol. I, p. 379:

Consult
1. To take counsel together, deliberate, confer.
2. To confer about, deliberate upon, consider.
3. To take counsel to bring about; to plan, devise, contrive.
4. To provide for by consultation; to have eye to.
5. To ask advice of, seek counsel from; to have recourse to for instruction or professional advice.

Consultation
1. The action of consulting or taking counsel together; deliberation, conference.

Exhibit 68 is entitled "This Document is the Property of the Government of Canada — Restricted — Guidance Notes for the Conduct of Cabinet Business (Revised June 1969)."

It will be recalled that counsel for the defendant initially claimed privilege for Exhibit 68 [guidance notes on the preparation of Cabinet documents] under s. 41(1) of The Federal Court Act but eventually said that any claim of confidentiality in regard to this "restricted document" was waived.

The document sets out the required format for a "Memorandum to the Cabinet" and one of the requirements of the format is that the document be signed by the minister who sponsors the memorandum.

On page 9 of the said document the following appears:

Subjects requiring consideration by the Cabinet are presented in the form of "Memoranda to the Cabinet." Upon receipt of the Privy Council Office they are registered and numbered and become Cabinet Documents for distribution to ministers in support of Cabinet/ Cabinet Committee meeting agenda items.

During the course of his evidence Teron made some astounding statements as to what constituted, in his phraseology, a "Cab. Doc." He asserted:
(a) "If it says 'Memo to Cabinet,' that is a 'Cab. Doc.' "
(b) "Any memo that says 'Memo to Cab.' means it is a 'Cab. Doc.' "
However when counsel for Rudnicki asked Teron if he would put the designation "Cab. Doc." on a comic book if it had the proper face sheet attached to it, Teron demurred and said "I would want to look at the contents."
(c) "When I say 'Cab. Doc.,' I mean Memorandum to Cabinet; within the corporation a 'Cab. Doc.' is a 'Memorandum to Cabinet' no matter what its stage of development."
(d) Teron on cross-examination was asked if he agreed with the following excerpt from Hansard, Commons Debates, House of Commons, for July 17, 1975 at p. 7696:

Mrs. Iona Campagnolo (Parliamentary Secretary to Minister of Indian Affairs and Northern Development): Madam Speaker, in replying to this question I should perhaps point out at the outset that a document does not become a cabinet document until it has been approved by the responsible minister, signed by him or her, and forwarded to the Privy Council office. The document being distributed at the meeting with the National Indian Brotherhood is not of this character. Each copy was clearly marked "Draft – for discussion purposes only."

Teron in reply to the question said that the parliamentary assistant was defining a "Privy Council Office cabinet document."
(e) Teron said "There is an honest difference of

opinion between Rudnicki and me as to what is meant by a 'Cab. Doc.'."

The evidence appears to be uncontradicted that persons at CMHC used the "Memorandum to Cabinet" format as a discipline so that the material would be properly organized in accordance with Exhibit 68, if in fact the proposal went on to the minister and on to the Cabinet.

In my view none of Exhibits 74, 75, 76, 77, 78, 79, 79A or 79B is a "Cabinet document" within the definition set out above in Exhibit 68 and as enunciated by Mrs. Campagnolo in the above quote from Hansard of July 17, 1975.

Exhibit 10 is a memorandum from the former president of CMHC, Mr. Hignett, and marked "Confidential."

The document lists various designations of classified material and states on page 2:

(c) Confidential — This would generally relate to those memoranda which are presently so classified except to the extent that this is changed by the adoption of the above classification.

Under the heading of "Restricted" it is stated:

This will apply to the following:

(iv) major policy proposals including reports by the Research Groups and the Policy Sector Teams.

No one has suggested during the course of this trial that the documents which have been marked "Confidential" should in fact have been marked "Restricted."

By whom is a document or memorandum designated "confidential?"

Teron stated:

1. "Each individual has responsibility — if it is to be kept confidential, he will so mark it and keep it so."
2. "Every one who initiates a document has authority to use the prescribed format."
3. "The chief of a division and those he designates to do so can put 'confidential' on a document."

I recall the following evidence as well:

(a) Gene Rheaume said that in government circles you often put "confidential" on something because that was the "easiest way to get things read."

(b) Legasse stated that in some government departments he had seen the word "confidential" "stamped on press clippings because they did not want the opposition to know what they considered significant in the morning news."

Legasse stated that sometimes, as a discipline, the word "confidential" was put on a document at the beginning of the process but that at other times it was only attached to the document just prior to the document going to the minister.

DRAFT FOR MINISTERIAL REVIEW

THIS DOCUMENT IS THE PROPERTY OF THE GOVERNMENT OF CANADA

CONFIDENTIAL

October 3, 1973

MEMORANDUM TO CABINET

TITLE   Housing Program for Métis and Non-Status Indians

Programme de logement pour les Métis et pour les Indiens non inscrits

I.   PROBLEM

1. Housing conditions among Métis and non-status Indians are extremely poor. Although some federal assistance has been given, existing NHA housing programs have not been adequate to meet the need for rehabilitation or replacement of substandard units.

II.   BACKGROUND

1. Substandard housing has contributed to the high infant mortality rate and the short life expectancy among Métis and non-status Indian people and has aggravated other social and economic problems.

2. Métis and non-status Indians are not eligible for the Department of Indian Affairs and Northern Development assistance given to Eskimos and status Indians. The annual rate of residential construction for Métis and non-status Indians is one unit per 1000 population, compared with 14 per 1000 for Eskimos and 10 per 1000 for status Indians. Métis and non-status Indians are acutely aware of these discrepancies, particularly when they live in the

On the evidence before me I find that at the meeting with the Native Council of Canada on September 12, 1973, the phrases "You'll be consulted every step of the way — it won't be something that you will read about in the newspapers — you'll have a hand in preparing the program" — were used by the minister and by Teron.

I find that the Native Council of Canada and the Policy Program Division of CMHC each properly assumed that the exercise they were involved in that was to take place between September 12, 1973, and September 21, 1973, (the deadline set by the minister) was to be a new type of joint venture; after the meeting of September 12, 1973, the Native Council of Canada on September 13, elected an Executive Working Committee to meet with Rudnicki and his group.

I find on the evidence before me that Rudnicki and his staff and the representatives of the Native Council of Canada logically concluded that the consultation process was one that involved disclosure by CMHC employees to the Native Council of Canada people as to what proposals the CMHC personnel were going to put forth to the minister.

171

> As far as the letter from Belcourt to the minister is concerned, in my view, Teron has no one to blame for that letter but himself; he said to Belcourt, when asked as to whether or not he should write the letter, "By all means" ... The day before personnel at the Policy Planning Division had unanimously told Belcourt not to write such a letter.

I do not accept Teron's theory that there was only to be disclosure after the policy had been approved by the Cabinet and then only before a public announcement was to be made. If Teron's analysis were correct, then I cannot imagine why the members of the Native Council of Canada were so eager to meet and discuss the matter and I do not know why they would continue to come back for discussions; if Teron's analysis of what consultation was to have been is correct, then I would agree with counsel for Rudnicki that "Truly the white man had spoken with a forked tongue."

I find it strange that no one from management of CMHC was called as a witness to substantiate any of Teron's theories about "Cab. Docs.," "consultation" or "confidentiality."

If the actions of Rudnicki in disclosing the policy proposals and the documents that contained such policy proposals was such a departure from acceptable behaviour, how is it that no one complained about his actions and why is it that Teron said nothing to Rudnicki or to anyone else after Belcourt telephoned Teron on or about September 20, 1973, and told Teron about his (Belcourt's) meeting with Rudnicki and of the Native Council of Canada's objections "to the paper."

I find it strange that someone on behalf of CMHC has not come forward at this trial with some notes or some minutes of many of these meetings which took place.

As far as the letter from Belcourt to the minister (Exhibit 42) is concerned, in my view, Teron has no one to blame for that letter but himself; he said to Belcourt, when asked as to whether or not he should write the letter, "By all means" Belcourt should write to the minister. The day before personnel at the Policy Planning Division had unanimously told Belcourt not to write such a letter.

If Teron was so upset about what Belcourt told him on the phone on the morning of October 10, why would he have said to Belcourt "By all means" go ahead and write to the minister.

Rudnicki did not ask any of the executive of CMHC for permission to reveal the policy proposals to the Native Council of Canada because he was the one who had been put in charge of the project by Teron; in my view, Rudnicki was merely doing what he had been authorized to do. If in the course of carrying out his mandate Rudnicki did show some error in judgment (which I do not find to be so), in my view such error in judgment was minor and not gross or repetitive.

If an employer dismisses an employee for cause, no notice need be given and no remuneration in lieu of notice need be paid.

In this case Exhibit 24 — the letter of dismissal — states that Rudnicki will be paid two months' salary "in lieu of notice."

During the course of argument I asked counsel for CMHC why the remuneration was paid if in fact the dismissal was for cause; McInenly replied that the remuneration was paid "purely as a gratuitous payment."

JUDGMENT

The plaintiff Rudnicki will have judgment against the defendant CMHC in the sum of $18,006.14.

The plaintiff Rudnicki will receive his taxed party-party costs of this action and the costs of the day for July 8, 1976, will be on the basis of as between a solicitor and his own client.

RELEASED: July 13, 1976

O'Driscoll, J.
Supreme Court of Ontario

About the contributors

George Baird is a Toronto-based architect. He lectures in the University of Toronto Department of Architecture. He is the co-editor of *Meaning in Architecture* and co-author of *On Building Downtown: Design Guidelines for the Core Area of the City of Toronto*. He is a member of the editorial board of *City Magazine*.

Michael Fish is a Montreal architect whose special interest is co-op housing and the conservation of older parts of the city of Montreal.

Kent Gerecke is chairman of the Department of City Planning at the University of Manitoba and is a member of the editorial board of *City Magazine*.

Donald Gutstein is a Vancouver-based writer and researcher. He is co-author of the booklet *Forever Deceiving You* and author of *Vancouver Ltd*. He is a member of the editorial board of *City Magazine*.

Marsha Hewitt teaches humanities in a Montreal CEGEP and is a free-lance writer.

James Lorimer is a specialist in urban affairs. He is the author of *A Citizen's Guide to City Politics, The Real World of City Politics, Working People* (with Myfanwy Phillips) and co-editor of *The City Book*. He is a member of the editorial board of *City Magazine*.

Desmond Morton teaches history at the University of Toronto. He is the author of *Mayor Howland, the citizens' candidate* and *NDP: the dream of power*.

John Sewell is a Toronto alderman. He is the most prominent critic of "old guard" politics and the development industry in Toronto city politics. He is the author of *Up Against City Hall*.

Index